DÉLICIEUX

THE RECIPES OF FRANCE

THE RECIPES
OF FRANCE

DÉLICIEUX

GABRIEL GATÉ

hardie grant books

Published in 2016 by Hardie Grant Books,
an imprint of Hardie Grant Publishing

Hardie Grant Books (Melbourne)
Building 1, 658 Church Street
Richmond, Victoria 3121
hardiegrantbooks.com.au

Hardie Grant Books (London)
5th & 6th Floors
52-54 Southwark Street
London SE1 1UN
hardiegrantbooks.co.uk

A Cataloguing-in-Publication entry is available from the catalogue
of the National Library of Australia at www.nla.gov.au
Délicieux
ISBN 9781743791950

Publisher: Pam Brewster
Design Manager: Mark Campbell
Design concept: Michelle Mackintosh
Typesetting & layout: Kerry Klinner
Production Manager: Todd Rechner
Colour reproduction by Splitting Image Colour Studio
Printed in China by 1010 Printing International Limited

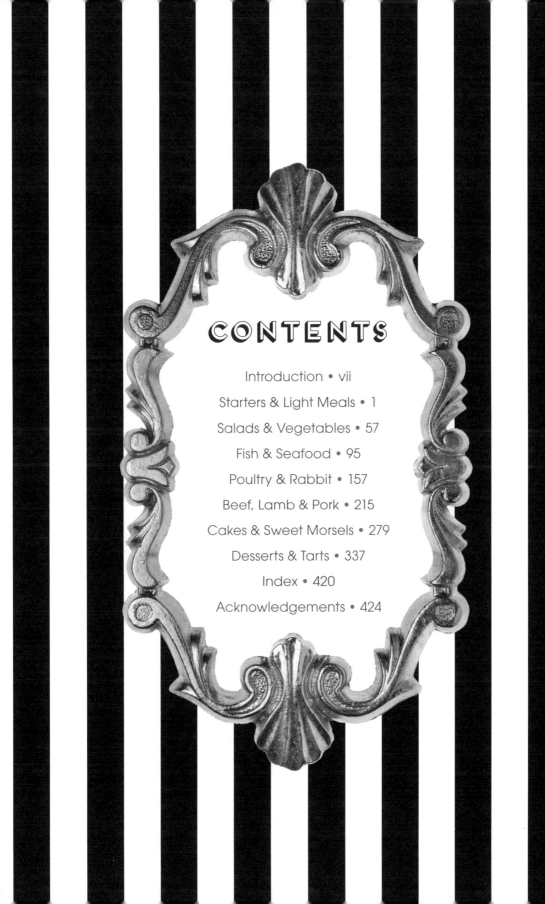

CONTENTS

INTRODUCTION

I was born in the picturesque and fertile Loire Valley region of France. Our family home was situated next to a large park surrounding a medieval château inhabited by a Duke and his family.

We had a small vineyard planted with red grape vines and an orchard of stone fruit and pear trees. My parents grew all the vegetables we needed for the eight of us, and my beautiful maternal grandmother, Pascaline, who lived with us, was the family cook. This was a real privilege as in her youth she had been the personal chef to a well-established local miller. We ate very well. It was a village cuisine and it inspired me to become a chef.

I became apprenticed to the extremely talented and charismatic Loire Valley chef, Albert Augereau who owned a Michelin-starred restaurant, and it was he who ignited my passion for fine French cuisine.

Nowadays I live with my family in Australia, but my work as a television chef, author, and leading gourmet tours of France takes me back twice a year. Every visit is an inspiration and a source of epicurean pleasure. I have toured and sampled food in every corner of France, from Normandy with its delicate Channel fish and seafood, and fine butter and cream; to Provence in the south, with its Mediterranean vegetables and olive oil; to Bordeaux with its illustrious red wines and renowned lamb; and Alsace with its great charcuterie and white wines.

I often stay in picturesque historic villages of which there are hundreds in France. After a leisurely start on the terrace of a brasserie enjoying a café au lait and croissant, I often visit a local farmers' market. French markets are very atmospheric and the food is local, fresh and seasonal. Some farmers still sell their home-made produce, just as previous generations have done for hundreds of years. Villagers loaded up with full baskets return home with a smile.

Making gâteaux and pâtisseries is a culinary art in which the French are leaders and I never fail to visit the local pâtisseries. Each region boasts its own creations using local ingredients. In the Ardèche region you find chestnuts used in cakes, mousses and ice-cream; in Provence almonds are used in many cakes; in Normandy it is pears and apples; in the south west it's Armagnac; and in the Alps wild berries.

Of course I taste and enjoy in moderation naturellement! I must leave room for dinner to taste the local specialities. I discover new chefs, new flavours, new and classic dishes – the possibilities are endless.

Délicieux: the recipes of France presents a broad selection of wonderful dishes resulting from my experiences as a chef, cookery teacher and lover of French food and travel. I have written and tested all the recipes and adapted them for the home cook, who can feel confident in preparing them successfully.

Happy cooking and bon appetit!

Gabriel Gaté
www.gabrielgate.com

Starters &
Light Meals

LYONNAISE CHEESE DIP WITH HERBS

Cervelle de Canut

FROM THE LYONNAIS-RHÔNE ALPS REGION

This dip was created in Lyons, the silk capital of France, in the 19th century, and the French title translates as 'silk worker's brain', meaning it is 'soft'. It's often served with hot baked potatoes but is lovely on toasted sourdough baguette with vegetable sticks.

250 g (9 oz) creamed cottage cheese or quark (in France it is called fromage frais)

50 ml (1¾ fl oz) crème fraîche

2 tablespoons extra-virgin olive oil

1 tablespoon red wine vinegar

1 garlic clove, finely chopped

salt

freshly ground pepper

1 medium shallot, finely chopped

2 tablespoons finely chopped parsley

3 tablespoons finely snipped chives

Place the cottage cheese in a salad bowl and mix in the crème fraîche.

Whisk in the olive oil, vinegar, garlic, salt and pepper, then stir in the shallot, parsley and chives.

Cover with plastic wrap and refrigerate for 2–3 hours before serving.

Serves 6–8

OYSTERS IN CHAMPAGNE SABAYON

Huîtres au sabayon de Champagne

FROM THE CHAMPAGNE REGION

It's fascinating to visit a Champagne cellar in France and then to taste the real thing where it is made. This oyster dish is one of my favourite appetisers.

50 g (1¾ oz) salted butter, melted

1 medium shallot, finely chopped

12 button mushrooms, finely chopped

salt

freshly ground pepper

12 freshly opened oysters

80 ml (2½ fl oz) Champagne

2 egg yolks

Preheat the oven to 250°C (480°F).

Heat one-third of the melted butter in a small frying pan. Stir in the shallots and cook on a low heat for 2 minutes. Add the chopped mushrooms and cook, stirring occasionally, for about 10 minutes until most of the moisture has evaporated. Season with salt and pepper.

Remove the oysters from the shells and put the shells aside on a baking tray. In a small saucepan, place 50 ml (1¾ fl oz) of the Champagne and bring to a low simmer. Gently stir in the oysters and turn off the heat.

Place the egg yolks and the remaining Champagne in a bowl. Place the bowl over a pan of simmering water (bain-marie) and beat the yolks and Champagne until light and fluffy. It takes a few minutes and the egg must not scramble.

Remove the bowl from the heat, slowly whisk in the remaining melted butter and season with salt and pepper.

Spoon a little mushroom mixture into each of the 12 oyster shells. Top with a drained oyster, then coat the oysters with the Champagne sauce.

Place the oysters in the hot oven for a few minutes until the sauce has lightly browned. Serve immediately.

Serves 2

FRENCH-STYLE ONION & ANCHOVY PIZZA

Pissaladière

FROM THE PROVENCE–CÔTE D'AZUR REGION | BY PHILIPPE MOUCHEL

The sunny Côte d'Azur on the coast of France next to Italy is typified by this pissaladière, a flavoursome French-style pizza much loved as a snack or as an appetiser served with drinks.

55 g (2 oz) salted butter

3 large brown onions, very thinly sliced

500 g (1 lb 2 oz) ready-to-use bread dough, or a large ready-to-use pizza base

3 tablespoons extra-virgin olive oil

20 anchovy fillets, drained of oil

25 black olives, pitted

25 small thyme sprigs, about 1 cm (½ in) long

freshly ground black pepper

Preheat the oven to 190°C (375°F). Line a baking tray with baking paper.

Heat the butter in a large, non-stick frying pan. Add the onions and cook on a low heat for about 20 minutes, stirring from time to time. Don't try to cook the onions too quickly or they will burn and taste unpleasant. Allow the onions to cool slightly before using.

If using bread dough, roll out to a thickness of about 5 mm (¼ in). Carefully lift the dough or pizza base onto the prepared tray. Brush with a little oil.

Spread the cooked onions on top of the dough or pizza base, leaving a margin of about 2 cm (¾ in) at the edges. Decorate with the anchovy fillets, making a criss-cross pattern. Arrange the olives and thyme sprigs in the spaces between the anchovies and season with a little black pepper.

Bake for about 15 minutes or until the pastry is brown and crisp and it smells wonderful. Cut into pieces and serve.

Serves 6–8 as an appetiser with pre-dinner drinks

SALMON TARTARE

Tartare de saumon

FROM THE AQUITAINE REGION

The Aquitaine region borders on the Atlantic Ocean just north of Spain. This superb entrée needs to be prepared with very fresh salmon. You can also use tuna for the same stunning result.

100 g (3½ oz) very fresh skinless salmon fillet

¼ large avocado, diced

2 tablespoons finely snipped chives

½ shallot, very finely chopped

2–3 drops Tabasco sauce

1 teaspoon finely grated lemon zest

1 tablespoon extra-virgin olive oil

1½ tablespoons salmon roe

2 tablespoons crème fraîche, whipped

Cut the salmon into 5 mm (¼ in) slices, then cut the slices into 5 mm (¼ in) sticks, then into 5 mm (¼ in) cubes.

In a bowl, gently combine the salmon with the avocado, half the chives, the shallot, Tabasco sauce, lemon zest and olive oil.

Place the PVC rings on two plates.

Spoon the salmon mix into each ring. Spread about 2 teaspoons of salmon roe on the plate around the edge of each ring, then spread a little crème fraîche on top of the salmon. Garnish the top with the remaining salmon roe and sprinkle with the remaining chives.

Carefully lift the PVC rings and serve.

Serves 2

SNAILS IN GARLIC & WALNUT BUTTER

Escargots au beurre d'ail et de noix

FROM THE MIDI-PYRÉNÉES REGION

For the French this is a very festive dish and each region has its own version — but they all contain lots of garlic. In the Midi-Pyrénées region walnuts are added for an extra crunch.

150 g (5½ oz) salted butter, softened

1 shallot, finely chopped

2 garlic cloves, finely chopped

3 tablespoons finely chopped parsley

80 g (2¾ oz) walnuts, finely chopped

salt

freshly ground pepper

1 tablespoon lemon juice

600 g (1 lb 6 oz) baby English spinach leaves, washed

60 ml (2 fl oz/¼ cup) pouring cream

48 cooked snails, rinsed and drained

25 g (1 oz/¼ cup) dry breadcrumbs

Preheat the oven to 180°C (350°F).

In a bowl, combine the softened butter, chopped shallot, garlic, parsley and walnuts. Season with salt, pepper and lemon juice. Place the mixture between two sheets of baking paper and roll into a square 5 mm (¼ in) thick. Cover in plastic wrap and place in the freezer to chill.

Place the spinach in a pot, cover with a lid and cook until just wilted. Drain the spinach and squeeze out the excess water.

Heat the cream in a pan. Stir in the spinach and season with salt and pepper.

Transfer the spinach to four individual gratin dishes and top each with 12 snails.

Remove the walnut butter from the freezer. Cut into four squares and place a piece on each serve of snails. Sprinkle breadcrumbs on top. Cook in the preheated oven for 10 minutes until hot. Serve immediately.

Serves 4

CHEESE SOUFFLÉ

Soufflé au fromage

FROM THE JURA REGION

The Jura mountain range bordering the Franche-Comté and Switzerland produces really flavoursome cheeses with lovely melting qualities. They are used frequently by local cooks in recipes such as this delicious soufflé.

30 g (1 oz) salted butter

30 g (1 oz) plain (all-purpose) flour

350 ml (12 fl oz) milk

¼ teaspoon freshly grated nutmeg

a good pinch of cayenne pepper

freshly ground black pepper

2 small egg yolks

55 g (2 oz) grated gruyère cheese

55 g (2 oz) grated emmental cheese

6 egg whites

a pinch of cream of tartar

Preheat the oven to 180°C (350°F). Butter and flour an 18 cm (7 in) soufflé mould.

Melt the butter in a saucepan over a medium heat. Whisk in the flour and cook for about 2 minutes. Slowly add the milk, whisking constantly until it forms a smooth white sauce. Cook gently for 3–4 minutes, then turn off the heat.

Mix in the nutmeg, cayenne pepper and a little black pepper. Add the egg yolks and grated cheese and mix in well. Transfer the soufflé base to a large bowl.

Whisk the egg whites with the cream of tartar until stiff. Mix a little of the beaten whites into the soufflé base to loosen the mixture, then gently fold in the remaining whites.

Pour the soufflé mixture into the prepared soufflé mould and smooth the surface. If you wish, you can decorate the surface with small, flat, diamond-shaped pieces of cheese for effect.

Bake for about 35 minutes, then serve immediately. Take care when carrying the hot soufflé to the table. To serve, spoon the soufflé onto warmed plates.

Serves 4

MARINATED SARDINES

Sardines à l'escabeche

FROM THE PROVENCE REGION

This traditional dish of sardines, marinated with vinegar, oil and herbs, is often associated with the historic Mediterranean Provençal city of Marseille. Marseille is famous for its daily fish market where sardines and other seafood are sold just hours after the catch.

12 fresh medium sardines

3 tablespoons lemon olive oil, plus a little extra for drizzling

salt

freshly ground black pepper

½ medium onion, very thinly sliced

1 medium baby carrot, thinly sliced

1 teaspoon coriander seeds

1 bay leaf

4 thyme sprigs

2 garlic cloves, unpeeled

60 ml (2 fl oz/ ¼ cup) good-quality white vinegar (I use Champagne vinegar)

125 ml (4 fl oz/½ cup) cold water

Clean the insides of the sardines, scale them and cut off the heads. Dry the sardines with paper towel.

Heat 2 tablespoons of the oil in a large frying pan and fry the sardines for 1–2 minutes on each side. Be careful not to overcook them. Season the sardines with salt and pepper and arrange them on a flat platter.

Heat the remaining oil in a separate frying pan. Add the onion, carrot, coriander seeds, bay leaf, thyme and garlic cloves and cook gently for 2 minutes. Add the vinegar and water, bring to the boil and simmer for 15 minutes.

Spoon the hot liquid, herbs and vegetables over the sardines. Allow to cool, cover with plastic wrap and refrigerate for 24 hours. The sardines will absorb the liquid.

Just before serving, drizzle the sardines with a little extra lemon olive oil.

Serves 4

BUCKWHEAT PANCAKES FROM BRITTANY

Galettes Bretonnes au Sarazin

FROM THE BRITTANY REGION | BY JEAN-MARIE BLANCHOT

These savoury buckwheat pancakes are the pride of Brittany's cuisine and I am very fond of them myself. They're usually prepared on special circular hotplates about 30 cm (12 in) in diameter, but at home you can use a very large non-stick frying pan.

250 ml (8½ fl oz/1 cup) cold water

½ teaspoon salt

200 g (7 oz) buckwheat flour

10 g (⅓ oz) salted butter, melted, plus extra unmelted butter

4 eggs

125 g (4½ oz) grated gruyère cheese

4–8 thin slices of ham

Place most of the water and all the salt in a large bowl and mix well. Add the flour and whisk to a smooth batter. It should fall like a ribbon when you lift the whisk. If necessary, add a little extra water.

Mix in the melted butter until well incorporated. Cover the batter and rest in the fridge for about 4 hours.

When ready to cook the pancakes, lightly grease a large non-stick frying pan with butter and heat over a medium heat. Pour in enough batter to cover the base very thinly. When the underside of the pancake is dry, lower the heat and rub the surface of the pancake with a piece of butter.

Break an egg in the centre and spread the white all over the pancake, keeping the yolk intact. Sprinkle with grated cheese and top with a slice or two of ham.

Using a spatula, carefully fold the sides of the pancake in towards the yolk to form a square. Cook for an extra minute or two, then transfer to a warm plate while you make the rest of the pancakes.

Serves 4

COUNTRY-STYLE PÂTÉ WITH PISTACHIOS

Pâté de campagne à la pistache

FROM THE BURGUNDY REGION | BY STÉPHANE LANGLOIS

Burgundy is one of the great gastronomic regions of France, with its superb wines and meat — including the charcuterie (smallgoods), such as this festive country-style pâté, which used to be made on the farm.

750 g (1 lb 11 oz) lean pork leg meat, cubed

350 g (12½ oz) pork fat, cubed

550 g (1 lb 4 oz) chicken livers, cleaned and trimmed

a handful of parsley leaves

½ brown onion, roughly chopped

40 g (1½ oz) salt (or less, to taste)

1 teaspoon ground white pepper

1 teaspoon mixed (pumpkin pie) spice

1 tablespoon chopped garlic

2 teaspoons dried thyme

60 ml (2 fl oz/¼ cup) cognac or brandy

2 tablespoons cornflour (cornstarch)

2 medium eggs

120 g (4½ oz) shelled pistachios

a few strips of thinly cut pork fat (optional)

10 g (⅓ oz) powdered gelatine

300 ml (10 fl oz) warm water

Preheat the oven to 90°C (195°F). Grease a 2-litre (68-fl oz/8-cup) terrine dish.

Mix together the pork, pork fat, chicken livers, parsley and onion. Put the mixture through a mincer then transfer to a bowl and stir in the salt, white pepper, spice, garlic and dried thyme. Add the cognac, cornflour, eggs and pistachio nuts and mix everything together thoroughly.

Tip the pâté mixture into the terrine dish and smooth the top. Decorate with a few strips of the thinly cut pork fat, if you wish, arranged in a criss cross pattern.

Place the terrine in a baking dish and pour in hot water to a depth of about 5 cm (2 in) to create a bain-marie. Bake for about 3 hours. When it is cooked, the temperature of the terrine will have reached 80°C (175°F) at its centre.

Remove the terrine from the oven and stand on a cool surface. Dissolve the gelatine in the warm water and pour over the terrine. Allow the terrine to cool, then refrigerate until ready to serve. Slice the terrine while still in the dish and serve with gherkins (pickles) and French bread.

Serves 12

BURGUNDY HAM TERRINE

Jambon de Bourgogne persillé

FROM THE BURGUNDY REGION	BY STÉPHANE LANGLOIS

This beautiful ham terrine is a speciality of Burgundy but it is loved all over France. It's usually served as a starter with baguette and gherkins (pickles).

2 litres (68 fl oz/8 cups) pork or chicken stock

1.3 kg (2 lb 14 oz) salted pork leg, including some skin

1 litre (34 fl oz/4 cups) clear chicken stock or water

60 g (2 oz) powdered gelatine

125 ml (4 fl oz/½ cup) red wine vinegar

125 ml (4 fl oz/½ cup) chardonnay or dry white wine

1 brown onion, finely chopped

30 g (1 oz/½ cup) chopped parsley

ground white pepper

In a stockpot, bring the stock to a simmer. Add the pieces of salted pork leg and simmer for about 2½ hours. The pork is now ham. Drain the ham, discard the cooking liquid and cool the ham on a dish.

While the ham is cooling down, heat the clear chicken stock in a saucepan and whisk in the gelatine until it has all dissolved. Add the vinegar and wine and allow to cool.

Preheat the oven to 150°C (300°F).

Ladle the chicken stock into a 2-litre (68–fl oz/8–cup) terrine dish, enough to cover 1 cm (½ in) of its base. Divide the chopped onion and parsley into four and add one-quarter to the dish.

Cut the cooled ham into slices 2 cm (¾ in) thick and season with a little white pepper. Finely shred the ham skin.

Place a layer of ham on top of the stock in the base of the terrine. Ladle in a bit more stock, then sprinkle with a quarter more onion and parsley and top with the shredded ham skin.

Top with another layer of ham, then ladle in more stock and add a quarter more onion and parsley. Add a final layer of ham and ladle in more stock to cover the ham by about 1 cm (½ in). Lastly, top with the remaining onion and parsley.

Place the terrine on a baking tray and into the preheated oven for about 20 minutes.

Remove from the oven and allow to cool, then refrigerate overnight to set.

Turn the terrine out before cutting it into 2 cm (¾ in) slices.

Serves about 10

CUCUMBER & SMOKED TROUT TERRINE

Terrine de truite fumée au concombre

FROM THE SAVOIE/ALPS REGION

Trout fishing and trout eating are popular activities in the alpine region where lakes, rivers and streams abound. This extremely light terrine is ideal as a first course for a special dinner party.

---

3 long cucumbers

2 tablespoons coarse salt

8 gelatine sheets or 1 x 7g (¼ oz) sachet powdered gelatine

freshly ground pepper

30 g (1 oz/½ cup) finely chopped dill

250 ml (8½ fl oz/1 cup) crème fraîche

a little extra-virgin olive oil

2 eggs, hard-boiled

3 smoked trout fillets, skinned

I use a 24 cm (9½ in) ring tin to mould the terrine.

Peel the cucumbers, then cut them in four lengthways. Remove the seeds and cut the cucumber into thin slices. Place in a bowl, toss with the coarse salt and put aside for 1 hour.

Place the gelatine sheets in a large bowl of cold water to soften for about 10 minutes.

Rinse and drain the cucumber. Pat it dry with paper towels or a clean tea towel. Blend the cucumber to a coarse purée, place in a bowl and season with pepper. Mix in the chopped dill.

Warm the crème fraîche in a small saucepan. Drain the softened gelatine sheets, squeezing them by hand to remove excess water, then add the gelatine sheets (or the powdered gelatine) to the warm crème fraîche, stirring to dissolve. Add this to the cucumber and mix well.

Brush the inside of the ring tin with olive oil and line the base with finely cut slices of hard-boiled egg. I use an egg slicer for more even results.

Pour about one-third of the cucumber preparation into the tin. Top with half of the trout fillets and another third of the cucumber mixture. Top with the remaining trout fillets and cucumber mixture.

Cover with plastic film and refrigerate for at least 6 hours.

Unmould the terrine carefully by dipping the mould briefly in hot water. Cut the terrine into 6 cm (2½ in) slices and serve.

Serves about 10

DUCK BALLOTINE

Ballotine de canard

| FROM THE VENDÉE REGION | BY PHILIPPE MOUCHEL |

*For this sophisticated terrine-style dish you will need a deboned duck.
If you are not sure how to do it, ask your poultry supplier to
debone it for you.*

600 g (1 lb 5 oz) minced (ground) duck leg meat

150 g (5½ oz) duck breast, diced

150 g (5½ oz) veal, diced

150 g (5½ oz) minced (ground) pork fat

50 g (1¾ oz) pistachio nuts

30 ml (1 fl oz) Madeira

30 ml (1 fl oz) cognac

120 ml (4 fl oz) dry white wine

salt

freshly ground pepper

1 teaspoon four-spice mix

1 duck, deboned

300 g (10½ oz) foie gras, cut into 2 cm (¾ in) chunks

1 litre (34 fl oz/4 cups) duck or chicken stock

In a bowl, thoroughly combine the minced duck leg with the diced duck breast, veal, pork fat, pistachio nuts, Madeira, cognac, dry white wine, a little salt and pepper and the four-spice mix. Cover and refrigerate overnight. This mixture is called forcemeat.

Place the deboned duck, skin side down, on several layers of plastic wrap. Spread the duck forcemeat on top of the deboned duck, leaving about 2 cm (¾ in) at the edge free of forcemeat.

Position the foie gras chunks lengthways along the centre, from the duck neck to the tail end of the duck. Carefully, but firmly, roll the deboned duck to enclose the forcemeat and foie gras. Then firmly wrap the duck parcel (ballotine) in the plastic wrap, securing the ends and centre with kitchen string.

In a large saucepan, bring the stock to almost a simmer, then immerse the ballotine into the stock to poach for about 2 hours. It's best if it does not boil.

Allow the ballotine to completely cool in the liquid, then refrigerate it.

Cut the ballotine into slices about 1 cm (½ in) thick and serve with gherkins (pickles), a little green salad drizzled with olive oil and some vegetable pickles.

Serves 6–8

YOUNG VEGETABLE SOUP

Potage aux primeurs

The French adore soup and this sort of vegetable potage is extremely popular in the countryside surrounding Paris, where many vegetables for the Parisian market are grown.

2 medium leeks

at least 1 cup celery leaves or 2 celery stalks

½ cos (romaine) lettuce

1½ litres (51 fl oz/6 cups) chicken stock

150 g (5½ oz) peas

2 tablespoons olive oil

20 g (¾ oz) butter

2 slices bread, cut into 2.5 cm (1 in) cubes

4 egg yolks

salt

freshly ground black pepper

Trim and wash the leeks and cut them into thin julienne strips, about 5 cm (2 in) long.

Shred the celery leaves (or thinly slice the stalks, if using). Wash and shred the lettuce leaves.

In a large saucepan, bring the chicken stock to the boil. Add the leeks, celery leaves, lettuce and peas and cook at a low boil for about 15 minutes, or until the vegetables are soft.

Meanwhile, heat the oil and butter in a frying pan and fry the bread cubes until lightly browned.

Place the egg yolks in a mixing bowl and whisk to combine. Slowly pour in about 250 ml (8½ fl oz/1 cup) of hot liquid from the soup, whisking continuously. Season with salt and pepper.

Take the soup off the heat, gradually whisk in the egg mixture, then season to taste. Ladle into deep soup bowls and serve the croutons separately.

Serves 4–6

ONION SOUP WITH PYRENEES CHEESE

Gratinée à la tomme des Pyrenées

In the Pyrenees they love to make this traditional, hearty soup using local onions and superb cheese, made with both goat's and sheep's milk. The sherry adds a beautiful flavour.

3 large brown onions

30 g (1 oz) butter

about 1.5 litres (51 fl oz/6 cups) strong chicken stock

salt

freshly ground black pepper

16 x 1 cm (½ in) slices of baguette

50 ml (1¾ fl oz) Xeres Spanish sherry

1 egg yolk

120 g (4½ oz) grated Tomme des Pyrenées cheese

Peel, halve and finely slice the onions.

Heat the butter in a large saucepan and cook the onions on gentle heat for about 10 minutes until very lightly browned and transparent.

Mix the stock into the onions. Season with salt and pepper, bring to the boil and boil for about 20 minutes.

Toast the baguette slices under the grill (broiler) (broiler).

Whisk the Xeres sherry and egg yolk together in a bowl.

Turn the heat off under the soup and mix the egg yolks and sherry into the soup. Ladle the soup into four bowls. Top with the toasted bread slices and sprinkle with grated cheese.

Place under the grill (broiler) for a few minutes until the cheese has melted and is golden brown.

Be careful – the soup is very hot.

Serves 4

CREAMY CELERIAC & ROQUEFORT SOUP

Velouté de celeri rave au Roquefort

FROM THE MIDI-PYRÉNÉES REGION

In this sophisticated soup the marriage of delicate celeriac and flavoursome and sharp roquefort is heavenly.

500 g (1 lb 2 oz) celeriac, peeled and cubed

2 potatoes, peeled and diced

salt

500 ml (17 fl oz/2 cups) milk

20 g (¾ oz) salted butter

150 g (5½ oz) Roquefort cheese, crumbled

freshly ground black pepper

3 tablespoons finely snipped chives

Place the celeriac and potatoes in a saucepan of salted water. Bring to the boil and cook until the vegetables are soft.

Drain the vegetables and return them to the saucepan, adding the milk and butter. Bring to a simmer and add the Roquefort cheese, stirring until it has all melted.

Turn off the heat and season with pepper. Blend the soup until it's very smooth.

Ladle the soup into bowls and sprinkle with chives.

Serves 3–5

MUSSEL & SAFFRON SOUP

Soupe de moules au saffran

FROM THE LANGUEDOC REGION | BY PHILIPPE MOUCHEL

The French Mediterranean coast in the Languedoc region is dotted with wonderful little fishing villages where you can enjoy hearty but delicately flavoured seafood soups and stews in the local restaurants.

1 kg (2 lb 3 oz) large very fresh mussels, scrubbed and beards removed

2 French shallots, thinly sliced

½ medium onion, thinly sliced

1 thyme sprig

1 bay leaf

a few parsley stalks

2 strips orange peel

250 ml (8½ fl oz/1 cup) dry white wine

3 tomatoes, peeled, seeded and diced

1 tablespoon cornflour (cornstarch)

2 tablespoons water

125 ml (4 fl oz/½ cup) pouring cream

a good pinch of saffron threads

30 g (1 oz) butter, cubed

freshly ground black pepper

4 tablespoons finely snipped chives

Put the mussels in a large saucepan and add the shallots and onion. Tie the thyme, bay leaf, parsley stalks and orange peel together with kitchen string and add to the pot. Pour in the wine and cover with a lid. Bring to the boil over a high heat and cook for a few minutes until the mussels have just opened.

Lift the mussels out of the cooking liquid into a bowl. Discard the onions and the herb bouquet. Taste the liquid and if it is too salty add a little water. Add the tomatoes and simmer for about 5 minutes. Meanwhile, remove the mussel meat from the shells and keep warm.

Mix the cornflour with the water then whisk into the simmering soup. Bring to the boil, add the cream and cook gently for a few minutes. Add the saffron, then blend until smooth. Stir in the butter until melted, then add plenty of pepper.

Divide the mussels among four bowls, pour on the soup and sprinkle with chives.

Serves 4

BEAUFORT OMELETTE

Omelette au Beaufort

FROM THE ALPS REGION

This omelette with local cheese is a common evening meal in the alps. It is usually served with a green salad.

10 g (¼ oz) salted butter

1 potato, peeled and diced

3 eggs

1 tablespoon crème fraîche

about 30 g (1 oz) shaved Beaufort cheese

salt

freshly ground black pepper

1 tablespoon finely snipped chives

2 teaspoons finely chopped tarragon

Heat half the butter in a small non-stick frying pan (or omelette pan) and cook the diced potatoes on a medium heat until cooked. Transfer the potatoes to a plate.

Beat the eggs in a bowl. Combine the beaten eggs with the crème fraîche and about two-thirds of the cheese. Season with salt and pepper.

Add the remaining butter to the frying pan on a high heat. Add the eggs and, using a fork, move the eggs in the pan so it cooks evenly. When the egg is almost set, top the centre with the cooked potatoes and most of the chives and tarragon. Fold the omelette and transfer to a plate.

Garnish with the remaining cheese and herbs.

Serves 1

CHEESE & HAM TOASTED SANDWICH

Crôque Monsieur

FROM THE PARIS REGION | BY PHILIPPE MOUCHEL

As a young chef in Paris, I often went out late at night after work to a cabaret and enjoyed a Crôque Monsieur while listening to live music. It smells delicious and is very popular.

8 slices of sandwich bread

8 slices of gruyère cheese, same size as the bread

8 thin slices of ham, same size as the bread

150 g (5½ oz) gruyère cheese, grated

100 g (3 ½ oz/1 cup) parmesan cheese, grated

60 ml (2 fl oz/¼ cup) pouring cream

2 egg yolks

salt

freshly ground pepper

Lay out four slices of bread and top each one with a slice of gruyère cheese. Then add a slice of ham, another slice of gruyère and, lastly, another slice of ham.

In a bowl, mix the grated gruyère with the grated parmesan, cream, egg yolks and a little salt and pepper.

Spread the remaining four slices of bread with half of the creamy cheese mixture. Carefully place the bread, cheese-side down, on top of the ham slices. Spread the remaining creamy cheese on top.

Place the Crôque Monsieur on a baking tray and bake in a hot oven or under the grill (broiler) until the cheese has melted inside and out.

Serves 4

CANTAL CREAM WITH WILD MUSHROOM TOASTS

Crème de Cantal et son toast de cèpes

FROM THE AUVERGNE REGION | BY FRANCIS DELMAS

Cantal cheese has been made in the mountainous region of Auvergne for more than a thousand years. This wonderful hard cheese, sharp and nutty, resembles a cheddar and is a great cheese to cook with.

80 g (2¾ oz) sugar

2 tablespoons water

80 g (2¾ oz) rhubarb, cut into 1 cm (½ in) pieces

1 teaspoon salted butter

100 ml (3 ½ fl oz) pouring cream

150 g (5½ oz) cantal cheese, grated

4 eggs

400 ml (13½ fl oz) hot milk

3 tablespoons extra-virgin olive oil

200 g (7 oz) cep mushrooms, sliced

freshly ground pepper

1 garlic clove, finely chopped

100 g (3½ oz) extra cantal cheese, cut into small pieces

6 × 1 cm (½ in) thick slices of baguette, 15 cm (6 in) long

12 cherry tomatoes

Preheat the oven to 140°C (275°F).

In a small saucepan, bring the sugar and water to the boil and cook until it is a light-brown caramel colour.

Pour the caramel into 6 x 100 ml (3½ fl oz) porcelain ramekins.

Cook the rhubarb in the butter in a small saucepan until soft, then spoon the rhubarb into the ramekins.

Combine the cream, grated cheese and eggs in a blender. Add the hot milk and blend again. Pour this custard into the ramekins and place them in a roasting pan. Add enough hot water to the pan to come halfway up the sides of the ramekins.

Cook the custards in the preheated oven for about 20 minutes or until set. Remove from the oven and allow to cool.

Heat half the olive oil in a frying pan and cook the mushrooms for a few minutes. Season with pepper and a little chopped garlic.

Alternate slices of mushroom and cantal cheese on the slices of baguette, then place under a grill and cook until the cheese has melted.

To unmould, run a knife blade around the inside edge of the ramekins and turn the cantal creams out onto plates. Top with a slice of cheese and mushroom toast, garnish with cherry tomatoes and drizzle the remaining olive oil over the top.

Serves 6

QUICHE LORRAINE

FROM THE LORRAINE REGION | BY PHILIPPE MOUCHEL

This is perhaps the best-known French dish outside France and can be easily varied by using different cheese, spices and herbs. It's a very traditional dish.

Pastry

125 g (4½ oz) salted butter, cut into pieces

1 egg yolk

a pinch of salt

300 g (10½ oz/2 cups) plain (all-purpose) flour

3 tablespoons water

juice of ½ lemon

Filling

2 egg yolks

2 whole eggs

100 ml (3½ fl oz) milk

300 ml (10 fl oz) pouring cream

salt

finely ground black pepper

2 pinches of freshly grated nutmeg

1 teaspoon salted butter

100 g (3½ oz) bacon, diced

100 g (3½ oz/¾ cup) grated gruyère cheese (or another cheese of your choice)

To make the pastry, place the butter, egg yolk and salt in a food processor and blend to combine. Add the flour, water and lemon juice and pulse to form a ball. Remove from the food processor, wrap in plastic wrap and refrigerate for at least 30 minutes before using.

Preheat the oven to 230°C (450°F). Grease a 22 cm (8¾ in) loose-based flan (tart) tin and line the base with baking paper.

Roll out the pastry on a floured surface and use to line the flan tin. Trim the edges and line the pastry with foil. Fill with pastry weights (or use rice or dried beans). Cook for 12 minutes, then carefully remove the foil and weights.

In a bowl, whisk together the yolks, whole eggs, milk and cream. Season to taste with salt, pepper and nutmeg.

Lower the oven temperature to 180°C (350°F).

Melt the butter in a frying pan and cook the bacon for 3 minutes, turning occasionally. Drain the bacon well then scatter over the blind-baked pastry shell. Sprinkle on the cheese then pour in the egg mixture.

Carefully transfer the quiche to the oven and cook for 20–25 minutes, or until the filling is set and the top is golden brown. When cooked, remove from the oven and leave for about 10 minutes before unmoulding.

Serves 6

LEEK TART

Flamiche aux poireaux

FROM THE NORTHERN REGION

Leeks are one of the most loved vegetables in France and the cool climate of northern France is perfect for their cultivation. This is my favourite savoury tart.

1 tablespoon vegetable oil

150 g (5½ oz) bacon, diced

30 g (1 oz) salted butter

3 medium leeks, white part only, thinly sliced

400 g (14 oz) savoury shortcrust pastry

4 large eggs

100 ml (3½ fl oz) milk

150 ml (5 fl oz) pouring cream

salt

freshly ground pepper

Preheat the oven to 220°C (430°F). You will need a 25 cm (10 in) loose-based flan (tart) tin.

Heat the oil in a wide non-stick pan and brown the bacon in it for 2–3 minutes. Transfer the bacon to a bowl.

Add the butter and the leeks to the pan and cook on a low heat for 10–15 minutes until the leeks are soft, stirring occasionally with a wooden spoon. Allow the leeks to cool.

Roll out the pastry to a thickness of about 4 mm (⅙ in). Line the tin with the pastry and prick the pastry about 30 times with a fork.

Spread the cold leeks and bacon over the pastry.

In a bowl, whisk together the eggs, milk and cream. Season with salt and pepper, then carefully pour the mixture over the leeks and bacon.

Place the tin on a baking tray and bake in the preheated oven for about 40 minutes until the pastry is cooked and filling set. Serve hot.

Serves 6–8

ZUCCHINI & SAINT MARCELLIN CHEESE FLAN

Flan de courgettes au Saint Marcellin

FROM THE RHÔNE-ALPES REGION

The creamy, flavoursome Saint Marcellin is a really popular French cheese and is much used in cooking. Serve this delicious dish with a salad.

4 small to medium zucchinis (courgettes)

1 tablespoon olive oil

salt

freshly ground black pepper

½ teaspoon curry powder

a little salted butter

2 Saint Marcellin cheeses, cut in half horizontally or 185 g (6½ oz) goat or brie-style cheese cut in 1 cm (½ in) slices

1 whole egg

1 egg yolk

120 ml (4 fl oz) crème fraîche

2 tablespoons finely snipped chives

Preheat the oven to 180°C (350°F).

Wash and trim the zucchinis and cut into thin slices.

Heat the oil in a large frying pan and cook the zucchini gently for about 10 minutes until soft. Season with salt, pepper and curry powder.

Use a little butter to grease four individual gratin dishes and spread the zucchini in the dishes. Top with a piece of Saint Marcellin cheese.

In a bowl, mix the whole egg and egg yolk with the crème fraîche and season with a little salt and pepper.

Pour this over the cheese and zucchini, and bake in the preheated oven for about 10 minutes.

Sprinkle with chives and serve.

Serves 4

ASPARAGUS & GOAT'S CHEESE TART

Tarte aux asperges et au fromage de chèvre

FROM THE LOIRE VALLEY REGION	BY PHILIPPE MOUCHEL

The sandy soil of the Loire Valley produces superb asparagus, and almost every restaurant in the region serves an asparagus dish in the two or three months leading up to the Tour de France.

400 g (14 oz) rolled puff pastry

2 egg yolks

1 teaspoon water

16 thin green asparagus spears, trimmed

2 tablespoons pouring cream

salt

freshly ground pepper

85 g (3 oz) fresh goat's cheese

Preheat the oven to 170°C (340°F). Line a baking tray with baking paper.

Cut the pastry into a rectangle about 10 x 30 cm (4 x 12 in) and place on the baking tray. Using the blade of a knife, lightly mark a 1 cm (½ in) border down both long sides of the pastry. Weight down the centre of the pastry (use baking paper with rice or small pastry weights) to stop it from rising when baked.

Lightly beat one of the egg yolks with the water and use to brush along the pastry edges. Bake for 15–20 minutes, or until the edges have risen and are golden brown.

Drop the asparagus spears into lightly salted boiling water for 2–3 minutes, then drain well.

Remove the baking paper and weights from the pastry. Lightly beat the remaining egg yolk with the cream and brush over the centre of the pastry. Season with salt and pepper. Top neatly with the cooked asparagus and spoon any remaining egg yolk and cream over the top. Dot with small pieces of goat's cheese and season with a little more salt and pepper. Return to the oven and bake for about 5 minutes, until the cheese is warm and lightly browned. Cut in half before serving.

Serves 2

GRATIN OF YABBIES

Gratin d'écrevisses

FROM THE ALPS REGION	BY PHILIPPE MOUCHEL

This stunning dish used to be served in many of the top three-star restaurants all over France. It's fairly rich but is a real classic and a great dish to learn and to serve for special occasions.

1.5 kg (3 lb 5 oz) cooked yabbies (or other crayfish)

60 ml (2 fl oz/¼ cup) olive oil

45 g (1½ oz) salted butter

3 French shallots, thinly sliced

1 fennel stalk

1 tablespoon tomato paste (concentrated purée)

1 tomato, diced

60 ml (2 fl oz/¼ cup) cognac

125 ml (4 fl oz/½ cup) Madeira

125 ml (4 fl oz/½ cup) white wine, plus 2 tablespoons extra

500 ml (17 fl oz/2 cups) crayfish or fish stock

1 bay leaf

2 thyme sprigs

Detach and reserve the yabby heads from the bodies and shell the yabby tails.

Heat 2 tablespoons of the oil in a heavy, cast-iron saucepan. When very hot, add the yabby heads and stir well for a couple of minutes, pressing on the heads from time to time to extract more flavour.

Add half the butter to the pan then add the shallots and fennel and stir well. Add the tomato paste and stir well. Stir in the diced tomato, cognac, Madeira and wine and bring to the boil. Add the stock, bay leaf and thyme and simmer for 20 minutes, uncovered. Stir in the cream and cayenne pepper and cook for a further 5 minutes.

Strain the yabby sauce through a chinois or very fine sieve into a saucepan, pressing on the shells to extract the maximum flavour. Simmer the sauce over a medium heat until reduced to about 325 ml (11 fl oz).

Place the egg yolks and the 2 extra tablespoons of wine in a medium bowl and sit it over a saucepan of simmering water. Whisk the yolks over the heat for about 5 minutes until light and fluffy. Remove the bowl from the saucepan and gradually add the melted butter, whisking continuously to form a creamy sauce. Whisk in the lemon juice.

80 ml (2½ fl oz/⅓ cup) pouring cream

a pinch of cayenne pepper

2 egg yolks

100 g (3½ oz) salted butter, warm and melted

juice of ¼ lemon

400 g (14 oz) cooked English spinach

1 garlic clove, chopped

salt

freshly ground black pepper

Melt a teaspoon of the remaining butter in a saucepan. Add the cooked spinach and garlic and warm through gently.

Melt the rest of the butter and the remaining 2 tablespoons of oil in a pan and gently reheat the yabby tails. Season to taste with salt and pepper and gently stir in the yabby sauce.

Arrange the spinach in a 25 cm (10 in) gratin dish. Top with the yabbies and sauce and place under a hot grill (broiler) (broiler) until lightly browned on top. Serve immediately.

Serves 4

MUSSEL GRATIN WITH SPINACH

Moules gratinées aux épinards

FROM THE NORTH COAST REGION	BY PHILIPPE MOUCHEL

*This mussel dish is out of this world, and so French,
with the flavour of garlic butter.*

1 tablespoon olive oil

125 g (4½ oz) salted butter

1 French shallot, finely chopped

20 mussels in their shells, thoroughly scrubbed and beards removed

10 parsley stalks, plus 3 tablespoons chopped parsley

60 ml (2 fl oz/¼ cup) dry white wine

2 garlic cloves, chopped

juice of ½ lemon

salt

freshly ground black pepper

200 g (7 oz) baby English spinach leaves

60 ml (2 fl oz/¼ cup) pouring cream

3 tablespoons dry breadcrumbs

Heat the oil and 1 teaspoon of butter in a large saucepan. Stir in the shallot and cook for 2 minutes. Add the mussels, parsley stalks and wine to the pan. Cover with a lid and cook for a few minutes until the mussels have just opened.

Place the rest of the butter in a small bowl, keeping 1 teaspoon in reserve. Add the garlic, chopped parsley, lemon juice and a little salt and pepper.

Heat the remaining teaspoon of butter in a large saucepan and cook the spinach until wilted. Drain well.

Heat the cream in a small saucepan and when it boils, stir in the wilted spinach.

Remove the mussel meat from the shells. Arrange 20 half-shells on a large plate or serving dish. Spoon a little of the creamed spinach into each shell and top with a mussel. Spoon a little herbed butter onto each mussel, then sprinkle lightly with breadcrumbs. Place under a hot grill (broiler) for a few minutes until the breadcrumbs are lightly browned. Serve immediately.

Serves 2

MUSSELS COOKED WITH WHITE WINE & HERBS

Moules marinières

FROM THE ATLANTIC-POITOU REGION | BY PHILIPPE MOUCHEL

A survey done a few years ago showed that the average French person's favourite dish was moules marinières. The French consider it an affordable festive dish to be enjoyed on the terrace of a seaside restaurant during the long days of summer.

2 tablespoons olive oil

2 French shallots, thinly sliced

1.5 kg (3 lb 5 oz) mussels, thoroughly scrubbed and beards removed

100 ml (3½ fl oz) dry white wine

a few parsley sprigs, plus 2 tablespoons chopped parsley

1 bay leaf

2 thyme sprigs

freshly ground black pepper

55 g (2 oz) salted butter, cut into small pieces

Heat the oil in a large saucepan over a gentle heat. Add the shallots and cook, stirring continuously, for a few minutes. Add the mussels, white wine, parsley sprigs, bay leaf and thyme, and season with pepper. Cover with a lid and steam the mussels for about 5 minutes, until they have all opened. Shake the pan a couple of times during the cooking.

Lift the mussels out of the pan into a large serving bowl. Bring the mussel juices to the boil and boil for 2 minutes. Add the butter and stir until melted. Stir in the chopped parsley, pour the liquid over the mussels and serve at once.

Serves 2–3

POACHED OYSTERS WITH POTATOES & CHIVE SAUCE

Huîtres pochées sauce ciboulette en pommes de terre

FROM THE VENDÉE REGION

Beautiful beaches and charming fishing ports line the Atlantic coast of the Vendée region. It is known for its seafood, and there are several islands not far from the mainland that produce some of France's finest oysters.

6 new potatoes

50 g (1¾ oz) salted butter, cut into small cubes

1 shallot, finely chopped

1 tablespoon white wine vinegar

125 ml (4 fl oz/ ½ cup) dry white wine

freshly ground pepper

1 teaspoon pouring cream

12 freshly opened oysters

2 tablespoons finely snipped chives

a few mixed green salad leaves and herbs

Cook the potatoes in salted boiling water until just done. Drain and peel the potatoes as soon as they can be handled. Place in warm water until ready to use.

Melt 1 teaspoon of butter in a small saucepan on a medium heat. Stir in the chopped shallot and cook on a medium heat for 1 minute. Add the vinegar and about 2 tablespoons white wine. Season with pepper and simmer until the liquid has almost evaporated.

Add the cream to the shallots and bring to a simmer. Whisk in the remaining butter, bit by bit, until creamy. Remove the pan from the heat.

Drain the potatoes. Cut each potato in half and scoop out a teaspoon of flesh from the centre. Remove the oysters from their shells.

Bring the remaining wine to a simmer in a second pan, then gently place the oysters in the pan, discarding the shells, and poach for about 20 seconds. Turn off the heat, drain the oysters and place in the sauce. Add the cut chives.

Divide the 12 potato halves between two plates. Top each potato half with an oyster and spoon over a little sauce. Garnish the plates with a few green leaves and serve.

Serves 2

CHEESE FONDUE LES ALPAGES

Fondue les alpages

| FROM THE ALPS REGION | BY BERNARD MURE-RAVAUD |

I had never eaten a great fondue until I tasted this dish prepared by a cheese master using wonderful cheeses. It's easy to make; the secret is to melt the cheese slowly. You will need a cheese fondue set.

400 g (14 oz) Beaufort cheese

200 g (7 oz) Abondance cheese

400 g (14 oz) Comté cheese

250 ml (8½ fl oz/1 cup) dry white wine

1 x one-day-old baguette, cut into 1 cm (½ in) slices

Trim the rind of all the cheeses and grate the cheeses very finely. Don't compress the grated cheese.

Place half the wine in a fondue pan on a low heat. Add about one-third of the cheese and stir using a wooden spoon as the cheese starts melting.

When the cheese is well on the way to melting, add half the remaining wine and half the remaining cheese, stirring as it continues to melt. Then add the remaining wine and cheese and stir again until it has almost melted.

Lift the cheese slightly from the pan, using a spoon, to give it a bit of elasticity. The cheese is ready when it is stretchy. This is now the fondue.

Do not allow the fondue to boil; it must not become too hot. Keep the fondue warm on a fondue burner.

Cut the baguette slices in half. Attach pieces of bread to fondue forks and dip the bread in the cheese, twisting the fork until the cheese sticks to the bread.

Serves 4–8

Salads &
Vegetables

GABRIEL
GATÉ

BEETROOT & WALNUT SALAD

Salade de betteraves aux noix

FROM THE PICARDY REGION

---

*The cold, fertile soil of Picardy is perfect for growing beetroot,
and baby beetroot have become a real gourmet item.
This is delicious served with a smooth goat's cheese.*

---

3 red baby beetroot
(beets)

3 yellow baby beetroot
(beets)

salt

freshly ground black
pepper

2 teaspoons raspberry
vinegar

½ teaspoon mustard

1½ tablespoons walnut
oil

2 tablespoons smooth
goat's cheese

2 tablespoons walnuts,
halved

2 tablespoons finely
snipped chives

Cook the cleaned baby beetroot in a saucepan of
salted boiling water for about 20 minutes or until tender.
Drain the beetroots and cool in cold water.

Peel and halve the beetroot. It's a good idea to use
gloves.

In a bowl, mix the vinegar with the mustard, a little salt
and pepper and the walnut oil.

If the goat's cheese is firm, soften it with a spoon, then
spread it in the centre of two plates.

Place the beetroot pieces attractively around the goat's
cheese and scatter the walnut pieces over the top.

Drizzle the dressing over the beetroot and sprinkle with
chives.

Serves 2

GOURMET CHEESE SALAD

Salade gourmande au fromage

FROM THE FRANCHE-COMTÉ REGION

This type of smart salad can be served for a light al fresco lunch. It's easy to present it attractively on plates. You can serve the dressing separately.

4 small cooked beetroots (beets), finely sliced

salt

freshly ground pepper

1 teaspoon dijon mustard

1 tablespoon raspberry vinegar or red wine vinegar

3 tablespoons walnut oil

1 small witlof (chicory/Belgian endive)

1 apple

2 tablespoons walnut pieces

about 80 g (2¾ oz) Comté cheese, cut into 12 thin slices

about 80 g (2¾ oz) Morbier cheese, cut into 12 thin slices

6 hard-boiled quail eggs, peeled and halved (optional)

2 tablespoons finely snipped chives

12 small edible flowers

Line four plates with the beetroot slices.

In a bowl, mix together a little salt, pepper, mustard and vinegar, then mix in the walnut oil.

Cut the witlof and apple into small sticks and place in a bowl. Mix in half the dressing and the walnut pieces.

Spoon some of the mixed salad in the centre of each plate on top of the beetroot and place the cheese slices around the salad. Garnish each plate with three halved quail eggs and spoon a little dressing on top of the cheese.

Sprinkle with chives and decorate with edible flowers.

Serves 4

POTATO GALETTES WITH WALNUT & ROQUEFORT CHEESE SALAD

Galettes de pomme de terre, salade de Roquefort aux noix

FROM THE LANGUEDOC REGION

This dish is so French — and so typical of the northern part of Languedoc, not far from where the famous Roquefort blue cheese is made. The use of duck fat to cook the potatoes is essential for the authentic flavour. It is available from specialist butchers, good delicatessens and some supermarkets.

1 garlic clove, finely chopped

salt

freshly ground pepper

1 tablespoon red wine vinegar

3 tablespoons olive oil

80 g (2¾ oz) mixed green leaves

60 g (2 oz) Roquefort cheese, broken into small pieces

4 shelled walnuts, very roughly chopped

2 medium potatoes

2 tablespoons chopped parsley

2 tablespoons duck fat

Place half the garlic in a large mixing bowl with a little salt and pepper and the vinegar and whisk together well. Whisk in the oil gradually. Add the green leaves, cheese and walnuts to the bowl and toss everything together gently.

Grate the potatoes onto a plate and pat dry with paper towel. Tip into a bowl with the remaining garlic and the chopped parsley. Season with salt and pepper and mix well.

Heat the duck fat in a 20 cm (8 in) frying pan. When the fat is hot, add the potato mixture to form a large galette about 1 cm (½ in) thick. Press with the back of a spoon or fork to flatten and cook on a medium heat for a few minutes. Carefully turn the galette over and cook the other side. (To turn the galette, slide it onto a plate, then invert the plate and slide the galette back into the pan.)

Cut the cooked galette in half or quarters and divide between two plates. Serve with the dressed salad.

Serves 2

ROSCOVITE SALAD WITH CAULIFLOWER & PRAWNS

Salade Roscovite

FROM THE BRITTANY REGION	BY PHILIPPE MOUCHEL

This classic Breton salad was named after the coastal town of Roscoff in Brittany. The locals adore cauliflower, which is just as important as the prawnss in this lovely salad. For an elegant presentation, use 10 cm (4 in) rings.

¼ cauliflower, cut into medium florets

12 cm (4¾ in) piece of cucumber, cut into cubes

2 potatoes, cooked in their skins and cubed

1 egg yolk

1 teaspoon dijon mustard

salt

freshly ground pepper

1 lemon

125 ml (4½ fl oz/½ cup) extra-virgin olive oil, plus 2 tablespoons extra

3 tablespoons pouring cream

3 tablespoons chervil leaves

3 tablespoons tarragon leaves

16 cooked prawns (shrimp), peeled and deveined

4 hard-boiled eggs, quartered

Cook the cauliflower florets in boiling salted water for a few minutes, until just tender. Drain and cool in cold water. Drain again and cut into smaller pieces.

Place the cauliflower, cucumber and potato in a bowl.

In a second bowl make a mayonnaise by whisking the egg yolk with the mustard, a little salt and pepper and a few drops of lemon juice. Slowly drizzle in the oil, whisking continuously until thick and creamy. Whisk in the cream and set aside.

Roughly chop two-thirds of the chervil and tarragon leaves, reserving the rest for garnish. Add to the vegetables and toss with the extra 2 tablespoons of oil.

Carefully spread 2 tablespoons of the creamy mayonnaise over each of the four plates. Place a PVC ring in the centre and spoon a few tablespoons of the vegetable salad into the rings. Lift the ring away carefully.

Divide the prawns and hard-boiled eggs among the plates, arranging them attractively around the vegetable salad. Scatter with the reserved chervil and tarragon on top and serve.

Serves 4

LIÈGEOISE SALAD WITH MUSSELS

Salade Liègeoise aux moules

FROM THE NORTHERN FRANCE/BELGIUM REGION

This delicious potato, bean and bacon salad is very popular in the north of France and was originally a speciality of Liège. Here I serve it with mussels, which the French adore. It can also be served on its own or with grilled meat or fish, and makes a lovely summer starter.

2 medium all-purpose potatoes

200 g (7 oz) green beans

500 g (1 lb 2 oz) mussels, cleaned

30 ml (1 fl oz) dry white wine or beer

salt

freshly ground pepper

2 bacon rashers, diced

1 tablespoon extra-virgin olive oil

1 shallot, finely chopped

½ small brown onion, finely chopped

2 tablespoons red wine vinegar

3 tablespoons chopped parsley

2 tablespoons finely snipped chives

In a saucepan, boil the potatoes in their skins until cooked, then drain. Add the beans to a saucepan of boiling water and continue boiling until cooked. Drain and refresh in cold water.

Place the mussels and the wine in a large saucepan, cover with a lid and bring to the boil. The mussels will open and be cooked in a few minutes. Shake the pan a few times during the cooking.

When all the mussels are open, drain the liquid and remove the mussels from the shells.

Peel and cube the potatoes, place in a bowl with the cooked beans and season with a little salt and pepper.

Cook the diced bacon in a non-stick pan for a few minutes, then transfer to a plate.

Add the olive oil to the pan and cook the chopped shallot and onion until soft and lightly browned. Stir in the vinegar and briefly bring to the boil. Add the cooked onion to the potatoes and beans and combine, then gently mix in the bacon and chopped parsley.

Season the mussels with pepper and chives.

Place a little of the Liègeoise salad on each plate, arrange the mussels around the salad and serve.

Serves 2

HERRING SALAD WITH POTATOES

Salade de harengs aux pommes de terre

FROM THE NORTHERN FRANCE REGION | BY PHILIPPE MOUCHEL

Forty years ago this was a popular salad served in working-class French restaurants. Marinated herring fillets in oil were an easy dish to prepare and it made a tasty, satisfying salad for workers. You'll find herring in oil in European-style delicatessens and gourmet stores.

salt

freshly ground pepper

1 tablespoon red wine vinegar

1 teaspoon dijon mustard

3 tablespoons vegetable oil

450–500 g (1 lb–1 lb 2 oz) cooked potatoes in their skins (kipflers are great)

1 tablespoon dry white wine

1 large shallot, finely chopped

2 tablespoons chopped parsley

2 tablespoons finely chopped tarragon leaves

4 herring fillets, marinated in oil and vegetables

In a bowl, mix together a little salt and pepper, the vinegar, mustard and oil to make a dressing.

Peel and slice the cooked potatoes. While they are still warm, mix them with the wine, then mix in the chopped shallot, dressing, chopped parsley and tarragon.

Spoon a little potato salad onto each plate then top with a herring fillet and a little vegetable garnish from the marinade. Season with a bit more black pepper and serve.

Serves 4

CRAYFISH & POTATO SALAD

Salade de langouste aux pommes de terre

| FROM THE ATLANTIC ISLAND REGION | BY PHILIPPE MOUCHEL |

The Atlantic coast south of the Loire River is dotted with many islands, one of which is Noirmoutier, which is famous for its shellfish and new-season potatoes. As a boy I enjoyed several summer holidays in Noirmoutier.

1 x 800 g (1 lb 12 oz) cooked crayfish

2–4 small new potatoes, cooked in their skins

125 g (4½ oz) green beans, cooked but firm

2 tomatoes, peeled, quartered and seeded

a few green salad leaves

juice of 1 lemon

sea salt

freshly ground black pepper

60 ml (2 fl oz/¼ cup) olive oil

2 tablespoons finely snipped chives

fresh herbs, to serve (optional)

Remove the crayfish from the shell and cut the tail meat into slices just less than 1 cm (½ in) thick.

Peel and slice the potatoes.

Arrange the crayfish and potato slices attractively on two plates. Garnish with a little bouquet of green beans and four tomato quarters. Top with salad leaves.

To make the dressing, whisk the lemon juice with a little salt and pepper then whisk in the olive oil. Add the chives and drizzle the dressing over the salad.

Garnish with extra fresh herbs if you wish, then serve.

Serves 2

CRAYFISH À LA PARISIENNE

Langouste à la Parisienne

FROM THE PARIS REGION | BY PHILIPPE MOUCHEL

During my younger days I worked in a wonderful Parisian seafood restaurant called Prunier where I learned to prepare this classic dish of crayfish with a diced vegetable and mayonnaise salad. This is Philippe's recipe and to present the dish he uses 10 cm (4 in) rings.

3 tablespoons diced turnips, about 6 mm (¼ in) square

3 tablespoons diced carrots, about 6 mm (¼ in) square

3 tablespoons diced beans, about 6 mm (¼ in) square

3 tablespoons diced potatoes, about 6 mm (¼ in) square

2 tablespoons peas

salt

1 egg yolk

2 tablespoons mustard

freshly ground black pepper

2 teaspoons vinegar

100 ml (3½ fl oz) olive oil, plus a little extra for drizzling

1 x 400 g (14 oz) cooked crayfish

a few cos (romaine) lettuce leaves

a few chives, to garnish

Cook the turnips, carrots, beans, potatoes and peas separately in boiling salted water until tender (either use separate saucepans or change the water for each vegetable). Drain each vegetable well then place on a clean cloth to absorb excess water.

In a bowl, mix the egg yolk with the mustard, a little salt and pepper and the vinegar. Gradually pour in the oil, whisking continuously, until you obtain a thick mayonnaise.

Place the cooked, drained vegetables in a bowl and mix in half the mayonnaise.

Remove the crayfish tail meat and cut it into 1 cm (½ in) slices.

To serve, place a PVC ring in the centre of each plate. Spoon in one-third of the vegetable mixture and flatten the surface with a spoon. Arrange a few overlapping slices of crayfish on top of the vegetables and carefully remove the PVC rings. Top with a few lettuce leaves and a small dollop of mayonnaise.

Drizzle on a little extra oil, sprinkle with a few chives and serve.

Serves 3

GOURMET YABBY SALAD WITH PEARS & WALNUTS

Salade gourmande d'écrevisses aux poires et aux noix

FROM THE DAUPHINÉE ALPS REGION

This is an outstanding starter, especially if you can source fresh yabbies. They have a uniquely delicate and sweet flavour and are a popular dish served in the top French restaurants of the Alps region. If yabbies are not available, try prawns (shrimp) or scampi.

about 28 cooked yabbies

2 teaspoons red wine vinegar

juice of ½ lemon

salt

freshly ground black pepper

3 tablespoons walnut oil

1 shallot, finely chopped

100 g (3 ½ oz) cooked baby green beans, cooled

45 g (1½ oz) mixed green salad leaves

60 g (2 oz) walnut halves

1 pear, just ripe

Shell, devein and clean the yabbies.

In a bowl, mix together the vinegar, lemon juice, a little salt, pepper, walnut oil and chopped shallot.

Add the green beans, the mixed green leaves, the walnut halves and the yabbies and mix gently together.

Halve and core the pear and slice thinly.

Form a circle of the pear slices in the centre of each plate. Gently spoon the salad on top of the pear slices and serve.

Serves 4

DUCK SALAD WITH GREEN BEANS & FOIE GRAS

Salade de canard aux haricots verts et au foie gras

FROM THE SOUTH WEST REGION

This type of gourmet French salad was served in the top restaurants forty years ago when I was working as a young chef. It's simple to prepare and so refined, especially if you can get some good quality foie gras.

---

2 boneless duck fillets, skin on

salt

freshly ground black pepper

1 tablespoon extra-virgin olive oil

150 g (5½ oz) green beans, topped and tailed

1 tablespoon red wine vinegar

3 tablespoons walnut oil

½ shallot, finely chopped

1 tablespoon chopped walnuts

1 tablespoon finely snipped chives

8 cherry tomatoes, halved

2 tablespoons foie gras, cut into small squares

Preheat the oven to 100°C (210°F).

Season the duck fillets with salt and pepper.

Heat the olive oil in an ovenproof frying pan on a medium heat, then cook the duck fillets, skin side down, for 2 minutes. Turn the duck fillets over, then place in the preheated oven to roast for about 12 minutes.

Remove the duck from the oven and allow to rest and cool for about 15 minutes.

Meanwhile, cook the green beans in a saucepan of salted boiling water until just done. Drain the beans and cool in cold water, then drain again.

Place a pinch of salt and a little black pepper in a bowl. Mix in the vinegar and walnut oil. Stir in the chopped shallot, walnuts and half the chives. Add the halved cherry tomatoes and the beans and mix gently.

Thinly slice the duck fillets and arrange in a circle on the plate. Spoon the bean salad into the centre and top with the foie gras squares.

Sprinkle with the remaining chives and serve.

Serves 2

SILVERBEET GRATIN

Gratin de blettes

FROM THE ALPS REGION

Many French people eat their main meal of the day at lunchtime, then for dinner they often have a satisfying vegetarian dish such as this lovely silverbeet gratin, an Alpine speciality that uses flavoursome local cheese.

8 silverbeet (Swiss chard) leaves with the stalks, well washed

55 g (2 oz) salted butter

salt

freshly ground pepper

¼ teaspoon freshly grated nutmeg

125 ml (4 fl oz/½ cup) cream

20 g (¾ oz) plain (all-purpose) flour

300 ml (10 fl oz) milk

a pinch of cayenne pepper

about 65 g (2¼ oz) finely grated gruyère cheese

3 tablespoons dry breadcrumbs

Separate the silverbeet stalks and leaves. Cut the stalks into 3 cm (1¼ in) pieces and shred the leaves.

Heat a third of the butter in a saucepan. Add the silverbeet stalks and stir for 3 minutes over a medium heat. Season with salt and pepper, cover with water and cook for about 15 minutes, or until soft. Drain well and set aside.

Heat another third of the butter in a different saucepan. Add the shredded silverbeet leaves and cook until wilted. Season with nutmeg, a little salt and pepper and half the cream. Set aside.

Melt the rest of the butter in a saucepan over a medium heat. Whisk in the flour and cook for 1 minute. Slowly add the milk, whisking constantly until it forms a smooth white sauce. Season with cayenne pepper, stir in the remaining cream and simmer for 2 minutes. Add the drained silverbeet stalks and mix in about 2 tablespoons of the gruyère cheese.

Spoon the cooked silverbeet leaves into a 25 cm (10 in) gratin dish. Pour on the white sauce, then scatter on the remaining cheese and top with the breadcrumbs. Place under a hot grill (broiler) (broiler) until lightly browned. Be careful when serving, it's very hot!

Serves 3–4

PROVENÇAL VEGETABLE BAKE

Tian aux légumes Provençals

FROM THE PROVENCE REGION

This excellent Provençal vegetable dish is typical of the region and a good example of how creative the locals are with their vegetables. 'Tian' is actually the name of the cooking dish used. You will need a large ovenproof dish, made of either porcelain or cast iron.

125 ml (4½ fl oz/½ cup) extra-virgin olive oil

1 large brown onion, thinly sliced

1 red or green capsicum (pepper), seeds removed, thinly sliced

2 medium eggplants (aubergines), halved and thinly sliced

1 garlic clove, finely chopped

4 medium zucchini (courgettes)

6 tomatoes, cut into 5 mm (¼ in) slices

salt

freshly ground black pepper

2 tablespoons finely chopped lemon thyme

2 tablespoons grated parmesan cheese

3 tablespoons dry breadcrumbs

Heat half the oil in a large, non-stick frying pan. Add the onion and cook, stirring continuously, for 2 minutes. Add the capsicum and cook for 2 minutes, stirring again. Add the eggplant and garlic and cook over low heat for about 20 minutes, or until the vegetables are soft.

Preheat the oven to 160°C (320°F).

Peel off the zucchini skin in vertical strips, 1 cm (½ in) apart, so that strips of skin remain. Cut the zucchini into 5 mm (¼ in) slices.

Transfer the cooked vegetables to an ovenproof dish. Arrange the zucchini and tomato slices on top of the vegetables in alternate, overlapping rows. Season with salt and pepper and sprinkle evenly with lemon thyme. Drizzle evenly with the remaining oil. Bake for about 30 minutes. Sprinkle with parmesan cheese and breadcrumbs and bake for a further 10 minutes.

Serves 6

BELGIAN WITLOF GRATIN

Endives au gratin

FROM THE NORTHERN FRANCE/BELGIUM REGION

This speciality of northern France is a popular winter dish that my mother would prepare every week for dinner for our family as a main meal. I remember not liking the bitterness of the witlof at first. I love it now.

4 medium witlof (chicory/Belgian endive)

80 g (2¾ oz) butter, cut into small pieces

salt

freshly ground pepper

4 tablespoons chopped parsley

50 g (1¾ oz) plain (all-purpose) flour

500 ml (17 fl oz/2 cups) milk

a pinch of grated nutmeg

a pinch of cayenne pepper

120 g (4½ oz) gruyère cheese, grated

4–8 thin slices of ham

Preheat the oven to 220°C (430°F).

Remove any damaged witlof leaves and trim the hard ends, keeping each witlof in one piece.

Place about 20 g (¾ oz) butter in a small saucepan. Add the witlof on top and season with salt and pepper. Sprinkle 2 tablespoons chopped parsley over the top and cover with a layer of baking paper. Place on a low heat and cook for 20–25 minutes, turning the witlof several times during the cooking. Transfer the cooked witlof to a plate and leave to cool slightly.

Melt the remaining butter in a saucepan on a medium heat. Whisk in the plain flour and cook for 2–3 minutes. Bit by bit, whisk in the cold milk until you obtain a smooth sauce. Cook for 2 minutes and season with salt, pepper, nutmeg and cayenne pepper and stir in 80 g (2¾ oz) grated gruyère cheese.

When the witlof is cool enough to handle, wrap each one in a slice or two of ham. Place in a greased gratin dish and spoon the sauce over the top. Sprinkle with the remaining chopped parsley and remaining gruyère.

Place in the preheated oven and cook for 10–15 minutes until golden brown. Take care, it's very hot!

Serves 4

Provence
Grenaille blanche
Charlotte
2.50
€ le kilo

CI
Grenaille
2
Provence
Roseval
le kg

Ardèche
Charlotte

CI

POTATO & REBLOCHON CHEESE GRATIN

Tartiflette au reblochon

FROM THE HAUTE-SAVOIE/ALPS REGION

This tasty gratin-style dish, often served in the alpine ski resorts, is a wonderful choice for a winter dinner and a popular party dish for young adults.

---

20 g (¾ oz) salted butter

2 brown onions, thinly sliced

250 g (9 oz) smoked bacon, diced

1.5 kg (3 lb 5 oz) all-purpose potatoes, cooked in their skins and cut in 1 cm (½ in) slices

salt

freshly ground pepper

3 tablespoons crème fraîche

1 reblochon cheese (or 450 g/1 lb of another washed-rind cheese), cut in half horizontally and then in half vertically

125 ml (4 fl oz/½ cup) dry white wine

2 tablespoons chopped parsley

Preheat the oven to 180°C (350°F).

Heat the butter in a frying pan and cook the onion for 3–4 minutes. Add the bacon and cook for a few more minutes before adding the potatoes. Stir well, season with salt and pepper and cook for about 5 minutes.

Butter a large gratin dish. Line the base of the dish with the potato preparation. Spoon the crème fraîche on top and finish with a layer of cheese. Pour the wine down the side of the dish.

Bake in the preheated oven for about 10 minutes or until it bubbles and the cheese has just melted.

Serve sprinkled with a little chopped parsley.

Serves 8–10

POTATO PURÉE WITH CHEESE

Aligot

FROM THE SOUTH AUVERGNE REGION | BY NICOLAS POELAERT

Thirty years ago this dish was really only known in the south of the mountainous region of Auvergne, but now that the world has gone crazy about mashed potato it's become very fashionable to serve aligot at foodie dinners all around the world.

250 g (9 oz) potatoes (desirée are good)

salt

40 g (1½ oz) salted butter

50 ml (1¾ fl oz) thickened cream

90 g (3 oz) strong-flavoured melting cow's milk cheese, such as gruyère, thinly sliced or grated (Nicolas used a Tomme cow's milk cheese)

Peel and quarter the potatoes. Place the potatoes in a saucepan filled with cold salted water and boil until tender.

Drain the potatoes and push them through a mouli into a saucepan, add the butter and cream.

Place the pan on a medium heat and, using a wooden spoon, stir in the cheese, stirring in one direction until the cheese has melted and the purée is elastic and stretches like a dough.

Aligot is often served with prosciutto-style ham and a green salad.

Serves 2–3

RATATOUILLE WITH LEMON CHANTILLY

Verrine de ratatouille Niçoise au chantilly citron

FROM THE NICE/RIVIERA REGION

Popular both in France and around the world, ratatouille is a speciality of the Mediterranean city of Nice.

60 ml (2 fl oz/¼ cup) extra-virgin olive oil

1 small onion, diced

1 tablespoon chopped thyme

1 garlic clove, chopped

1 red capsicum (pepper), diced

1 green capsicum (pepper), diced

1 medium eggplant (aubergine), diced

1 medium zucchini (courgette), diced

salt

freshly ground pepper

3 tomatoes

250 ml (8½ fl oz/1 cup) crème fraîche

juice of ½ lemon

2 tablespoons pitted black olives, diced

6 niçoise olives (small, like ligurian olives)

Heat the olive oil in a saucepan. Add the onion and thyme and stir on a medium heat for 2 minutes. Stir in the chopped garlic, the red and green capsicums and cook for a few minutes. Add the eggplant, stir for a few minutes, then add the zucchini. Stir well and season with salt and pepper.

Halve the tomatoes and squeeze out the seeds. Discard the tomato seeds, dice the flesh and add to the other vegetables. Stir well and simmer for about 15 minutes or until the vegetables are soft. Transfer to a bowl, allow to cool and refrigerate when cold.

In a bowl, season the crème fraîche with salt and pepper and whip until almost firm. Add the lemon juice and continue whipping until the chantilly is firm.

Transfer the ratatouille into six glasses. Top with the diced, pitted olives, pipe the cream on top and garnish with an olive.

Serves 6

SAVOY POTATO GRATIN

Gratin Savoyard

I am a cheese lover and the cheeses from the Alps really satisfy me with their beautiful nutty flavour. The local gruyère and Beaufort are great cooking cheeses, and in this classic gratin the savoyard cheese is the star. Alpine families love this classic potato dish, which is very easy to make and delicious. It's usually served at dinner with a salad or at Sunday lunch as part of a feast.

1.5 kg (3 lb 5 oz) all-purpose potatoes of regular shape (desiree are good)

salt

freshly ground pepper

nutmeg, grated

80 g (2¾ oz) butter

150 g (5½ oz) gruyère cheese, grated

150 g (5½ oz) Beaufort cheese, grated

375 ml (12½ fl oz/ 1½ cups) chicken stock

Preheat the oven to 200°C (400°F).

Peel the potatoes, cut them into 3 mm (⅛ in) slices and place in a bowl with salt, pepper and a little grated nutmeg. Mix well together.

Generously grease a medium to large ovenproof gratin dish with one-third of the butter. Place half the potato slices neatly in the dish and top with the grated gruyère cheese. Cover with the remaining potatoes, taking time to make a regular pattern with the slices. Sprinkle the beaufort cheese on top and dot with knobs of the remaining butter.

Carefully pour the chicken stock into the dish.

Bake in the preheated oven for 15 minutes, then lower the heat to 150°C (300°F) and cook for a further 45 minutes or until the potatoes are soft.

Serves 6–8

BABY BEETROOT WITH BURNED CARROT PURÉE

Petites betteraves à la purée de carottes brûlées

| FROM THE NORTHERN FRANCE REGION | BY NICOLAS POELAERT |

Beetroot and other root vegetables are grown in the north of France. They have gained enormous popularity in the last 20 years and this delicious dish is a good example of modern French cuisine.

2 medium carrots

salt

freshly ground pepper

2 tablespoons extra-virgin olive oil

8 baby beetroot (beets)

10 g (¼ oz) salted butter

a selection of herbs and flowers from the garden (chervil, tarragon, parsley)

Place the carrots on a grill plate or under the grill (broiler) to burn the skin off. When the skin is dark, put the carrots in a steamer and cook until tender.

Transfer the carrots to a blender, season with salt, pepper and the olive oil and blend to a very smooth purée. The purée will be very dark and have a smoky flavour.

Wash the beetroot well and trim the leaves and roots. Cook beetroot in salted boiling water until tender. Peel and quarter the beetroot.

Heat the butter in a saucepan and toss the beetroot in the butter.

Spread a little carrot purée on each plate. Top with the beetroot pieces and garnish with the herbs and flowers.

Serves 2

BAKED HARICOT BEANS WITH SMOKED BACON

Haricots blancs des Pyrénées au lard fumé

FROM THE PYRÉNÉES REGION

This lovely baked bean recipe, cooked with charcuterie like tasty bacon and sausage to boost the flavour, is a perfect example of a traditional French family dish.

150 g (5½ oz/¾ cup) dried haricot beans

½ onion, sliced

2 garlic cloves, crushed

2 thyme sprigs, chopped

100 g (3½ oz) smoked bacon

1 spicy Spanish-style sausage

1 tablespoon extra-virgin olive oil

1 teaspoon tomato paste (concentrated purée)

2 tablespoons dry white wine

30 g (1 oz) salted butter

2 tablespoons chopped parsley

1 extra garlic clove, finely chopped

freshly ground black pepper

Place the dried haricot beans in a bowl. Cover with plenty of cold water and soak overnight.

Drain the beans, place in a saucepan and cover with cold water. Add the onion, crushed garlic and thyme and bring to the boil. Simmer for about 1 hour until the beans are tender.

Drain the cooked beans and discard the onion and garlic.

Cut the bacon and sausage into slices 1 cm (½ in) thick.

Heat the olive oil in a frying pan and cook the bacon for 1 minute. Add the sausage and cook for 2 minutes. Stir in the tomato paste, the beans and white wine and cook gently for a few minutes.

Stir in the butter, chopped parsley and extra garlic and season with black pepper.

Serves 2–3

Fish & Seafood

SCALLOPS THE PARISIAN WAY

Coquilles St Jacques à la Parisienne

FROM THE PARIS REGION | BY PHILIPPE MOUCHEL

The French are very fond of scallops and this delicate dish is a popular family favourite for Sunday lunch. If you have the chance to visit Paris, go to one of the many produce markets and admire the outstanding fish available. This dish looks lovely when presented on empty, clean scallop shells.

12 fresh scallops, cleaned and briefly rinsed

8 mushrooms, sliced

250 ml (8½ fl oz/1 cup) strong fish stock

20 g (¾ oz) salted butter

20 g (¾ oz) plain (all-purpose) flour

60 ml (2 fl oz/¼ cup) pouring cream

1 egg yolk

juice of ½ lemon

salt

freshly ground pepper

60 g (2 oz) finely grated gruyère cheese

2 tablespoons dried breadcrumbs

Place the scallops in a saucepan with the mushrooms. Add the stock and place over a medium heat. Bring to a low simmer and cook for 20 seconds. Drain the scallops and mushrooms, and reserve and cool the stock. Divide the scallops and mushrooms among four clean scallop shells and set aside.

Melt the butter in a small saucepan over a medium heat. Whisk in the flour and cook for 2 minutes. Slowly add the cool stock, whisking constantly until it thickens. Stir in 2 tablespoons of the cream and cook for a further 2 minutes.

In a small bowl, mix the egg yolk with the rest of the cream. Remove the sauce from the heat and whisk in the cream and egg mixture. Stir in the lemon juice and season with salt and pepper.

Spoon some sauce over the scallops and mushrooms in the shells. Sprinkle with a little grated cheese and breadcrumbs. Place under a hot grill (broiler) (broiler) until golden brown. (Alternatively, place the shells in a hot oven.) Serve immediately.

Serves 4

PAN-FRIED SCALLOPS WITH CAULIFLOWER

Coquilles St Jacques à la purée de chou-fleur

FROM THE BRITTANY REGION

The scallops of Brittany are out of this world.

100 g (3½ oz) cauliflower

10 g (¼ oz) salted butter

salt

freshly ground black pepper

juice of ½ lemon

2 tablespoons olive oil

1 tablespoon roasted hazelnut pieces

1 teaspoon finely chopped tarragon

½ teaspoon vegetable oil

200 g (7 oz) fresh scallops

Steam the cauliflower until tender. Drain and blend the cauliflower to a purée with the butter and a little salt and pepper.

In a bowl, combine the lemon juice, a little salt and pepper, the olive oil, hazelnuts and tarragon.

Heat the vegetable oil in a non-stick frying pan and cook the scallops for about 20 seconds on each side over a high heat.

Drop the scallops into the dressing and toss gently.

Spoon the cauliflower purée onto two plates and top with the scallops and dressing.

Serves 2

SCALLOP MOUSSE WITH PRAWN SAUCE

Mousseline de coquilles St Jacques sauce crevette

FROM THE NORTHERN FRANCE REGION

The fish and seafood from the cold waters of the Channel are superb, and this scallop mousse is a very delicate dish suitable for the finest dinner party. You need four 125 ml (4 fl oz/½ cup) buttered soufflé moulds.

350 g (12½ oz) cleaned scallops, without the roe

2 eggs

200 ml (7 fl oz) cream

salt

freshly ground black pepper

8 prawns (shrimp) with the shells

1 tablespoon olive oil

1 French shallot, finely chopped

10 fennel seeds

3 tablespoons tomato passata (puréed tomatoes)

100 ml (3½ fl oz) dry white wine

a little chilli powder

4 tablespoons finely snipped chives

Preheat the oven to 140°C (275°F).

Blend the scallops to a purée. Add the eggs and blend well. Mix in 100 ml (3½ fl oz) of the cream and season with salt and pepper. Spoon the mousse into the prepared soufflé moulds and place the moulds on a baking tray. Pour 2 cm (¾ in) of hot water into the tray around the mould and bake in the preheated oven for 20 minutes.

Peel and clean the prawns and cut each into three pieces.

Heat the oil in a pan and cook the prawn shells on a high heat for a few minutes. Add the shallot and fennel seeds and cook for 2 minutes. Add the tomato passata and the wine. Bring to the boil and simmer for 5 minutes.

Add the remaining cream to the pan, stir well and cook for a few minutes. Strain the sauce, then return it to the pan and gently cook the prawn pieces in the sauce. Season with salt, pepper and chilli powder.

Unmould each scallop mousse onto four plates. Spoon a little prawn sauce over the top and garnish with pieces of prawn. Sprinkle with chives and serve.

Serves 4

SCAMPI & ARTICHOKE CRÊPES

Crêpes aux langoustines et aux artichauts

FROM THE BRITTANY REGION

*The charming region of Brittany is known for its delicious seafood.
The Bretons love their crêpes and this dish is a superb example
of the regional taste.*

150 g (5½ oz/1 cup) plain (all-purpose) flour

salt

freshly ground pepper

1 egg

250 ml (8½ fl oz/1 cup) milk

80 g (2¾ oz) butter

2 tablespoons finely snipped chives

1 egg yolk mixed with 1 tablespoon water

juice of ¼ lemon

2 tablespoons whipped cream

60 g (2 oz/½ cup) cooked cauliflower florets

220 g (8 oz/1 cup) cooked artichoke hearts, cut into small pieces

12 cooked scampi (10 peeled)

Place the flour, salt and pepper in a bowl. Make a well in the centre and pour the egg and half the milk into the well. Whisk the egg and milk together, then gradually incorporate the flour, slowly adding the rest of the milk to form a smooth, thin mixture. Rest this batter for 15 minutes.

Melt a teaspoon of butter in a crêpe pan. When it begins to foam, whisk the melted butter into the crêpe batter. Stir in half the chives as well.

Ladle enough crêpe batter into the pan to lightly coat the base. Cook the first side then turn the crêpe to cook the other side. Cook three more crêpes in the same way.

Place the egg yolk and water in a small bowl resting over a pan of simmering water. Beat the yolk and water until it becomes light and fluffy, then remove from heat.

Melt half the remaining butter, without boiling it, and then bit by bit whisk it into the egg yolk in the bowl. Season with lemon juice and fold in the whipped cream. This is called a mousseline sauce.

Reheat the cauliflower, artichokes and scampi in the remaining butter. Add the remaining chives.

On each crêpe, place two or three scampi tails and some vegetables. Top with a little sauce and fold each crêpe.

Serve two crêpes per person, garnished with one un-shelled scampi.

Serves 2

YABBIES IN PUFF PASTRY

Ecrevisses en chausson

| FROM THE ALPS REGION | BY PHILIPPE MOUCHEL |

Yabbies are very popular in France and are found on the menus of the best French restaurants, especially around the Alps region where there are lots of freshwater streams.

2 rectangles rolled puff pastry, 8 x 12 cm x 3 mm thick (3 x 4 in x ⅛ in thick)

1 egg yolk

2 teaspoons cold water

6 cm (2½ in) piece carrot

6 cm (2½ in) piece leek

6 cm (2½ in) piece celery

1 teaspoon olive oil

40 g (1½ oz) salted butter

2 tablespoons pouring cream

2 teaspoons finely chopped tarragon

2 teaspoons finely chopped parsley

6 thin slices truffle

12 cooked yabbies, shelled

salt

freshly ground black pepper

Preheat the oven to 180°C (350°F). Line a baking tray with baking paper. Place the puff pastry rectangles on the prepared baking tray. Using the tip of a knife, lightly mark a smaller rectangle inside each pastry rectangle, forming a 5 mm (¼ in) border.

Mix the egg yolk and water together and brush over the pastry. Bake for 15–18 minutes, or until lightly browned and risen. It should rise at least 2 cm (¾ in) if the pastry is good quality.

Thinly slice the carrot, leek and celery, then cut into thin julienne strips. Heat the oil and butter in a small saucepan over a medium heat. Add the vegetables and cook for a few minutes until soft. Add the cream, tarragon and parsley, then add the truffle slices and yabbies and reheat. Season to taste with salt and pepper.

Cut the smaller rectangle out of each cooked pastry rectangle and set this 'lid' aside. Remove any excess pastry from the centre to create a cavity. Divide the yabby and vegetable mixture between the pastry cases, replace the pastry lids and serve straight away.

Serves 2

YABBY TURNOVERS WITH TRUFFLE

Chausson d'écrevisses aux truffes

FROM THE ALPS REGION

Yabbies are a much-loved delicacy in the Alps region, where they are found in its many streams and lakes. Prawns could also be used in this recipe.

1 carrot

1 celery stalk, 20 cm (8 in) long

3 large mushrooms

40 g (1½ oz) butter

2 teaspoons red wine vinegar

salt

freshly ground pepper

8–12 shelled and cleaned yabbies, depending on size

4 rounds of rolled puff pastry, about 12 cm (4 in) diameter x 3 mm (⅛ in) thick

1 egg yolk mixed with 1 teaspoon water

10 g (¼ oz) fresh truffle, cut into fine sticks

Preheat the oven to 200°C (400°F).

Cut the carrot, celery and mushrooms into batons about 4 cm (1½ in) long x 2 mm (¹⁄₁₃ in) thick.

Heat the butter in a frying pan. Add the vinegar and bring to the boil. Add the vegetables and stir-fry until they are soft but still a bit crunchy, then remove from the heat. Season the vegetables with salt and pepper, then briefly stir in the yabbies. Allow to cool.

Lay the puff pastry rounds on the bench and brush the edges with a little diluted egg yolk.

In the centre of each pastry round, place 1 tablespoon of vegetables, two or three yabbies and a little of the fresh truffle. Fold the pastry rounds over, into the shape of a turnover, and seal the edges by pressing with a fork. Brush the top with the remaining diluted egg yolk and make a light criss-cross pattern on top with a fork.

Bake the turnovers in the preheated oven for about 20 minutes until the pastry is well cooked.

Serves 4

RED MULLET WITH TAPENADE & FENNEL SALAD

Filets de rouget poêlé à la tapenade, salade de fenouil

FROM THE PROVENCE REGION | BY PHILIPPE MOUCHEL

Red mullet is a really tasty fish and greatly loved by gourmets. It goes well with strongly flavoured ingredients such as olives, anchovies and fennel. I love it.

80 g (2¾ oz) black olives, pitted

1 teaspoon capers, rinsed

3 anchovy fillets

60 ml (2 fl oz/¼ cup) olive oil

1 garlic clove, finely chopped

3 basil leaves, finely chopped, plus 3 whole leaves

juice of 1 lemon

1 bulb baby fennel, trimmed and thinly sliced

¼ medium red (Spanish) onion, thinly sliced

4 cherry tomatoes, quartered

2 sprigs fennel leaves, chopped (or use dill)

salt

freshly ground black pepper

6 red mullet fillets

To make the tapenade, combine the olives, capers and anchovy fillets in a small food processor and blend to a paste. Continue blending while adding 1½ tablespoons of the oil. Transfer the paste to a bowl and stir in the garlic, chopped basil and a little less than half of the lemon juice. Set aside.

Place the fennel, red onion and cherry tomatoes in a bowl. Roughly tear the whole basil leaves and add them to the bowl with the chopped fennel leaves. Season with a little salt and pepper, half of the remaining oil and the remaining lemon juice. Mix well and set aside.

Heat the remaining oil in a non-stick frying pan over a medium–high heat and cook the red mullet fillets, skin side down, for 2 minutes. Turn the fish and cook for 10 seconds.

Divide the salad between two plates. Arrange three fish fillets on each salad and top with a little tapenade. Serve immediately.

Serves 2

FISH QUENELLES

Quenelles de poisson

| FROM THE LYONNAIS REGION | BY PHILIPPE MOUCHEL |

Philippe Mouchel, a talented chef and my good friend, learned to make fish quenelles when he worked with the world-famous French chef Paul Bocuse in Lyon. This is Philippe's classic and delicious recipe. The quenelles have a unique texture and a wonderful crayfish flavour.

250 ml (8½ fl oz/1 cup) milk

75 g (2¾ oz) salted butter

4 egg yolks

125 g (4½ oz) plain (all-purpose) flour

250 g (9 oz) delicate white fish fillets

1 egg white

100 g (3½ oz) veal kidney fat, cut into very small pieces (available from good butchers)

a pinch of freshly grated nutmeg

salt

freshly ground pepper

400 ml (13½ fl oz) crayfish bisque (make your own or buy a can)

100 g (3½ oz) crayfish meat, cut into small pieces

Bring the milk and butter to the boil in a medium saucepan. In a bowl, mix the egg yolks with the flour. Add to the milk mixture and whisk until it thickens and forms a mass (called a 'panade'). Transfer the panade to a bowl to cool.

Place the fish and egg white in a food processor and blend to a purée. Add the veal kidney fat and pulse briefly. Add the cool panade gradually, pulsing to incorporate, then season with nutmeg, salt and pepper. Transfer to a bowl and refrigerate for at least 1 hour.

Bring a large, wide saucepan of water to a very gentle simmer. Using two large oval spoons, carefully mould some of the mixture into the traditional oval quenelle shape (practice makes perfect!). You should get 6–8 quenelles from the mixture. Place the quenelles in the hot water to poach for 6–8 minutes, then drain on paper towel.

Preheat the oven to 200°C (400°F). Gently heat the crayfish bisque.

Transfer the quenelles to several small ovenproof dishes – aim for two quenelles per person. Spoon in the crayfish bisque so it comes three-quarters of the way up the quenelles, and garnish with a little crayfish meat. Bake for 10 minutes, then serve.

Serves 3–4

CRAYFISH GRATIN

Langouste gratinée

FROM THE LANGUEDOC-ROUSSILLON REGION

The coast around the Languedoc-Roussillon region abounds in superb shellfish and this crayfish gratin is a famous French classic. It's fairly easy to prepare but make sure the crayfish is freshly cooked and has not been frozen.

2 x 700 g (1 lb 9 oz) cooked crayfish

80 g (2¾ oz) butter

2 shallots, finely chopped

2 tablespoons plain (all-purpose) flour

100 ml (3½ fl oz) dry white wine

500 ml (17 fl oz/2 cups) milk

salt

freshly ground pepper

a pinch of cayenne pepper

25 g (1 oz/¼ cup) grated parmesan or gruyère cheese

50 g (1¾ oz/½ cup) fine breadcrumbs

Preheat the oven to 220°C (430°F).

Cut each cooked crayfish in half lengthways. You can ask your fishmonger to do it for you if you prefer. Carefully remove the flesh from the tail. Detach and discard the intestine. Dice the flesh into 1.5 cm (½ in) squares and refrigerate until required.

Place the four half-crayfish shells in a gratin dish for later.

Heat half the butter in a small saucepan. Add the shallots and stir until almost golden. Stir in the flour and cook on a low heat for a few minutes.

Whisk in the white wine. When it is well incorporated, gradually whisk in the milk and cook on a low heat for 5 minutes. Season with salt, pepper and cayenne pepper.

Gently mix in the crayfish pieces and the parmesan and heat for 2 minutes.

Spoon the crayfish and sauce into the empty crayfish shells. Sprinkle the top evenly with breadcrumbs and dot a little of the remaining butter here and there. Place in the preheated oven and brown the top of the crayfish. It will take about 10 minutes. Serve immediately.

Serves 4

CRAYFISH À L'ARMORICAINE

Langouste à l'Armoricaine

FROM THE BRITTANY REGION	BY ELISABETH KERDELHUÉ

This is a Breton crayfish dish. For me, when prepared by a master chef, it remains one of the greatest classic French dishes. The prawn stock can be made ahead of time. This recipe makes about 500 ml (17 fl oz/2 cups) and it keeps well in the freezer.

60 ml (2 fl oz/¼ cup) olive oil

shells from 20 medium prawns (shrimp)

750 ml (25½ fl oz/3 cups) cold water

3 parsley sprigs

salt

freshly ground black pepper

1 thyme sprig

a few parsley sprigs

½ bay leaf

1 x 1 kg (2 lb 3 oz) uncooked crayfish, cut into 8 pieces

2 French shallots, chopped

1 garlic clove, chopped

1 tablespoon cognac

To make the prawn stock, heat half the oil in a saucepan and stir-fry the prawn shells over a high heat for 3–4 minutes. Add the water, parsley and a little salt and pepper. Return to the boil and simmer for 15 minutes, stirring occasionally.

Strain the stock through a sieve, pressing on the prawn shells to extract as much flavour as possible. Set aside until ready to use.

Use kitchen string to tie the thyme, parsley and bay leaf together to make a bouquet garni.

Heat the remaining oil in a heavy saucepan. Add the crayfish pieces and sauté for 1 minute. Turn them over and sauté for a further 1–2 minutes, or until the shells have turned red. Remove the crayfish pieces from the pan.

Add the shallots and garlic to the pan and stir over a medium heat for a couple of minutes. Return the crayfish pieces to the pan and stir well. Add the cognac to the pan, remove the pan away from the stove and carefully flame the crayfish mixture. Return the pan to the stove. Add the wine, stock, tomatoes, bouquet garni, tomato paste and cayenne to the pan and stir gently. Cover and simmer for 10 minutes.

100 ml (3½ fl oz) dry white wine

250 ml (8½ fl oz/1 cup) prawn stock (or use a good strong fish stock)

2 tomatoes, diced

1 teaspoon tomato paste (concentrated purée)

a pinch of cayenne pepper

2 tablespoons pouring cream

20 g (¾ oz) butter

1 tablespoon tarragon leaves, finely chopped

Transfer the crayfish pieces to a serving dish and keep warm.

Pour the sauce and any pieces of shell into a sieve set over a saucepan and press down to extract the juices. Stir in the cream and butter and reheat gently. Just before serving, add the tarragon and season with salt and pepper.

Spoon the sauce over the crayfish and serve. It's lovely served with boiled potatoes.

Serves 2

CRAYFISH STEW

Civet de langouste

FROM THE COAST OF LANGUEDOC-ROUSSILLON REGION | BY PHILIPPE MOUCHEL

This special crayfish stew has a real taste of the Mediterranean region, especially when made using Banyuls, a local fortified wine that is very popular as an aperitif.

60 ml (2 fl oz/¼ cup) extra-virgin olive oil

½ brown onion, chopped

3 tomatoes, peeled, seeded and diced

1 garlic clove, chopped

1 bay leaf

4 parsley sprigs

1 x 500 g (1 lb 2 oz) crayfish tail in the shell, cut into 6 pieces

salt

freshly ground pepper

20 g (¾ oz) salted butter

2 teaspoons cognac

80 ml (2½ fl oz/⅓ cup) Banyuls

a pinch of cayenne pepper

4 thin slices prosciutto-style ham, roughly torn

a few chervil sprigs

Heat 1 tablespoon of the oil in a non-stick saucepan. Add the onion and cook over a medium heat for a few minutes. Add the tomatoes, garlic, bay leaf and parsley, then cover the pan and cook over a low heat for 30 minutes.

Season the crayfish pieces with a little salt and pepper.

Heat 2 more tablespoons of oil in a frying pan and cook the crayfish pieces on all sides for a few minutes. Add the butter and when it has melted, baste the crayfish. Add the cognac, bring to the boil, remove the pan away from the stove and flame. Return the pan to the stove, add the Banyuls, bring to the boil and flame once more (again, do this away from the stove). Remove the crayfish pieces from the pan, then boil the liquid until reduced by half.

Add the tomato mixture to the pan and season with cayenne pepper, salt and pepper. Bring to a simmer, return the crayfish pieces to the pan and simmer in the sauce for a few minutes.

Add a few pieces of ham to the sauce and warm gently. Spoon a little sauce onto two plates and divide the crayfish pieces between them. Top each serve with a few pieces of ham, drizzle on the remaining olive oil and garnish with chervil.

Serves 2

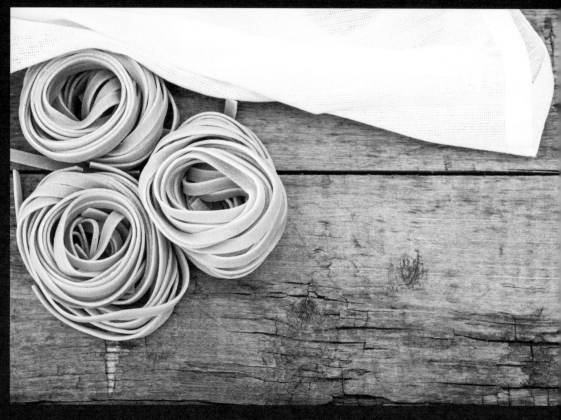

CORSICAN CRAYFISH WITH LINGUINE

Langouste de Corse aux linguine

FROM THE CORSICA REGION

The Corsicans, whose island is in the middle of the Mediterranean Sea, are very fond of seafood and crustaceans. They are skilled fishermen and their recipes are richly flavoured. They call crayfish the 'queen of crustaceans'.

1 cooked crayfish, about 800 g (1 lb 12 oz)

60 ml (2 fl oz/¼ cup) extra-virgin olive oil

1 onion, finely chopped

10 fennel seeds

10 cumin seeds

1 small chilli, cut in half lengthways, seeds removed

1 teaspoon tomato paste (concentrated purée)

1 teaspoon plain (all-purpose) flour

1 teaspoon brandy

75 ml (2½ fl oz) dry white wine

3 tomatoes, diced

salt

freshly ground pepper

150 g (5½ oz) linguine

6 basil leaves

½ garlic clove, chopped

Remove the meat from the crayfish legs and body and cut the body meat into bite-sized pieces. Refrigerate until required. Cut the shells into small pieces.

Heat half the olive oil in a heavy medium saucepan. Add the crayfish shells and onion and cook on a medium heat, stirring for a few minutes. Stir in the fennel and cumin seeds and the chilli, then add the tomato paste and flour. Stir well. Add the brandy and wine and stir until the liquid is combined.

Stir in the tomatoes, season with salt and pepper and simmer for 15 minutes. Then strain the sauce into a saucepan.

Cook the pasta in boiling salted water for a few minutes, then drain.

Heat the crayfish meat in the sauce for a few minutes.

Chop the basil leaves and mix them in a bowl with the remaining olive oil and the chopped garlic.

Place half the linguine on each plate and top with the crayfish meat and sauce. Drizzle with the basil olive oil and serve.

Serves 2

RICH BASQUE FISH STEW

Ttoro

---

*Basque cooking is influenced by both French and Spanish cuisine.
It is full of colour and strong flavours, such as olive oil, chilli and saffron.*

1.5 kg (3 lb 5 oz) firm, whole white fish

60 ml (2 fl oz/¼ cup) olive oil

1 small leek, thinly sliced

1 small onion, thinly sliced

½ small capsicum (pepper), diced

½ long red chilli, thinly sliced

2 tomatoes, finely diced

1 garlic clove, crushed

1 thyme sprig

2 parsley sprigs

a pinch of saffron threads

150 ml (5 fl oz) dry white wine

salt

freshly ground black pepper

55 g (2 oz) plain (all-purpose) flour

12 scampi

500 g (1 lb 2 oz) mussels, thoroughly scrubbed and beards removed

4 tablespoons chopped parsley

4 slices toasted bread, rubbed with raw garlic

Ask your fishmonger to clean and scale the fish, and to cut it into 5 cm (2 in) pieces. Ask them to remove the fish heads and to cut them into pieces also.

Heat 2 tablespoons of the oil in a large saucepan. Add the leek, onion and fish heads. Cook over a medium heat for 5 minutes, stirring occasionally.

Add the capsicum, chilli, tomatoes, garlic, thyme, parsley and saffron and stir well. Add the wine and bring to the boil. Add enough water to cover and season with salt and pepper. Bring to a simmer and cook for 30 minutes, uncovered.

Pat the fish pieces dry and coat lightly with flour.

Heat the remaining oil in a large saucepan and fry the fish pieces for about 1 minute on each side. Add the scampi, then the mussels. Strain the fish stock into the pan, shake well and cover with a lid. Cook over a medium heat until the mussels have opened.

Ladle the stew into deep soup plates. Sprinkle with chopped parsley and serve with the garlic toasts.

Serves 6

BOUILLABAISSE FISH STEW

Bouillabaisse

FROM THE PROVENCE REGION

This fish stew speciality of Marseille is traditionally made with a selection of rock fish. When well made it is one of my favourite French dishes. It is traditionally served with fried slices of baguette and a garlic mayonnaise.

---

2 tablespoons extra-virgin olive oil

1 medium onion, chopped

10 cumin seeds

20 fennel seeds

1 small red chilli, thinly sliced

1 bulb fennel, cut into 8 wedges

1 kg (2 lb 3 oz) tomatoes, peeled, seeded and chopped

1 litre (34 fl oz/4 cups) fish stock

salt

freshly ground black pepper

a large pinch of saffron threads

2 kg (4 lb 6 oz) firm white fish, cleaned and heads removed

16 prawns (shrimp), shelled and deveined

16 new potatoes, peeled and cooked

2 garlic cloves, chopped

Gently heat the oil in a casserole dish. Add the onion, cumin seeds, fennel seeds and chilli and fry for 1 minute. Add the fennel wedges and fry for 1 minute. Add the tomatoes and stir for 1 minute. Add the fish stock and season with salt, pepper and saffron. Bring to the boil, then boil for 10 minutes.

Add the whole fish to the casserole dish and simmer for 10 minutes. Add the prawns and simmer for a further 5 minutes.

Transfer the fish and vegetables to a platter and garnish with boiled potatoes.

Stir the garlic into the cooking liquid and transfer to a soup tureen.

Diners serve themselves by placing the seafood and potato into deep soup plates and ladling the liquid over the top.

Serves 8

Note: French people love fish, and to obtain the maximum flavour, they always cook fish on the bone when making bouillabaisse. Then, as they eat it, they patiently remove the bones from the flesh.

BRITTANY FISH MEDLEY

Cotriade

FROM THE BRITTANY REGION

Cotriade is a traditional coastal Breton fish and potato soup and every family has their own recipe. It's made using whole fish, cut into pieces rather than fillets, and it is best to include at least three different types of fish.

80 g (2¾ oz) salted butter

1 onion, chopped

1 leek, chopped

2 garlic cloves, chopped

3 thyme sprigs

6 medium all-purpose potatoes, peeled and quartered

1 litre (34 fl oz/4 cups) cold water

salt

freshly ground pepper

1.5 kg (3 lb 5 oz) whole fish (e.g. monkfish, flathead, john dory, whiting), cleaned and cut into 3 cm (1¼ in) pieces

12 mussels, scrubbed and beards removed

4 tablespoons chopped parsley

Gently heat the butter in a large saucepan. Add the onion and stir for 2 minutes. Add the leek and garlic and stir for a further 2 minutes. Add the thyme and potatoes and stir for another minute. Cover with the litre of cold water, season with salt and pepper, bring to the boil and cook for 5 minutes.

Add the fish pieces and shake the saucepan. Simmer for about 5 minutes.

Add the mussels, cover with a lid and cook for 2–3 minutes until the mussels have opened.

Serve the stew in large bowls and sprinkle with parsley.

Serves 4

NORMANDY FISH CASSEROLE

Marmite Dieppoise

FROM THE NORMANDY REGION

Normandy is synonymous with outstanding seafood. The French really know how to handle fish and love to eat it. It's not uncommon for a small coastal village to have two or three seafood shops selling the local catch. This seafood stew is named after the fishing town of Dieppe.

---

16 mussels, scrubbed and beards removed

30 ml (1 fl oz) dry white wine

50 g (1¾ oz) salted butter

1 leek, white part only, thinly sliced

½ onion, finely chopped

1 celery stalk, diced

50 ml (1¾ fl oz) dry apple cider

600 g (1 lb 5 oz) firm fish fillets (e.g. monkfish, flathead)

8–12 prawns, shelled and deveined

12 scallops

125 ml (4 ½ fl oz/½ cup) cream

salt

freshly ground pepper

12 chervil sprigs

Place the cleaned mussels in a saucepan with the dry white wine, cover with a lid and bring to the boil. The mussels will open after a few minutes. Shake the mussels around and when they are all open, strain the liquid into a bowl. Remove the mussels from the shells and place in the mussel juice.

Heat the butter in a wide saucepan on a medium heat and cook the leeks, onion and celery for a few minutes until soft. Pour in the apple cider and bring to the boil. Place the fish fillets, prawns and scallops on top and add the mussel juice. Cover with baking paper to keep in the juices and simmer for a few minutes until the fish is just cooked.

Carefully lift the cooked fish and seafood onto individual warm plates or a warm platter.

Add the cream to the pan and bring to the boil, cooking until the sauce thickens. Season with salt and pepper, then stir in the mussels, reheating for a few seconds.

Coat the fish and seafood with the sauce and mussels, garnish with chervil sprigs and serve.

Serves 4

MONKFISH FRICASSÉE

Bourride Sétoise

FROM THE LANGUEDOC-ROUSSILLON REGION | BY ALAIN GEGNANI

This local speciality of the picturesque seaside town of Sète, which borders the Mediterranean Sea, is popular because it's so tasty but also because the French love the texture and flavour of monkfish.

1 teaspoon dijon mustard

1 egg

1 egg yolk

1 teaspoon red wine vinegar

100 ml (3½ fl oz) extra-virgin olive oil, plus extra 2 tablespoons

6 silverbeet (Swiss chard) leaves, without the stalk

1 small leek, white part only, cut into pieces

1 small celery stalk, cut into pieces

1 carrot, cut into pieces

1 kg (2 lb 3 oz) monkfish tail, cut into 16 pieces

85 ml (2¾ fl oz) Noilly Prat vermouth

salt

freshly ground pepper

a pinch of cayenne pepper

a pinch of saffron

3 garlic cloves, finely chopped

8 slices of baguette, 10 cm (4 in) long × 2 cm (¾ in) thick, toasted

In a small blender, place the mustard, whole egg, egg yolk and vinegar and blend for 10 seconds. Bit by bit, add the olive oil, blending until thick. This is a type of mayonnaise. Transfer the mayonnaise to a bowl.

Place the silverbeet leaves, leek, celery and carrot in the blender and mix until well chopped but not quite puréed.

Heat the extra 2 tablespoons of olive oil in a frying pan. Add the chopped vegetables and stir for a few seconds. Add the monkfish pieces and stir on a medium heat for a few seconds. Add the Noilly Prat and season with salt, pepper, cayenne pepper and saffron. Bring to the boil, cover and cook for about 8–10 minutes, turning the fish every minute or so.

Transfer the fish pieces onto four warm plates. Turn off the heat under the pan and slowly stir in two-thirds of the garlic and all the mayonnaise to thicken the sauce.

Spoon the sauce over the fish and serve with the toasted bread brushed with the remaining garlic.

It's lovely served with steamed potatoes.

Serves 4

TROUT WITH PINE NUTS & CAPERS

Truite Grenobloise

FROM THE ALPS REGION | BY PHILIPPE MOUCHEL

I cooked this beautiful trout dish hundreds of times when I was a young chef working in Paris. It's very easy to do at home.

60 ml (2 fl oz/¼ cup) olive oil

2 slices bread, cut into 1 cm (½ in) cubes

2 fresh trout, thoroughly cleaned inside and out

salt

freshly ground black pepper

3 tablespoons plain (all-purpose) flour

85 g (3 oz) salted butter

3 tablespoons pine nuts

3 tablespoons capers

1 lemon, peeled and cut into segments

juice of ½ lemon

3 tablespoons chopped parsley

Heat half the oil in a frying pan and fry the bread cubes until golden. Drain on paper towel.

Season the fish with salt and pepper and dust all over with a little flour.

Heat the remaining oil in another frying pan and cook the fish for 4 minutes on each side. Add one-third of the butter to the pan and baste the fish. Transfer the fish to a serving plate and keep warm.

Add the remaining butter to the pan. Stir in the pine nuts and cook for 1 minute until golden brown. Add the capers, lemon segments and lemon juice and reheat. Add the chopped parsley and spoon the sauce over the trout. Scatter the croutons on top and serve.

Serves 2

POACHED TROUT
WITH HOLLANDAISE SAUCE

Truite au bleu hollandaise

FROM THE ALPS REGION | BY PHILIPPE MOUCHEL

The beautiful streams and lakes in the Alps region are teeming with trout, so it has become the speciality of the area. The French often prefer their fish poached rather than pan-fried or deep-fried.

3 litres (101 fl oz/12 cups) cold water

1 medium onion, thinly sliced

1 medium carrot, thinly sliced

a few parsley stalks

1 bay leaf

2 thyme sprigs

10 peppercorns

2 very fresh river trout (not rainbow trout), thoroughly cleaned, inside and out

small handful of parsley leaves

60 ml (2 fl oz/¼ cup) white vinegar

Hollandaise sauce

85 g (3 oz) salted butter

1 egg yolk

2 teaspoons hot water

salt

freshly ground black pepper

1 teaspoon lemon juice

Put the water in a large saucepan over a medium heat and add the onion and carrot. Use kitchen string to tie the parsley stalks, bay leaf and thyme sprigs together to make a bouquet garni and add to the pan with the peppercorns. Bring to the boil and cook for 10 minutes.

Meanwhile, make the hollandaise sauce. Melt the butter in a small saucepan over a low heat until warm, but not hot. Combine the egg yolk and hot water in a bowl set over a saucepan of hot water. Season with a little salt and pepper and whisk for a few minutes until light and fluffy. Remove the bowl from the heat, then very slowly add the warm melted butter, whisking continuously until well incorporated. Stir in the lemon juice.

Carefully place the trout in the hot poaching liquid and heat until close to boiling point. Reduce the heat and poach the fish for 10 minutes. Turn off the heat, add the parsley and leave to stand for 3 minutes.

Heat the vinegar in a small saucepan. Carefully lift the two trout onto a flat dish and spoon on the hot vinegar, which gives them a blueish tinge.

Arrange the trout in deep serving plates with some of the vegetables and 2–3 tablespoons of the cooking liquid. Drizzle on a little hollandaise sauce and serve the remaining sauce in a small bowl on the side.

Serves 2

BAKED TROUT
WITH HERBS & BACON

Truite rôtie aux herbes et lardons

FROM THE MIDI-PYRÉNÉES REGION

The streams of the Pyrénées teem with trout that can be seen swimming in the water from the river bank. I've adapted this classic baked trout recipe by adding small apple cubes and walnuts. It's superb.

---

1 trout, about 1 kg (2 lb 3 oz), cleaned and scaled

90 ml (3 fl oz) extra-virgin olive oil

4 thyme sprigs, finely chopped

salt

freshly ground pepper

2 bay leaves

3 garlic cloves

3 thin slices of lemon

½ apple, peeled, cored and cut into 3 mm (⅛ in) cubes

8 walnut halves, finely chopped

juice of ½ lemon

3 bacon rashers, cut into small strips

3 tablespoons finely snipped chives

Preheat the oven to 140°C (275°F).

Pat the trout dry with paper towel and place on a baking tray lined with baking paper.

In a bowl, mix 3 tablespoons of the olive oil with the chopped thyme and a little salt and pepper. Brush the inside and outside of the trout with this flavoured oil.

Insert the bay leaves, whole garlic cloves and lemon slices inside the fish. Place the fish in the preheated oven for about 30 minutes or until cooked, basting occasionally to keep the fish moist.

Meanwhile, mix together in a bowl the remaining oil, diced apple, chopped walnuts, lemon juice and season with salt and pepper.

Just before the trout is ready, cook the bacon for a few minutes in a small frying pan.

Carefully transfer the trout to a serving platter. Spoon a little of the apple and walnut preparation on top, sprinkle with bacon pieces and chives and serve.

Serves 4

BAKED TROUT WITH GRUYÈRE CHEESE

Truites à la Savoyarde

FROM THE ALPS REGION

The icy streams of the French Alps are full of trout, and this dish with gruyère cheese is a family staple.

2 tablespoons very soft salted butter

2 rainbow trout, cleaned and scaled

50 ml (1¾ fl oz) dry white wine

1 egg

50 ml (1¾ fl oz) crème fraîche

salt

freshly ground black pepper

80 g (2¾ oz) freshly grated gruyère cheese

Pre-heat the oven to 150°C (300°F).

Butter a gratin dish large enough to hold the two trout. Place the trout in the dish and brush them with butter. Add the white wine, then bake the fish in the pre-heated oven for 5 minutes.

In a small bowl, beat the egg with the crème fraîche. Season with a little salt and pepper and pour the sauce over the fish.

Sprinkle evenly with the gruyère cheese.

Bake in the oven for a further 15 minutes.

Serves 2

BAKED GURNARD & FENNEL PURÉE

Grondin rôti à la purée de fenouil

FROM THE MARSEILLE/PROVENCE REGION

The capital of Provence, Marseille, is famous for its seafood cuisine, which is wonderfully colourful and flavoursome. Flathead, john dory or monkfish could also be used in this dish.

60 ml (2 fl oz/¼ cup) extra-virgin olive oil

1 shallot, finely chopped

2 garlic cloves, chopped

2 small fennel bulbs, each cut into 4 wedges

2 parsley sprigs

2 thyme sprigs

2 tablespoons pernod

60 ml (2 fl oz/¼ cup) dry white wine

a pinch of saffron

2 tomatoes, chopped

salt

freshly ground pepper

350 g (12½ oz) gurnard fillets

2 tablespoons chopped parsley

Preheat the oven to 140°C (275°F).

Heat half the olive oil in an ovenproof dish. Stir in the shallot and garlic, then add the fennel wedges and cook for 2 minutes. Add the parsley and thyme and stir well. Add the pernod and wine and bring to the boil. Add the saffron and tomatoes and season with salt and pepper. Stir well and simmer for 5 minutes.

Top with the fish fillets, drizzle the remaining olive oil over the fish and bake in the preheated oven for about 5 minutes or until the fish is almost cooked. Transfer the fish to a warm plate and cover with foil.

Remove the fennel wedges from the dish and blend them to a purée. Strain the tomato sauce.

Spoon a little of the fennel purée onto each plate. Top with a fish fillet and coat with the tomato sauce. Sprinkle with parsley and serve.

Serves 2

MACKEREL THE FLEMISH WAY

Maquereau à la Flamande

FROM THE NORTHERN FRANCE REGION

The north of France benefits from the cold waters of the Channel, where some of the finest and tastiest fish are caught. Mackerel is a popular family meal as it's usually inexpensive and filling.

100 g (3½ oz) salted butter, at room temperature

2 tablespoons finely chopped parsley

1 tablespoon finely chopped dill

1 shallot, finely chopped

1 tablespoon finely snipped chives

juice of ½ lemon

salt

freshly ground pepper

a pinch of nutmeg

2 fresh mackerels, cleaned and gutted

2 lemon wedges

In a bowl, mix 80 g (2¾ oz) of the butter with the parsley, dill, shallot, chives, lemon juice, a little salt and pepper and a pinch of nutmeg.

Fill the two mackerels with this herb butter. Place each mackerel on a piece of baking paper large enough to wrap the fish in. Brush the fish on both sides with the remaining butter (melted) and season with salt and pepper.

Wrap each fish in the baking paper and tie the parcels with kitchen string at each end and in the middle.

Place the fish on a hot grill plate or the flat plate of a barbecue and cook for about 10 minutes, turning the fish once, until it is cooked.

Carefully unwrap the fish and transfer onto plates. Spoon the hot melted herb butter over the fish and serve garnished with a lemon wedge.

Serves 2

ROAST SNAPPER WITH MONTPELLIER BUTTER

Daurade rôtie au beurre de Montpellier

FROM THE LANGUEDOC REGION

The sunny city of Montpellier in southern France is a lovely place to visit. There's a great tradition in the region of blending seafood with the produce of the land. Montpellier butter is a very tasty accompaniment and goes well with fish.

---

1 kg (2 lb 3 oz) snapper (or other firm white fish), scaled and cleaned

sea salt

freshly ground black pepper

3 tablespoons olive oil

2 French shallots, thinly sliced

2 teaspoons fennel seeds

4 parsley sprigs

80 ml (2½ fl oz/⅓ cup) dry white wine

Montpellier butter

55 g (2 oz) salted butter, softened

1 tablespoon chopped parsley

1 tablespoon chopped chervil

6 tarragon leaves, thinly sliced

1 small gherkin (pickle), finely chopped

6 capers, finely chopped

1 anchovy fillet, finely chopped

juice of ¼ lemon

freshly ground black pepper

To make the Montpellier butter, place the butter in a bowl and add the herbs, gherkin, capers, anchovy, lemon juice and a little pepper. Mix with a fork until just combined. Spoon onto a piece of foil, roll up into a neat log and refrigerate until firm.

Preheat the oven to 200°C (400°F).

Make several 1 cm (½ in) deep cuts in the thickest part of both sides of the fish and season with sea salt and pepper.

Pour half the oil in a baking dish large enough to hold the fish. Scatter half the shallots, half the fennel seeds and all the parsley sprigs on the base of the dish. Place the snapper on top and scatter on the remaining shallots and fennel seeds. Drizzle the wine and remaining oil over the fish, cover with foil and bake for 25 minutes.

To serve, discard the parsley stalks and carefully lift the snapper flesh away from the bones. Serve with a slice of Montpellier butter. It's lovely with a tomato salad.

Serves 2

PERCH FILLET WITH ASPARAGUS & CHABLIS SAUCE

Filet de perche sauce au Chablis et aux asperges

FROM THE BURGUNDY REGION

If you are a food and wine lover, Burgundy is one of the top French regions to visit, and Chablis is a most charming village nestled amongst the chardonnay vineyards.

55 g (2 oz) salted butter

1 French shallot, finely chopped

2 button mushrooms, thinly sliced

2 x 200 g (7 oz) perch fillets, or other lean, flaky-textured fish such as rockfish or red snapper

salt

freshly ground black pepper

3 tablespoons chablis

6 fat asparagus tips

2 tablespoons pouring cream

4 chervil sprigs

Melt a quarter of the butter in a frying pan over a medium heat. Add the shallot and stir for 30 seconds. Add the mushrooms. Top with the fish fillets, season with salt and pepper and pour the chablis around the fish.

Cover the pan with foil or a lid and steam over a low heat until just done. It only takes 6–8 minutes.

Meanwhile, steam the asparagus tips until tender.

Transfer the fish and mushrooms to a serving dish or two plates and cover with foil. Bring the cooking liquid to the boil and cook for 2 minutes. Whisk in the remaining butter. When it has all melted, add the cream and asparagus tips to the sauce.

Top the fish with the asparagus and spoon on the sauce. Garnish with chervil sprigs and serve.

Serves 2

PAN-FRIED SALMON WITH BUTTER SAUCE

Saumon poêlé au beurre blanc

FROM THE LOIRE VALLEY REGION | BY PHILIPPE MOUCHEL

Beurre blanc was the star sauce during my apprenticeship in the Loire Valley and chef Albert Augereau was a master at preparing it. This classic sauce has become less popular because of its butter content, but it's so delicious! The reduction part of the sauce may be made ahead of time, but the cream and butter should not be added until you are ready to serve as the sauce does not reheat well.

2 medium potatoes

10 asparagus spears, trimmed

1 tablespoon vegetable oil

2 salmon cutlets

2 teaspoons salted butter

salt

freshly ground black pepper

Beurre blanc sauce

1 large French shallot or ½ medium white onion, finely chopped

60 ml (2 fl oz/¼ cup) dry white vinegar

60 ml (2 fl oz/¼ cup) dry white wine

1 teaspoon cracked pepper

1 teaspoon pouring cream

100 g (3½ oz) very cold butter, cut into small cubes

To make the beurre blanc sauce, combine the shallot, vinegar, wine and pepper in a small saucepan. Bring to a simmer and cook for 5–10 minutes, or until almost all the liquid has evaporated. Set aside.

Steam the potatoes and asparagus separately, until tender. Meanwhile, heat the oil in a frying pan and cook the salmon for 2 minutes on each side. Add the butter to the pan and when it has melted, baste the salmon. Season with salt and pepper.

While the salmon is cooking, gently reheat the shallot reduction. Add the cream and bring to the boil. Lower the heat to a minimum and whisk in the butter, piece by piece. During this time the sauce must be whisked constantly. It should hold together and be creamy and smooth.

Arrange the salmon on two plates with the asparagus and potatoes. Serve the sauce either on the side of the plate or separately in a sauce boat.

Serves 2

PAN-FRIED SALMON WITH SHALLOTS

Saumon poêlé aux échalottes

FROM THE PYRÉNÉES REGION | BY PHILIPPE MOUCHEL

I first visited the Pyrénées region only a few years ago. It's a beautiful area of France with stunning mountains and valleys, lively markets and rustic, flavoursome food.

3 shallots, finely chopped

3 tablespoons sherry vinegar

60 ml (2 fl oz/¼ cup) dry white wine

salt

freshly ground pepper

2 salmon fillets, skin on

1 tablespoon extra-virgin olive oil

20 g (¾ oz) salted butter

1 tablespoon finely chopped tarragon leaves

chives

Place the shallots in a saucepan with the sherry vinegar and dry white wine and season with salt and pepper. Bring to a simmer and cook until almost all the liquid has evaporated.

Season the salmon fillets with salt and pepper.

Heat the olive oil in a non-stick pan and cook the fish, skin side down, for about 5 minutes. Turn the fish over and remove the pan from the heat.

Return the shallot reduction to the heat, add the butter and tarragon and stir until the butter has melted.

Spread some of the shallot sauce on each plate. Top with the salmon, skin side down, and spread a bit more sauce on top. Garnish with chives.

It's lovely served with steamed potatoes.

Serves 2

BLUE EYE AND SCALLOPS WITH BUTTER SAUCE

Cabillaud et coquilles St Jacques au beurre blanc

FROM THE BRITTANY/LOIRE VALLEY REGIONS

The west of France, with the Channel and the Atlantic Ocean, has a wonderful repertoire of excellent fish dishes. I am a native of Western France and when I was young my mother usually preferred to serve a fish dish such as this for special occasions rather than a meat dish.

60 g (2 oz) salted butter, cut into cubes

1 French shallot, finely chopped

2 tablespoons white wine vinegar

100 ml (3½ fl oz) dry white wine

freshly ground black pepper

1 zucchini (courgette)

2 blue eye fillets (or other firm, white fish), skinned

200 g (7 oz) fresh scallops, cleaned

salt

1 teaspoon pouring cream

1 dill sprig

Melt 1 teaspoon of the butter in a small saucepan over a low heat. Add the shallot and stir for 1 minute. Add the vinegar and 3 tablespoons of the wine, season with black pepper and simmer until the liquid has nearly evaporated. Set aside.

Cut the zucchini into thin slices, and then into thin julienne strips.

Melt another teaspoon of the butter in a medium frying pan over a medium heat. Add the zucchini and stir for 20 seconds. Add the fish, cook for 1 minute, then add the scallops. Season with salt and pepper. Add the remaining wine, cover with foil or a lid and cook over a low heat for about 2 minutes. Turn the fish over and cook for a further 2 minutes.

Add the cream to the shallot mixture. Place the pan over a low heat and slowly whisk in the remaining butter, cube by cube, until melted and smooth.

Place the fish fillets on two warmed plates. Top with a little zucchini, then a few scallops. Spoon on some of the butter sauce, garnish with dill and serve.

Serves 2

BLUE EYE WITH OYSTERS IN A CREAMY CIDER SAUCE

Cabillaud aux huîtres sauce au cidre

FROM THE NORMANDY REGION

This lovely but simple dish makes the most of the amazing seafood Normandy has to offer. If you can't get blue eye, use a firm white-fleshed fish, such as snapper or barramundi.

10 g (¼ oz) salted butter

1 shallot, finely chopped

1 small carrot, cut into long julienne strips

1 stalk of celery, cut into long julienne strips

2 medium mushrooms, cut into long julienne strips

2 x 150 g (5½ oz) blue eye fillets

60 ml (2 fl oz/¼ cup) apple cider

salt

freshly ground black pepper

3 tablespoons pouring cream

6 very fresh natural oysters

2 tablespoons chopped parsley

Heat the butter in a frying pan. Stir in the shallot, the carrot, celery and mushrooms.

Make two spaces in the pan and place the fish fillets in the spaces. Pour the cider over the top and season with salt and pepper. Cover with foil and cook on a low heat for 10 minutes.

Transfer the drained vegetables and fish onto two plates and keep warm.

Boil down the cooking liquid in the frying pan for about 30 seconds before adding the cream and boiling until the sauce has a creamy texture.

Add the drained oysters to the sauce and simmer for 20 seconds. Add the chopped parsley.

Spoon the oysters and sauce over the fish.

Serves 2

JOHN DORY
WITH A CREAMY SEAFOOD SAUCE

St Pierre sauce Normande

| FROM THE NORMANDY REGION | BY PHILIPPE MOUCHEL |

The cold waters of the English Channel are ideal for producing delicate fish and seafood, and most coastal towns and villages of Normandy have one or more excellent seafood restaurants serving delicious dishes like this one.

12 mussels, thoroughly scrubbed and beards removed

3 tablespoons white wine

2 teaspoons butter

2 French shallots, finely chopped

150 g (5½ oz) mushrooms

2 small john dory or other flat fish, gutted, skinned and heads removed

250 ml (8½ fl oz/1 cup) fish stock

salt

freshly ground black pepper

2 lemon slices

a few parsley stalks

4 medium prawns (shrimp), shelled and deveined

4 large oysters

1 egg yolk

3 tablespoons cream

juice of ¼ lemon

2 tablespoons chopped parsley

Place the mussels in a saucepan with the white wine. Cover with a lid and cook over a high heat for a few minutes until the mussels have opened. Remove the mussel meat from the shells and set aside. Strain the cooking juices into a bowl.

Put the butter, shallots, mushrooms, fish, mussel juices and stock in a wide saucepan or frying pan and season with salt and pepper. Place the lemon slices on the fish and add the parsley stalks to the pan. Bring to a very slow simmer, cover with a lid and poach for 5 minutes. Turn the fish over and simmer for a few minutes more. Carefully lift the fish onto a warm plate and cover with foil.

Transfer the mushrooms to a separate saucepan with a few tablespoons of the cooking liquid. (Set aside the pan with the remaining cooking liquid.) Add the prawns, oysters and mussel meat to the mushrooms. Cover the pan with a lid and steam over a high heat for 1 minute.

Return the pan with the reserved cooking liquid to the heat and boil until reduced by half.

In a small bowl, whisk together the egg yolk and cream. Pour into the reduced liquid, whisking continuously, until it thickens slightly. It is best to do this away from the heat.

Strain the sauce into the cooked seafood and mushrooms. Add the lemon juice and season to taste. Spoon over the fish, sprinkle with chopped parsley and serve.

Serves 2

JOHN DORY WITH ASPARAGUS & A CHAMPAGNE SAUCE

St Pierre aux asperges sauce Champagne

FROM THE CHAMPAGNE REGION	BY PHILIPPE MOUCHEL

Every French chef learns to make a Champagne sauce and I vividly recall the first time I made one — as a young chef working in a seafood restaurant in Paris. It's a lovely sauce to serve with fish. Only a little Champagne is used in the sauce, so you can drink what's left over!

50 g (1¾ oz) mushrooms, sliced

1 shallot, finely sliced

40 g (1½ oz) salted butter

6 parsley sprigs

2 thyme sprigs

2 x 180 g (6½ oz) john dory fillets

salt

freshly ground black pepper

150 ml (5 fl oz) Champagne

2 teaspoons extra-virgin olive oil

6 asparagus spears, trimmed and peeled

125 ml (4 fl oz/½ cup) thickened cream

about 10 tarragon leaves

Preheat the oven to 170°C (340°F).

Place the sliced mushrooms in an ovenproof pan with the sliced shallot, a quarter of the butter, the parsley and thyme. Top with the john dory fillets, season with salt and pepper and pour over the Champagne.

On top of the stove, bring the pan to a simmer then cover with a lid and put into the preheated oven to bake for about 10 minutes.

Heat the olive oil and half the remaining butter in a pan and cook the asparagus for about 1 minute. Add 1–2 tablespoons water and steam-cook the asparagus until just tender.

Lift the fish and mushrooms from the cooking liquid and place in a dish. Strain the cooking liquid into a small saucepan and boil down by at least half. Add the cream, return to the boil and simmer until creamy. Whisk remaining butter into the sauce.

Place three asparagus spears on each plate. Top with a fish fillet and coat the fish with the delicious Champagne sauce.

Garnish with tarragon leaves and serve.

Serves 2

GABRIEL
GATÉ

Poultry &
Rabbit

SAUTÉED CHICKEN WITH TARRAGON CREAM SAUCE & CARROTS

Poulet sauté à la crème d'estragon et aux carottes

FROM THE LYON/CENTRAL FRANCE REGIONS

One of the highlights of French cooking is its wonderful variety of poultry dishes. Chicken with tarragon is so French and is often served as a main course at Sunday lunch for the extended family.

1 tablespoon extra-virgin olive oil

8 pieces chicken on the bone (thighs or drumsticks)

2 French shallots, finely chopped

60 ml (2 fl oz/¼ cup) dry white wine

5 medium carrots, thinly sliced

20 g (¾ oz) salted butter

60 ml (2 fl oz/¼ cup) water

salt

freshly ground pepper

60 ml (2 fl oz/¼ cup) pouring cream

3 tablespoons tarragon leaves

Heat the oil in a wide, non-stick saucepan and brown the chicken pieces on all sides. Add the shallots, then stir and cook over a low heat for 5 minutes. Add the wine to the pan and bring to a simmer. Cover with foil and a lid and cook over a low heat for about 20 minutes.

Meanwhile, put the carrots in a saucepan with the butter and water and season with salt and pepper. Cover the pan and cook for about 10 minutes, or until the carrots are tender.

When ready to serve, add the cream to the chicken and bring to a simmer uncovered, turning the chicken pieces around in the sauce. Stir in 2 tablespoons of the tarragon leaves.

Divide the carrots among four plates and top each with two pieces of chicken. Spoon a little sauce over the top, garnish with the remaining tarragon leaves and serve.

Serves 4

ROAST POUSSIN WITH FRENCH LENTILS

Poussin rôti aux lentilles du Puy

FROM THE CENTRE OF FRANCE/MASSIF CENTRAL REGION

The delicious and delicate green lentils from the town of Le Puy-en-Velay are world famous and loved by all, from the most humble cook to the top French chefs.

2 poussins (baby chickens)

2 tablespoons olive oil

2 thyme sprigs, finely chopped

freshly ground black pepper

French lentils

2 teaspoons salted butter

30 g (1 oz) bacon, finely chopped

¼ onion, finely chopped

2 thyme sprigs

a few parsley sprigs

½ bay leaf

½ carrot, diced

3 tablespoons diced celery

140 g (5 oz/¾ cup) puy lentils

1 garlic clove

375 ml (12½ fl oz/ 1½ cups) chicken stock

salt

freshly ground black pepper

3 tablespoons chopped parsley

To prepare the lentils, heat the butter in a saucepan. Add the bacon and fry for 1 minute. Add the onion, stir well and fry for 1 minute.

Use kitchen string to tie the thyme, parsley and bay leaf together.

Add the carrot and celery to the pan and stir well. Add the herbs, lentils and whole garlic clove. Add the stock and bring to a simmer. Cover with a lid and cook over a low heat for about 40 minutes, or until the lentils are tender.

The lentils may be prepared ahead of time and gently reheated. Season with salt and pepper and stir in the chopped parsley just before serving.

Rub the poussins all over with the oil and the chopped thyme. Season with pepper, cover and refrigerate until 10 minutes before cooking.

Preheat the oven to 160°C (320°F).

Place the poussins in a small roasting tin and roast for about 35 minutes, turning the birds a couple of times during the cooking. Rest for 10 minutes before carving and serve with the lentils.

Serves 2–4

BRESSE CHICKEN WITH MOREL MUSHROOMS

Poulet de Bresse aux morilles

FROM THE FRANCHE-COMTÉ REGION

The chickens from around the town of Bourg-en-Bresse are considered by many to be the finest in France for flavour and texture. Select the best-quality chicken you can find for this dish. Dried morels are readily available from good supermarkets and delicatessens. They need to be rinsed and soaked before using. Fresh morels are usually fairly clean, but brush away any visible dirt.

10 g (¼ oz) dried morels or 100 g (3½ oz) fresh morels

10 baby carrots

20 g (¾ oz) salted butter

2 corn-fed chicken breast fillets

salt

freshly ground black pepper

1 French shallot, finely chopped

3 tablespoons strong veal stock

2 tablespoons pouring cream

2 tablespoons chopped parsley

juice of ¼ lemon

Preheat the oven to 130°C (250°F).

If using dried morels, put them in a bowl and cover with lukewarm water. Stir to wash the grit off. Carefully lift the morels from the water and transfer them to a clean bowl. Cover with cold water and leave to soak for 15 minutes.

Put the carrots in a saucepan with a little water and cook until just tender.

Heat the butter in a non-stick frying pan and brown the chicken fillets for 2 minutes on each side. Season with salt and pepper. Transfer to a small ovenproof dish and bake for 15 minutes.

Add the shallot to the frying pan and stir for 1 minute. Drain the morels, reserving the liquid. Add to the pan, season with salt and pepper and sweat for 5 minutes over a medium heat. Add the soaking liquid and bring to a simmer. Add the stock and cream and simmer until the liquid has reduced by half.

Add the chicken and carrots to the morel sauce. Baste the chicken with the sauce for 30 seconds. Add the chopped parsley and lemon juice, stir and serve.

Serves 2

CHICKEN FRICASSÉE WITH ARTICHOKES

Poulet aux artichauts

FROM THE PROVENCE REGION

The sun shines abundantly at the border of the northern part of Provence, and the local artichokes and tomatoes make a superb, delicate accompaniment to the region's many fine chicken dishes.

3 small globe artichokes

1 slice lemon

1 tablespoon extra-virgin olive oil

2 chicken drumsticks on the bone, skin on

2 chicken thighs on the bone, skin on

salt

freshly ground black pepper

1 teaspoon coriander seeds

½ teaspoon fennel seeds

½ small brown onion, finely chopped

1 teaspoon tomato paste (concentrated purée)

3 tablespoons dry white wine

2 tomatoes, finely diced

2 tablespoons chopped parsley

Cut two-thirds off the top of the artichokes, using a serrated knife. Then use a paring knife to carefully trim away all the leaves so you are left with the artichoke heart. Trim the artichoke stalks, leaving about 2 cm (¾ in). Using a melon baller or spoon, remove the hairy part of the heart, then cut the heart into quarters. Rub the clean artichoke pieces with a slice of lemon to prevent discolouring, then place them in a bowl of cold water until required.

Heat the oil in a medium frying pan and brown the chicken pieces for 2 minutes on each side. Season the chicken with salt and pepper.

Drain the artichoke pieces, add them to the pan and stir for 2 minutes. Add the coriander and fennel seeds and stir briefly, then add the onion and cook for 3 minutes. Stir in the tomato paste and white wine and bring to the boil. Stir in the tomatoes and bring to a simmer. Cover with a lid and cook over a low heat for 15–20 minutes.

To serve, spoon a little sauce and some artichoke pieces onto two plates. Top with the chicken pieces, sprinkle with parsley and serve.

Serves 2

CHICKEN FRICASSÉE WITH CHESTNUTS

Fricassée de poulet aux marrons

FROM THE RHÔNE VALLEY REGION | BY PHILIPPE MOUCHEL

The French love the unique texture and flavour of chestnuts, and chicken with chestnuts is a great French classic. During my youth in France, we often collected large quantities of chestnuts from the local forest.

1 chicken, cut into pieces, skin on

salt

freshly ground pepper

60 ml (2 fl oz/¼ cup) extra-virgin olive oil

3 tablespoons salted butter

2 garlic cloves, whole

4 thyme sprigs

1 bay leaf

3 celery stalks, cut into sticks about 5 cm (2 in) long x 1 cm (½ in) wide

250 g (9 oz) peeled chestnuts

150 ml (5 fl oz) rich chicken stock

a few celery leaves

Preheat the oven to 170°C (340°F).

Season the chicken pieces with salt and pepper.

Heat 2 tablespoons of olive oil in an ovenproof saucepan. Add 1 tablespoon of butter and brown the chicken pieces on all sides. Stir in the garlic cloves and add the herbs. Bake in the preheated oven for about 10 minutes.

Transfer the chicken to a plate and keep warm. Discard the herbs and remove the excess fat from the pan.

Add the celery stalks, peeled chestnuts and 1 tablespoon of butter and stir well for 2 minutes.

Return the chicken pieces to the pan, add the stock and return the pan to the oven to bake for 10 minutes.

Transfer the chicken to serving plates.

Add the remaining butter and 1 tablespoon of olive oil to the cooking juices and vegetables in the pan and boil down for about 2 minutes to reduce the sauce.

Serve the chestnuts, celery and sauce around the chicken. Garnish with celery leaves and drizzle the remaining olive oil over the top.

Serves 4

CHICKEN WITH CHAMPAGNE & MUSHROOM SAUCE

Poulet au Champagne et champignons

FROM THE CHAMPAGNE-ARDENNES REGION

The extraordinary sparkling wines of the Champagne region are famous and loved the world over, and in cooking the wines impart delicate flavour. This lovely dish is easy to make for a special occasion.

2 tablespoons olive oil

8 pieces of chicken, on the bone

2 French shallots, finely chopped

1 tablespoon cognac

salt

freshly ground black pepper

½ bottle Champagne or sparkling white wine

600 g (1 lb 5 oz) mixed mushrooms

125 ml (4 fl oz/½ cup) cream

3 tablespoons finely snipped chives

12 asparagus spears, sliced and steamed

Heat 1 tablespoon of olive oil in a heavy-based saucepan and cook the chicken pieces for a few minutes on a medium heat, turning, until browned all over. Stir in the shallots and cook for about 5 minutes.

Add the cognac and stir well. Season with salt and pepper, then add the Champagne. Bring to a simmer, cover with foil and a lid and simmer for 20 minutes.

Heat the remaining olive oil in a large frying pan on a high heat and cook the mushrooms for 3–4 minutes or until softened and golden.

Transfer the chicken pieces with the mushrooms to a bowl and cover to keep warm.

Bring the cooking juices to the boil and cook for 10–15 minutes or until reduced to about 125 ml (4 fl oz/½ cup). Add the cream and simmer for 2–3 minutes or until slightly thickened.

Return the chicken pieces and mushrooms to the sauce and heat for 5 minutes until warmed through.

Spoon the mushrooms onto four plates and top each with two pieces of chicken. Spoon the sauce over the chicken and sprinkle with chives.

It's lovely with steamed asparagus.

Serves 4

GRANDMÈRE'S CHICKEN CASSEROLE

Poulet cocotte grandmère

FROM THE BRESSE REGION

The region of Bresse is famous for producing some of the tastiest chicken in France and this easy, delicious local recipe is one of our children's favourite dishes.

---

40 g (1½ oz) salted butter

3 tablespoons vegetable oil

4 free-range chicken drumsticks, skin on

4 free-range chicken thighs, skin on

salt

freshly ground pepper

1 brown onion, diced

1 bay leaf

2 tablespoons rosemary sprigs

150 g (5½ oz) bacon, diced

125 ml (4½ fl oz/½ cup) white Macon wine or another dry white wine

180 g (6½ oz/2 cups) button mushrooms, washed

4 medium all-purpose potatoes, cubed

3 tablespoons chopped parsley

Heat the butter and 1 tablespoon of the oil in a wide heavy frying pan and brown the chicken pieces for a few minutes. Season with salt and pepper, add the onion, bay leaf and rosemary and stir well. Add the bacon and cook for a few minutes.

Add the white wine and bring to the boil. Stir in the mushrooms then cover with foil and a lid. Cook on a low heat for about 30 minutes.

Heat the remaining oil in a heavy frying pan and cook the potato cubes for about 15 minutes or until they are almost done. Transfer the potatoes to the chicken dish and mix gently. Cook for a further 5 minutes to combine the flavours.

Serve two pieces of chicken on each plate with the vegetables. Garnish with parsley.

Serves 4

CHICKEN & CAPSICUM CASSEROLE WITH OLIVES

Poulet aux poivrons et olives

FROM THE NORTH OF PROVENCE REGION

With its beautiful flavour of herbs, capsicum and olives, this dish is a great example of Provençal cuisine.

1 tablespoon olive oil

8 chicken drumsticks, skin on

12 baby potatoes, peeled

2 tablespoons chopped rosemary

1 onion, diced

salt

freshly ground black pepper

3 capsicums (peppers) of different colour, finely sliced

16 black olives

Preheat the oven to 180°C (350°F).

Heat the olive oil in a wide, non-stick frying pan over a medium–high heat. Add the chicken pieces and brown them for a few minutes. Add the potatoes and brown them for 2 minutes. Sprinkle the rosemary over and stir in the onion. Season with salt and pepper and cook for a few minutes before transferring to a baking dish.

Bake the chicken in the preheated oven for about 20 minutes.

Meanwhile, add the sliced capsicum to the pan and cook on a medium heat for about 20 minutes, stirring occasionally.

Return the chicken and potatoes to the saucepan and stir in the black olives until all the ingredients are warmed through.

Serves 4

CHICKEN & PRAWN CASSEROLE

Poulet aux gambas

FROM THE LANGUEDOC-ROUSSILLON REGION

It's very Mediterranean to cook chicken and prawns together, especially with spices such as chilli and saffron (as in a paella). Gambas are large prawns — they are fleshy and succulent.

60 ml (2 fl oz/¼ cup) extra-virgin olive oil

1 brown onion, chopped

4 chicken pieces on the bone (thighs are good)

salt

freshly ground pepper

1 mild green chilli, thinly sliced

2 large tomatoes, peeled, seeded and chopped

3 tablespoons vermouth

a pinch of saffron threads

8 raw king prawns (jumbo shrimp), shells on

40 g (1½ oz/¼ cup) pine nuts, roasted and finely chopped

3 tablespoons chopped parsley

2 garlic cloves, chopped

Heat 1 tablespoon of the oil in a frying pan and cook the onion over a low heat for 5 minutes.

Season the chicken pieces with salt and pepper. Heat another 2 tablespoons of oil in a wide saucepan and brown the chicken pieces all over. Add the onion to the pan, together with the chilli, tomato, vermouth and saffron. Bring to a simmer, cover with a lid and cook for 20 minutes. Turn the chicken pieces over once during the cooking.

Heat the remaining oil in a large frying pan and cook the prawns for 1 minute on each side. Add the prawns to the pan with the chicken, stir gently and cook for 2 minutes more. Stir in the pine nuts, parsley and garlic and serve immediately.

Serves 4

CHICKEN CASSEROLE COOKED IN RIESLING

Poulet au riesling

FROM THE ALSACE REGION

The white wines of Alsace made with riesling grapes are outstanding and, in true French tradition, a region with great wine also offers wonderful gastronomy. This dish is a fine example of a festive Alsatian dish.

12 parsley stalks

1 bay leaf

2 thyme sprigs

4 chicken drumsticks (skin on or off)

4 chicken thighs (skin on or off)

salt

freshly ground black pepper

1 tablespoon olive oil

20 g (¾ oz) butter

2 French shallots, chopped

2 tablespoons cognac or brandy

200 ml (7 fl oz) Alsace riesling

a little grated nutmeg (optional)

300 g (10½ oz) baby mushrooms

juice of ½ lemon

100 ml (3½ fl oz) pouring cream

2 egg yolks

3 tablespoons chopped parsley

Use kitchen string to tie the parsley stalks, bay leaf and thyme together. Season the chicken pieces with salt and pepper. Heat the oil and half the butter in a large heavy-based saucepan. Brown the chicken pieces over a high heat for 2–3 minutes. Add the shallots, shake the pan and cook for 2 minutes.

Add the cognac to the pan, stir well, remove the pan away from the stove, then carefully flame the chicken pieces. When the flame dies down, add the wine, nutmeg and herbs. Return the pan to the stove, bring to a slow simmer, cover with a lid and cook for about 25 minutes.

Meanwhile, melt the remaining butter in a frying pan. Sauté the mushrooms until just tender. Add them to the chicken and simmer for 3 minutes. Stir in the lemon juice.

In a medium bowl, whisk together the cream and egg yolks. Pour in 250 ml (8½ fl oz/1 cup) of the hot cooking liquid from the chicken, whisking continuously. Pour the mixture back into the pan and stir gently over a low heat for a few minutes (it must not boil). Discard the bouquet garni, add the chopped parsley and serve.

Serves 4

CHICKEN CASSEROLE VALLÉE D'AUGE

Poulet Vallée d'Auge

FROM THE NORMANDY REGION

The popularity of this dish doesn't surprise me. The sweetness of the cooked apples and creamy sauce is a real winner, and it is an easy-to-prepare dish for a special occasion.

---

90 g (3 oz) butter

8 chicken pieces, on the bone, skin on

20 ml (¾ fl oz) Calvados liqueur

salt

freshly ground pepper

3 shallots, cut into quarters

150 ml (5 fl oz) cider

250 g (9 oz) mushrooms

2 apples

210 ml (7 fl oz) cream

Heat one-third of the butter in a large cast-iron pan and brown the chicken pieces on all sides. Then pour in the Calvados. Season with salt and pepper. Add the shallots and cider and shake the pan. Bring to a simmer and then cover with foil and a lid and cook on a low heat for 30 minutes.

Meanwhile, heat another third of the butter in a separate frying pan and cook the mushrooms for a few minutes.

Peel, halve and core the apples. Cut each half into four segments.

Heat the remaining butter in a large pan and cook the apple segments until soft.

Add the mushrooms to the chicken, then add the cream and mix well. Bring to a simmer and cook for about 5 minutes.

Serve the chicken and sauce on a large platter surrounded by the apple pieces.

Serves 4

CHICKEN MARENGO WITH OLIVES

Poulet Marengo aux olives

FROM THE CORSICA REGION

Napoleon Bonaparte's cook created this dish for the emperor after the Battle of Marengo in northern Italy. Bonaparte won the battle and enjoyed this Franco-Italian-style meal. It's delicious served with delicate broad beans.

60 ml (2 fl oz/¼ cup) extra-virgin olive oil

8 chicken pieces, on the bone, skin on

3 tablespoons finely chopped shallots

2 tablespoons finely chopped lemon thyme

4 thin strips of orange zest

100 ml (3½ fl oz) dry white wine

500 g (1 lb 2 oz/2 cups) peeled, diced tomatoes

30 olives

salt

freshly ground pepper

20 broad beans (fava), shelled, blanched and skin removed

2 tablespoons chopped parsley

Preheat the oven to 160°C (320°F).

Heat half the olive oil in a frying pan and brown the chicken pieces, skin side down, for a few minutes. Transfer the chicken to a roasting tray and finish cooking in the preheated oven for about 15 minutes.

Remove the chicken fat from the roasting tray. Add the remaining oil, shallots, thyme and orange zest and stir for a few minutes. Stir in the wine and bring to the boil. Add the tomatoes, stir well and cook for 10 minutes.

Add the chicken pieces and olives to the sauce, season with salt and pepper, and heat through on a low heat.

Serve the chicken and the sauce with broad beans, sprinkled with chopped parsley.

Serves 8

POACHED CHICKEN WITH VEGETABLES

Poule au pot

FROM THE BÉARN/PYRÉNÉES REGION | BY ELIZABETH KERDELHUÉ

The French, me included, adore their poule au pot. In the depths of winter it is really lovely comfort food. Poule au pot is easy to prepare and very healthy. The tasty cooking broth is served separately as a soup, to which small pasta is sometimes added.

1.8 kg (4 lb) free-range chicken, skin on or off, according to taste

a few thyme sprigs

a few parsley sprigs

1 bay leaf

1 medium brown onion

3 cloves

8 black peppercorns

salt

freshly ground black pepper

4 medium carrots

4 medium turnips

2 leeks, cut into 10 cm (4 in) lengths

2 celery stalks, cut into 10 cm (4 in) lengths

2 teaspoons mustard

2 tablespoons red wine vinegar

125 ml (4 fl oz/½ cup) olive oil

6 gherkins (pickles), thinly sliced

2 tablespoons chopped parsley

Put the chicken in a large pot, cover with water and place it on a medium heat.

Use kitchen string to tie the thyme, parsley and bay leaf together to make a bouquet garni. Stud the onion with the cloves and add to the pot with the bouquet garni and peppercorns. Season with salt and pepper.

Add the vegetables to the pot, bring to a simmer and cook for about 50 minutes. Remove surface foam from time to time with a large spoon or skimmer.

In a small bowl, mix the mustard with a little salt and pepper. Whisk in the vinegar, then add the oil, whisking continuously. Stir in the gherkins and parsley.

Transfer the chicken and vegetables to a platter and serve with the dressing either poured over the top or in a separate bowl. Serve the broth separately, with or without pasta.

Serves 4

CHICKEN BURGUNDY

Coq au vin

FROM THE BURGUNDY REGION

This is one of the first classic French dishes I learned to prepare as an eighteen-year-old chef in Paris. There are several versions of the dish and if you have time you can marinate the chicken in the wine overnight.

---

20 baby onions

55 g (2 oz) salted butter

100 g (3½ oz) bacon, thinly sliced

250 g (9 oz) mushrooms

8 chicken pieces on the bone (e.g. 4 drumsticks and 4 thighs)

sea salt

freshly ground black pepper

2 tablespoons cognac

1 heaped tablespoon plain (all-purpose) flour

400 ml (13½ fl oz) good-quality red wine

1 thyme sprig

a few parsley sprigs

1 bay leaf

1 clove

2 tablespoons tomato paste (concentrated purée)

2 tablespoons chopped parsley

Put the onions in a saucepan with plenty of cold water, bring to the boil, cook for 2 minutes then drain well.

Melt half the butter in a large ovenproof saucepan or casserole dish. Add the onions and brown them over a medium heat for a few minutes. Add the bacon and stir well for 2 minutes. Add the mushrooms and cook for 4–5 minutes until the mushrooms are soft. Transfer the onions, bacon and mushrooms to a dish.

Add the remaining butter to the pan and brown the chicken pieces over a high heat for a few minutes. Season with salt and pepper and stir well. Drain off excess fat into a bowl and discard.

Add the cognac to the pan, remove the pan away from the stove and carefully flame the chicken pieces. Stir well, then sprinkle on the flour. Pour in the red wine and shake the pan.

Use kitchen string to tie the thyme, parsley and bay leaf together to make a bouquet garni. Add to the pan, together with the garlic and tomato paste, return the pan to the heat and stir well. Bring to a slow simmer, cover with a lid and cook for about 20 minutes.

Turn the chicken pieces over, add the mushrooms, bacon and onions to the pan and simmer for a further 10 minutes. Check the seasoning, sprinkle with chopped parsley and serve.

Serves 4

Note: If you prefer a thicker sauce, pour it into a separate saucepan and boil until reduced to your liking.

GRILLED DUCK WITH SAUTÉED POTATOES & CURLY SALAD

Canard grillé, pommes de terre sautées, salade frisée

FROM THE LANGUEDOC REGION | BY PHILIPPE MOUCHEL

This duck recipe is very simple to prepare and a lovely example of a rustic French dish that can be served when a couple of friends come to dinner.

3 duck legs

1 tablespoon sea salt

freshly ground black pepper

3 teaspoons finely grated lemon zest

2 tablespoons goose fat (available from good delicatessens)

2 large potatoes, peeled and cut into 1 cm (½ in) cubes

2 garlic cloves, 1 crushed and 1 finely chopped

1 red (Spanish) onion, cut into long thin pieces

100 g (3½ oz) mushrooms, quartered

1 tablespoon chopped thyme

1 tablespoon rosemary leaves

20 g (¾ oz) salted butter

1 teaspoon dijon mustard

1 tablespoon cherry vinegar or other vinegar

3 tablespoons olive oil

3 cups curly endive (frisée), roughly torn

3 thyme sprigs, to garnish

Preheat the grill (broiler) to high.

Rub the duck legs all over with sea salt, paying special attention to the skin side. Place the duck legs on a rack set in a roasting tin. Season the duck skin with pepper and lemon zest. Place under the hot grill and cook until the skins have browned a little. Turn off the grill element and set the oven temperature to 200°C (400°F). Cook the duck legs for about 30 minutes.

Meanwhile, heat the goose fat in a large frying pan. Add the potato and stir over a medium heat for 2–3 minutes. Add the crushed garlic and the onion and stir for 2 minutes. Season with salt and pepper. Add the mushrooms and cook for about 8 minutes, or until the potatoes and mushrooms are tender. Add the thyme, rosemary and butter.

In a large salad bowl mix the chopped garlic clove with the mustard, cherry vinegar and a little salt and pepper. Whisk in the oil. Add the curly endive to the bowl and toss well in the dressing.

Divide the potatoes among three plates. Top with a duck leg, garnish with a sprig of thyme and serve with the endive salad.

Serves 3

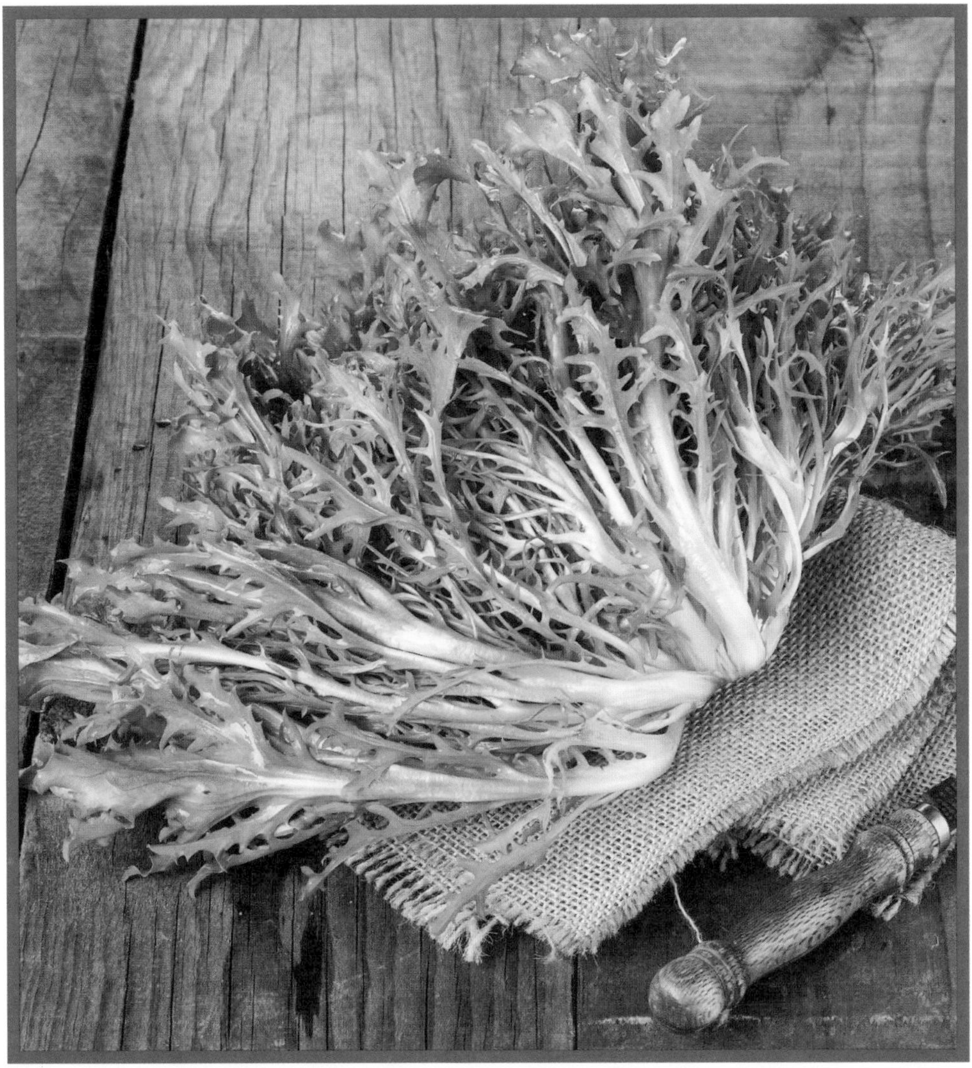

DUCK FILLET WITH PORCINI MUSHROOMS & GREEN PEPPERCORN SAUCE

Filet de canard aux cèpes, sauce au poivre vert

FROM THE AQUITAINE/DORDOGNE REGION

For special occasions, duck is the meat most commonly served in the Dordogne region. Porcini (cèpe) mushrooms are usually considered the best type of mushroom.

2 tablespoons olive oil

2 duck fillets

150 g (5½ oz) porcini mushrooms, washed and cut into bite-sized pieces

1 shallot, finely chopped

1 garlic clove, finely chopped

2 tablespoons chopped parsley

sea salt

freshly ground black pepper

1 tablespoon green peppercorns

2 tablespoons cognac

60 ml (2 fl oz/¼ cup) strong beef stock

1 tablespoon cream

Heat half the oil in a saucepan over a medium heat. Cook the duck fillets, skin side down, for about 8 minutes, then turn the fillets over and cook for a further 2 minutes or until cooked through.

While the duck is cooking, drop the mushrooms in boiling water. Cook for 2 minutes, then drain.

Heat the remaining olive oil in a non-stick pan over a medium–high heat. Stir in the chopped shallot and cook for 2 minutes.

Add the mushrooms and cook for a few minutes. Stir in the garlic and parsley and season with sea salt and pepper.

Transfer the duck fillets to a plate and keep warm.

Discard the duck fat from the saucepan and add the green peppercorns. Stir in the cognac and bring to the boil. Add the stock, return to the boil and cook for about 20 seconds. Then add the cream and stir well for about 10 seconds.

Slice the duck into three or four pieces. Transfer the duck pieces to a serving plate, garnish with the mushrooms and spoon the sauce over the duck.

Serves 2

ROAST DUCK FILLET WITH CHERRIES

Canard aux cerises

FROM THE PYRÉNÉES REGION

---

*The scenery in the Pyrénées mountain ranges is stunning.
Fruit groves thrive in the valleys between the peaks, and during the hot
summers the local sweet cherries make a superb accompaniment to duck,
one of the most popular festive dishes of the region.*

2–3 medium potatoes, peeled and quartered

salt

80 ml (2½ fl oz/⅓ cup) milk

20 g (¾ oz) salted butter

2 duck breast fillets, skin on

freshly ground black pepper

1 tablespoon olive oil

2 tablespoons port or red wine

2 tablespoons fresh orange juice

2 tablespoons veal glaze (available from good butchers and delicatessens)

12–20 cherries, pitted just before using

2 tablespoons chopped parsley

Preheat the oven to 150°C (300°F).

Boil the potatoes in lightly salted water until tender, then drain well.

Bring the milk and butter to the boil in a medium saucepan. Push the drained potatoes through a mouli or sieve into the hot milk. Stir well. Set the potato purée aside and keep warm.

Meanwhile, use a sharp knife to score the skin of the duck fillets in a criss-cross pattern. Season with salt and pepper.

Heat the oil in small roasting tin and brown the duck fillets, skin side down, for about 3 minutes. Turn the fillets over, then transfer to the oven for about 10 minutes.

When the duck fillets are cooked, transfer them to a warm plate and cover with foil.

Discard the excess fat from the pan, then add the port and bring to the boil.

Add the orange juice and bring to a simmer. Add the veal glaze, return to a simmer, then add the pitted cherries and heat them through.

Just before serving, gently reheat the potato. Divide the potato between two deep plates and arrange a duck fillet on top. Garnish with cherries, spoon on the sauce, sprinkle with chopped parsley and serve.

Serves 2

DUCK LEG WITH PRUNES

Cuisse de canard rôtie aux pruneaux

FROM THE PYRÉNÉES/SOUTH WEST REGION

The production of duck liver pâté is big in the South West and duck meat is plentiful. It is common family fare prepared in many different ways. This easy recipe is ideal for a special occasion.

---

2 duck legs, skin on

1 tablespoon extra-virgin olive oil

sea salt

½ teaspoon cracked pepper

½ teaspoon fennel seeds, crushed

1 large carrot, peeled and sliced

40 g (1½ oz) salted butter

1 shallot, finely chopped

2 tablespoons red wine

60 ml (2 fl oz/¼ cup) rich chicken stock

10 prunes

Preheat the oven to 180°C (350°F).

Rub the duck legs with olive oil and season the skin with salt, pepper and crushed fennel seeds.

Place the duck legs in a small roasting tray and bake in the preheated oven, skin side up, for about 30 minutes, basting from time to time.

Meanwhile, steam the carrot in a little water until cooked. Drain the carrot, blend to a purée, stir in half the butter and season to taste.

Transfer the duck to a plate and cover with foil. Drain the duck fat from the tray, then add the shallots and cook for a few minutes. Add the red wine, stir and bring to the boil, evaporate most of it. Add the stock and bring to a simmer, then add the prunes and simmer for a further few minutes.

Stir in the remaining butter. Add the duck legs to the sauce and coat them.

Place a little carrot purée on each plate. Top with the duck, spoon the sauce and prunes on top and serve.

Serves 2

DUCK WITH TURNIPS

Canard aux navets

FROM THE PYRÉNÉES REGION

Many years ago, duck was only available whole and it was mostly eaten at restaurants, but now it's easy to buy in a variety of cuts, and duck has become a common and much-loved family treat.

2 turnips

125 ml (4 fl oz/½ cup) water

20 g (¾ oz) salted butter

2 duck breast fillets, skin on

1 teaspoon fennel seeds

salt

freshly ground pepper

1 shallot, finely chopped

1 tablespoon cognac

2 tablespoons veal glaze

2 tablespoons extra water

Peel the turnips and cut each into six segments. Using a paring knife, trim the turnips into large olive shapes, the size of a date.

Place the turnips, the water and half the butter in a saucepan and cook on a medium heat until the turnips are soft and the water has evaporated. By that time, the turnips will be glazed by the butter.

Meanwhile, season the skin of the duck fillets with fennel seeds and a little salt and pepper.

Heat a heavy frying pan. Place the duck, skin side down, in the hot pan and cook on a medium heat for about 8 minutes. Turn the duck over and cook for a further 2 minutes. Transfer the duck fillets to a warm plate and cover with foil.

Discard the duck fat from the pan. Put the shallots into the pan and cook for 2 minutes.

Add the cognac and flame it before adding the veal glaze and 2 tablespoons of water. Simmer for 1 minute, then stir in the remaining butter.

Reheat the turnips in the sauce.

Cut each duck fillet into three pieces and serve on warm plates with the turnips and sauce.

Serves 2

DUCK CASSEROLE IN RED WINE
Daube de canard

FROM THE GASCOGNE/PYRÉNÉES REGION | BY PHILIPPE MOUCHEL

A casserole of duck legs cooked slowly in red wine and flavoured with aromatic herbs, orange zest and vegetables is called a 'daube'. It is one of my favourite dishes to enjoy with a good red wine on a cold winter's evening.

3 duck legs

250 ml (8½ fl oz/1 cup) good-quality red wine

1 medium onion, diced

1 medium carrot, diced

2 garlic cloves, crushed

2 thyme sprigs

1 bay leaf

a few pieces orange zest

salt

freshly ground pepper

a little olive oil

500 g (1 lb 2 oz) baby carrots

2 tablespoons chopped parsley

Put the duck legs in a bowl with the wine, onion, carrot, garlic, thyme, bay leaf and orange zest. Cover with plastic wrap and marinate overnight in the refrigerator.

Preheat the oven to 160°C (320°F).

Remove the duck legs from the marinade and pat them dry with paper towel. Season with salt and pepper. Heat a little oil in a cast-iron saucepan or casserole dish and brown the duck legs on all sides. Use a slotted spoon to remove the vegetables and herbs from the marinade. Add them to the pan and stir for a few minutes. Pour in the marinade, stir and bring to a low simmer. Cover the pan with a lid and bake in the oven for about 1½ hours.

Meanwhile, steam the baby carrots for a couple of minutes.

When the duck legs are almost cooked, remove them from the pan and strain the sauce, discarding the herbs and vegetables. Return the duck legs to the pan and pour in the sauce. Add the carrots, cover the pan and return to the oven for 15 minutes.

Serve each duck leg topped with carrots. Spoon the sauce over the top and serve sprinkled with chopped parsley.

Serves 3

CASSOULET

Cassoulet is a hearty dish of confit duck, baked beans and various pork cuts. It is one of the most popular French winter classics and features on restaurant menus in most family restaurants between Montpellier and Bordeaux. Confit duck and duck fat are available from butchers and good delicatessens.

1 tablespoon duck fat (or butter or olive oil)

40 g (1½ oz) diced celery

40 g (1½ oz) diced carrot

40 g (1½ oz) diced onion

1 garlic clove

200 g (7 oz/1 cup) coco or haricot beans, soaked overnight in cold water

3 tablespoons dry white wine

1 teaspoon tomato paste (concentrated purée)

1 bay leaf

2 thyme sprigs

salt

freshly ground black pepper

1 tablespoon olive oil

1–2 Toulouse sausages, or good-quality pork sausages

200 g (7 oz) cooked pork knuckle

200 g (7 oz) cooked pork belly

2 confit duck legs

50 g (1¾ oz/½ cup) dried breadcrumbs

3 tablespoons chopped parsley

Preheat the oven to 150°C (300°F).

Heat the duck fat in an ovenproof dish over a medium heat. Add the vegetables and garlic clove and sauté for a few minutes. Drain the soaked beans and add them to the dish. Add the wine, stir well and bring to the boil. Add enough water to cover and bring to a simmer. Add the tomato paste, bay leaf and thyme and season with a little salt and pepper. Cover with a lid and cook for 1–1½ hours, or until the beans are almost cooked.

Heat the oil in a frying pan and brown the sausages all over. Add them to the ovenproof dish, along with the pork knuckle, pork belly and duck legs. Shake the dish to distribute the beans evenly, then sprinkle on the breadcrumbs.

Return the dish to the oven and cook, uncovered, for 30 minutes until the breadcrumbs are crisp and brown.

Sprinkle with chopped parsley and serve. French people love to eat cassoulet with mustard but my wife doesn't!

Serves 2–3

BAKED QUAIL WITH GRAPES & CHESTNUTS

Cailles aux raisins et aux marrons

FROM THE AQUITAINE REGION

I like to serve this very simple but special dish to my gourmet friends. Quail meat is tender and delicate, and the grapes and chestnuts provide a lovely contrast of textures.

2 teaspoons oil

40 g (1½ oz) salted butter

4 quails, butterflied

1 French shallot, finely chopped

2 bacon rashers, chopped

100 ml (3½ fl oz) white wine from Bergerac

100 ml (3½ fl oz) strong chicken stock

12 raw chestnuts, peeled

salt

freshly ground black pepper

about 25 grapes

2 tablespoons chopped parsley

Heat the oil in a heavy-based saucepan over a medium-high heat. Add half the butter and cook the quails for 3–4 minutes each side or until browned all over.

Add the shallot and bacon and cook for 1 minute, stirring well. Add the white wine, bring to the boil and cook for 1 minute. Add the stock and chestnuts and season with salt and pepper. Cover with a lid and cook on a low heat for 10 minutes.

Meanwhile, drop the grapes into boiling water for a second or two, then drain and peel them. Remove the quails and chestnuts from the pan and boil down the cooking juices to about 60 ml (2 fl oz/¼ cup). Stir in the remaining butter. Return the quails and chestnuts to the pan with the grapes and reheat for 5 minutes.

Serve the quails with the chestnuts, grapes and sauce, and sprinkle chopped parsley over the top.

Serves 2–4

Note: Tinned or frozen chestnuts are available from gourmet food stores and select grocers.

ROAST GUINEA FOWL WITH SPINACH & PEARS

Pintade rôtie aux épinards et aux poires

FROM THE PYRÉNÉES REGION

I'm always a bit surprised that outside France few restaurants serve guinea fowl. In France it's a popular Sunday lunch treat and this recipe is delicious.

---

3 rosemary sprigs, about 10 cm (4 in) long

4–5 garlic cloves, whole

1 guinea fowl, about 1 kg (2 lb 3 oz)

salt

freshly ground pepper

1 tablespoon extra-virgin olive oil

30 g (1 oz) salted butter

½ brown onion, diced

70 g (2½ oz/½ cup) diced celery

2 just ripe pears (Williams pears are good)

100 g (3½ oz/2 cups) spinach leaves, washed

2 tablespoons pouring cream

2 tablespoons dry white wine

75 ml (2½ fl oz/¼ cup) cold water

2 finely chopped mint leaves

Preheat the oven to 160°C (320°F).

Place the rosemary and garlic cloves in the cavity of the guinea fowl and season the bird with salt and pepper.

Heat the oil and 10 g (¼ oz) butter in a flameproof baking pan and brown the guinea fowl on each side for 1–2 minutes. Place the onion and celery around the bird, then roast it in the preheated oven for about 45 minutes, basting once or twice during the cooking.

Meanwhile, peel, halve and core the pears. Cut each half into four segments.

Heat 10 g (¼ oz) butter in a wide frying pan and cook the pears for a few minutes on each side.

Cook the spinach in a saucepan of boiling water until wilted. Drain the spinach and press by hand to extract the excess water.

Add the cream to the pears, stir in the spinach and reheat.

Remove the guinea fowl from the baking pan and keep warm.

Add the wine to the baking pan and bring to a simmer. Add the water and boil for about 2 minutes. Strain the juices into a small saucepan and stir in the remaining butter and the mint leaves.

Portion the guinea fowl into eight pieces. Put some spinach and pear onto each plate and top with three or four pieces of guinea fowl. Spoon a little sauce over the top and serve.

Serves 2

RABBIT STEW WITH PRUNES

Lapin aux pruneaux

FROM THE BÉARN/PYRÉNÉES REGION | BY PHILIPPE MOUCHEL

Rabbit was an extremely popular meat during my youth in rural France. My family kept rabbits in the backyard, and we fed them with vegetable scraps and used the manure to fertilise our vegetable garden.

18 pitted prunes

375 ml (12½ fl oz/1½ cups) good-quality red wine

1 tablespoon honey

1 cinnamon stick

1 star anise

1 x 1.5 kg (3 lb 5 oz) rabbit, cut into 6–8 pieces

salt

freshly ground black pepper

1 tablespoon olive oil

20 g (¾ oz) salted butter

1 small brown onion, diced

1 small carrot, diced

3 thyme sprigs

1 slice pain d'épice (spiced honey bread)

3 tablespoons chopped parsley

Preheat the oven to 150°C (300°F).

Put the prunes in a bowl. Combine the wine, honey, cinnamon stick and star anise in a saucepan. Bring to the boil then pour over the prunes.

Season the rabbit pieces with salt and pepper. Heat the oil and half the butter in an ovenproof saucepan or casserole dish and brown the rabbit pieces all over. Tip any excess fat out of the pan and add the remaining butter. Stir in the onion and carrot, cover with a lid and cook for a few minutes.

Add the soaked prunes, together with their soaking liquid and spices. Finally, add the thyme and pain d'épice, which will soften and thicken the sauce as it cooks. Cover the pan and cook for about 2 hours, stirring a couple of times during cooking. When cooked, the rabbit meat should fall away from the bones.

Sprinkle with chopped parsley and serve.

Serves 6

RABBIT CASSEROLE WITH CAPSICUM & OLIVES

Lapin aux poivrons et aux olives

FROM THE NORTHWEST PROVENCE REGION	BY PHILIPPE MOUCHEL

Wild Provençal herbs and wild rabbits are both plentiful around the incredible Mont Ventoux, one of the highest mountains in the north of Provence.

1 red capsicum (pepper)

6 baby onions, peeled

6 rabbit pieces, on the bone

salt

freshly ground black pepper

60 ml (2 fl oz/¼ cup) extra-virgin olive oil

4 garlic cloves

2 bacon slices, cut into batons

20 black olives

1 small red chilli, roughly chopped

1 rosemary sprig, roughly chopped

100 ml (3½ fl oz) dry white wine

250 ml (8½ fl oz/1 cup) strong chicken or rabbit stock

Preheat the oven to 200°C (400°F).

Wrap the capsicum in foil and bake in the oven for about 20 minutes. Remove from the oven, carefully open the foil and, when cool enough to handle, peel the capsicum. Cut it in half, remove the seeds and cut each half into three pieces.

Reduce the oven temperature to 160°C (320°F).

Put the onions in a saucepan with plenty of cold water and bring to the boil. Boil for 2 minutes then drain well.

Season the rabbit with salt and pepper. Heat 2 tablespoons of the oil in a cast-iron casserole dish and brown the rabbit. Add the capsicum, onions, garlic, bacon, olives, chilli and rosemary. Stir well, cover and cook over a low heat for 10 minutes.

Add the wine to the pan, bring to the boil and cook until the liquid is reduced to about 2 tablespoons. Add the stock, bring to a simmer, cover with a lid and bake in the oven for about 1½ hours, or until the rabbit is cooked.

Lift the rabbit pieces onto a serving plate. Add the remaining 2 tablespoons of olive oil to the pot with the sauce and vegetables. Bring to the boil and cook for a few minutes to thicken it.

Spoon the vegetables and sauce over the rabbit and serve.

Serves 2

RABBIT
WITH A DIJON MUSTARD SAUCE

Lapin à la moutarde de Dijon

FROM THE BURGUNDY REGION

Dijon, the capital of Burgundy, is a great city to visit, not only for its splendid architecture, but because of its world-famous mustard.

---

6 rabbit hind legs

a little sea salt

freshly ground black pepper

a little plain (all-purpose) flour for dusting

2 tablespoons olive oil

20 g (¾ oz) salted butter

a few thyme sprigs, chopped

150 g (5½ oz) bacon, finely chopped

1 bay leaf

2 garlic cloves, crushed

1 medium brown onion, chopped

150 ml (5 fl oz) dry white wine

200 g (7 oz) mushrooms, halved or quartered, depending on size

2 tablespoons dijon mustard

2 tablespoons pouring cream

1 egg yolk

2 tablespoons chopped parsley

Preheat the oven to 150°C (300°F).

Season the rabbit legs with a little salt and pepper and dust with a little flour.

Heat the oil and butter in an ovenproof casserole dish over a medium heat and brown the rabbit legs all over. Add the thyme, bacon, bay leaf, garlic and onion and stir well for 3–5 minutes. Stir in the wine, then add the mushrooms and stir again. Cover with a lid and cook for 1–1½ hours.

Transfer the casserole dish to the stove top over a low heat. In a bowl, whisk together the mustard, cream and egg yolk. Slowly stir this mixture into the hot casserole, taking care not to let the sauce boil. Cook over a low heat for 5 minutes for the mustard flavour to infuse the rabbit.

Divide the rabbit pieces among six plates, spoon on the sauce and sprinkle with chopped parsley. Serve with your choice of vegetables.

Serves 6

WILD RABBIT WITH MUSHROOMS

Lapin de Garenne aux champignons

FROM THE SOUTH OF THE LOIRE/CENTRE REGION | BY PHILIPPE MOUCHEL

Wild rabbit abounds in the forested rural regions south of the Loire. In autumn and winter, rabbits feature on the table of many farmhouses and the favourite accompaniment is wild mushrooms. I prepare this dish using field mushrooms mixed with a few Swiss browns and shiitake mushrooms.

1 wild rabbit (about
1 kg/2 lb 3 oz), cut into
8 pieces

salt

freshly ground pepper

2 tablespoons olive oil

55 g (2 oz) butter

3 garlic cloves, peeled
and crushed

3 French shallots, diced

1 celery stalk, diced

400 g (14 oz) mixed
mushrooms, quartered

150 ml (5 fl oz) dry white
wine

250 ml (8½ fl oz/1 cup)
strong veal or rabbit
stock

1 thyme sprig

10 green peppercorns

1 tablespoon tarragon
leaves

Preheat the oven to 150°C (300°F).

Season the rabbit with salt and pepper. Heat the oil in a cast-iron saucepan or casserole dish and brown the rabbit on all sides. Add about a third of the butter to the pan, then the garlic, shallots, celery and about 10 of the quartered mushrooms. Stir well, cover and cook over a low heat for about 5 minutes.

Add the wine to the pan, bring to the boil and boil for 2 minutes. Add the stock, thyme and peppercorns, cover with a lid and bake for about 2 hours, or until the rabbit is tender, stirring once or twice during the cooking.

Fifteen minutes before you are ready to serve, heat another third of the butter in a frying pan. Add the remaining mushrooms and sauté until just tender. Set aside and keep warm.

Transfer the rabbit pieces to a dish, and cover with foil to keep warm.

Reduce the sauce by half, then stir in the remaining butter. Spoon the sauce and mushrooms over the rabbit pieces, garnish with tarragon leaves and serve.

Serves 3

WILD RABBIT STEW COOKED IN GAILLAC WINE

Civet de lapin au vin de Gaillac

FROM THE SOUTH WEST REGION

The scenery of the Tarn valley around the town of Albi in the South West is quite superb. The local food is rustic and the Gaillac wines are strong and fruity, complementing the gamey flavour of this dish.

1 wild rabbit, cut into portions

1 carrot, sliced

125 g (4½ oz/1 cup) sliced celery

about 10 parsley sprigs

2 thyme sprigs

1 bay leaf

2 shallots, sliced

1 teaspoon cracked pepper

½ bottle red Gaillac wine or another full-bodied red wine

75 g (2¾ oz/½ cup) diced bacon

2 tablespoons plain (all-purpose) flour

salt

180 g (6½ oz/2 cups) quartered mushrooms

20 g (¾ oz) salted butter

2–3 tablespoons chopped parsley

Place the rabbit pieces in a wide bowl with the carrots, celery, parsley, thyme, bay leaf, shallots and cracked pepper. Add the red wine, stir briefly, cover with plastic wrap and marinate overnight in the fridge.

The next day, preheat the oven to 140°C (275°F). Drain the rabbit pieces and strain the red wine marinade into a bowl, reserving the vegetables and herbs.

Stir-fry the bacon in a non-stick frying pan for 1 minute and then transfer to a plate.

Place the rabbit pieces in the non-stick pan and cook, stirring, for a few minutes. Add the flour and stir for 2–3 minutes. Stir in the marinade liquid and bring to a simmer. Pour the vegetables and herbs over the rabbit. Season with salt, cover with foil and a lid, and cook in the preheated oven for about 2 hours.

A little before serving, cook the mushrooms in butter for a few minutes, then add the mushrooms and bacon to the rabbit. Reheat for a few minutes. Spoon some of the rabbit stew onto each plate and garnish with chopped parsley.

This is delicious served with boiled potatoes.

Serves 3

HARE & RED WINE STEW

Civet de lièvre au vin d'Arbois

I have always liked the richness of hare meat. When I was a boy, my grandmother often cooked hare during the winter hunting season. Hare can be ordered from a good poultry shop.

1 hare, about 1 kg (2 lb 3 oz), cut into portions (2 front legs, 2 back legs and the body cut into 4 pieces)

1 brown onion, sliced

1 medium carrot, sliced

3 garlic cloves, crushed

1 bay leaf

2 cloves

3 thyme sprigs

2 tablespoons brandy

625 ml (22 fl oz/2½ cups) red Arbois wine or another medium-bodied red wine

2 tablespoons vegetable oil

20 g (¾ oz) salted butter

salt

freshly ground pepper

1½ tablespoons plain (all-purpose) flour

3 tablespoons chopped parsley

Place the hare pieces in a bowl with the onion, carrot, crushed garlic, bay leaf, cloves, thyme, brandy and red wine. Cover the bowl with plastic wrap, refrigerate and leave to marinate overnight.

The next day, preheat the oven to 140°C (280°F).

Drain the hare pieces on kitchen paper. Strain the liquid into a bowl, reserving the vegetables and herbs.

Heat the oil and butter on a medium heat in a flameproof casserole dish and brown the hare pieces on all sides. Season with salt and pepper and stir in the vegetables and herbs, cook for a few minutes. Dust with flour and stir well. Stir in the marinade liquid and bring to a simmer. Cover with foil and a lid and bake in the preheated oven for about 2½ hours.

Transfer the cooked hare pieces to a platter. Strain the rich sauce over the meat, discarding the vegetables and herbs. Sprinkle the meat with chopped parsley.

I love it served with pasta such as pappardelle.

Serves 4–5

Beef, Lamb & Pork

POACHED BEEF WITH SPRING VEGETABLES

Boeuf à la ficelle aux légumes du printemps

FROM THE PARIS/ÎLE-DE-FRANCE REGION

This wonderful classic French dish of tender eye fillet poached slowly in a rich broth is served with the sweetest spring vegetables.

1 litre (34 fl oz/4 cups) rich beef broth or stock, well seasoned with salt and pepper

12 baby carrots, peeled

8 bite-size pieces of celery

3 broad beans (fava), shelled

2 x 180 g (6½ oz) pieces of beef eye fillet from the middle

1 tablespoon finely chopped herbs (e.g. parsley, dill or chervil)

Bring the rich broth to a simmer in a small saucepan. Add the carrots and celery pieces and the shelled broad beans to the broth, cook for 1 minute, then remove the broad beans using a slotted spoon. Cool the broad beans in cold water, peel them and place in another small saucepan.

When the carrots and celery are cooked, transfer them to the broad beans, with a little of the beef broth.

Neatly tie each slice of beef with two rounds of kitchen string. Place the meat in the simmering rich stock and poach for 5–8 minutes, depending on how cooked you like your meat to be. When cooked, transfer the meat to a plate and remove the string.

Serve this dish in deep plates. Arrange the warm vegetables in each plate plus about 4 tablespoons of broth.

Cut each piece of meat in half and place in the centre of the vegetables. Garnish the vegetables with fresh herbs.

It is lovely served with salt, pepper and mustard.

Serves 2

BEEF SHIN STEWED WITH CARROTS

Jarret de boeuf aux carottes

FROM THE LIMOUSIN REGION

The Limousin region in central France is famous for its breed of cattle, which produces some of the tastiest beef in France. Share this wonderful winter classic with good friends over a bottle of your best red.

2 tablespoons extra-virgin olive oil

1 shin of beef with the bone, trimmed of fat

½ brown onion, diced

2 bacon rashers, diced

1 medium carrot, diced

70 g (2½ oz/½ cup) diced celery

3 garlic cloves, crushed

1 clove

1 tablespoon plain (all-purpose) flour

1 tablespoon tomato paste (concentrated purée)

250 ml (8½ fl oz/1 cup) rich beef stock

100 ml (3½ fl oz) dry white wine

bouquet garni, made up of a few sprigs of parsley, thyme and a bay leaf tied together with kitchen string

salt

freshly ground pepper

8 medium carrots, peeled

chopped parsley

Preheat the oven to 120°C (250°F).

Heat the olive oil in a large, non-stick frying pan and brown the beef shin for a few minutes. Transfer the shin to a large, cast-iron pan.

Add the onion and bacon to the non-stick pan and stir for 1 minute. Add the diced carrot and celery, the garlic and clove and stir for a couple of minutes. Stir in the flour and tomato paste, then add the beef stock, wine and the bouquet garni. Season with salt and pepper. Bring to the boil and stir well.

Transfer to the cast-iron pan with the meat. Cover the pan with foil and a lid and cook in the preheated oven for about 3 hours, turning the meat over once or twice.

Add the carrots and stir briefly. Cover the pan again and finish cooking in the oven for a further hour or so.

Transfer the beef, carrots and sauce to a warm platter and garnish with chopped parsley to serve.

Serves 4–6

EYE FILLET STEAK WITH BÉARNAISE SAUCE

Tournedos sauce béarnaise

FROM THE PYRÉNÉES/BÉARN REGION | BY PHILIPPE MOUCHEL

The delicious béarnaise sauce that is served with this steak was named after the region of Béarn in the north-west of the Pyrénées. If you prefer, cook the steaks on a barbecue.

4 x 150 g (5½ oz) eye fillet steaks (or another steak of your choice)

salt

freshly ground black pepper

1 tablespoon olive oil

1 teaspoon butter

Béarnaise sauce

2 French shallots, finely chopped

2 tablespoons white wine vinegar

2 tablespoons tarragon leaves

2 tablespoons white wine

4 black peppercorns, crushed

125 g (4½ oz) salted butter, cut into small cubes

2 egg yolks

salt

freshly ground black pepper

To make the béarnaise sauce, combine the shallots, vinegar, half the tarragon, the white wine and peppercorns in a saucepan. Bring to a simmer and cook until the liquid has reduced to about 1 tablespoon.

Meanwhile, melt the butter in a small saucepan over a low heat.

Place the egg yolks in a medium metal or glass bowl and whisk in the shallot reduction. Sit the bowl over a saucepan of hot water, taking care that the bowl doesn't touch the water. Keep the pan over a low heat, as the water must be hot but not boiling. Continue whisking the yolks briskly until they become thick and foamy. After about 5 minutes they should have doubled in volume.

Remove from the saucepan and very slowly pour in the melted butter, whisking continuously until well incorporated. The finished sauce should be creamy but not too runny. Add the rest of the tarragon and season with salt and pepper.

Season the steaks with salt and pepper. Heat the oil in a frying pan and cook the steaks over a high heat for 3–5 minutes on each side, or to your liking. Towards the end of the cooking, add the butter to the pan and baste the steaks. Season with salt and pepper and serve on hot plates. Serve the sauce separately.

Serves 4

ROAST BEEF FILLET WITH FRENCH-STYLE PEAS

Rôti de boeuf et petits pois à la Française

| FROM THE LIMOUSIN REGION | BY PHILIPPE MOUCHEL |

The Limousin region in the heart of France is famous for its superb cattle breed of the same name. The garnish of peas cooked with lettuce is a classic and much loved by the French.

1 x 600 g (1 lb 5 oz) beef eye fillet, tied with kitchen string

salt

cracked black pepper

1 tablespoon olive oil

45 g (1½ oz) salted butter

1 French shallot, chopped

100 ml (3½ fl oz) red wine

2 tablespoons veal glaze (available from good butchers and delicatessens)

3 tablespoons water

1 thyme sprig

Preheat the oven to 180°C (350°F).

Season the beef with salt and pepper. Heat the oil and 1 tablespoon of the butter in a roasting tin, then brown the meat on all sides, basting well. Transfer to the oven for 15–20 minutes, or until cooked to your liking. Remove the string, wrap the meat in foil and leave to rest for 10 minutes.

Tip the cooking fat out of the roasting tin then add another tablespoon of butter. Add the shallot and stir over a medium heat for 2 minutes. Add the red wine and boil until reduced to about 2 tablespoons. Add the veal glaze and water and bring to the boil. Season with a little cracked pepper and add the thyme. Tip the sauce into a smaller saucepan and keep hot.

French-style peas

1 tablespoon olive oil

55 g (2 oz) salted butter

1 medium brown onion, sliced

1 cos (romaine) lettuce heart, washed and cut into bite-sized pieces, plus a few extra small cos lettuce leaves for garnish (optional)

3 prosciutto slices, cut into pieces

1 garlic clove, finely chopped

500 g (1 lb 2 oz) peas

1 thyme sprig

250 ml (8½ fl oz/1 cup) chicken stock

To prepare the French-style peas, heat the oil and 2 tablespoons of the butter in a saucepan. Add the onion and cook for 5 minutes. Add the lettuce, prosciutto, garlic, peas, thyme and chicken stock and simmer for 10 minutes.

When ready to serve, reheat the beef in a frying pan with the remaining butter for 1–2 minutes. Carve into 8 slices. Divide the peas among four plates and top with slices of beef. If you wish, add a little extra butter to the hot sauce, then spoon it over the beef. Garnish with lettuce leaves, if using, and serve at once.

Serves 4

BEEF FILLET WITH TRUFFLES & FOIE GRAS

Filet de boeuf aux truffes et foie gras

FROM THE PÉRIGORD REGION

Every year French gourmets look forward to the truffle season, which starts with the first frost and finishes with the last (that is, from November to February). If you are able to source a fresh truffle, then do try this classic dish.

2 medium potatoes, peeled and quartered

salt

60 ml (2 fl oz/¼ cup) milk

55 g (2 oz) salted butter

2 x 200 g (7 oz) eye fillet steaks

2 teaspoons cracked black pepper

2 teaspoons olive oil

1 small French shallot, finely chopped

2 tablespoons Madeira

60 ml (2 fl oz/¼ cup) strong veal stock

10 g (¼ oz) black truffle, thinly sliced

2 x 20 g (¾ oz) foie gras slices

Boil the potatoes in lightly salted water until tender, then drain well.

Bring the milk to the boil in a medium saucepan. Push the drained potatoes through a mouli or sieve into the hot milk. Stir well, then mix in 2 tablespoons of the butter. Set the potato purée aside and keep warm.

Season the steaks with cracked pepper and salt. Heat the oil and 1 teaspoon of the remaining butter in a small frying pan. Fry the steaks over a high heat for 3–5 minutes on each side, or to your liking. Transfer the steaks to a warm plate and cover with foil.

Add another teaspoon of butter to the pan. Add the shallot and stir for 2 minutes over a medium heat. Add the Madeira and bring to the boil. Add the stock, return to the boil and boil for 1 minute. Add the rest of the butter and season to taste. Stir in the sliced truffles.

Just before serving, gently reheat the potato. Divide the potato between two plates and place a steak on top. Arrange a slice of foie gras on top of each steak, spoon on a little sauce and serve.

Serves 2

BEEF RIB EYE WITH RED WINE SAUCE & VEGETABLE PURÉE

Côte de boeuf sauce au vin rouge purée de légumes

FROM THE LIMOUSIN/CENTRE REGION

If you're looking for a great dish to serve with a special bottle of red wine, this is it. It's easy to prepare, but take care not to overcook the beef, and make sure you rest it for at least 5 minutes before carving.

---

2 teaspoons olive oil

1 beef rib eye, 400–500 g (about 1 lb)

250 g (9 oz) peas

2 small carrots, cut into small pieces

30 g (1 oz) salted butter

salt

freshly ground pepper

1 French shallot, finely chopped

2 tablespoons red wine

60 ml (2 fl oz/¼ cup) strong beef stock

Preheat the oven to 200°C (400°F).

Heat the oil in a roasting tin and brown each side of the rib eye for about 2 minutes. Transfer to the oven and cook for 10–15 minutes, or to your liking.

Cook the peas and carrots in boiling water in separate saucepans. Drain each well, then blend each separately with a little of the butter to form a purée. Season with salt and pepper and keep them warm in the saucepans.

When the rib eye is cooked, transfer it to a warm plate, cover with foil and leave to rest for about 5 minutes.

Melt the remaining butter in the roasting tin. Add the shallot and cook over a low heat for 2 minutes. Add the red wine and bring to the boil. Add the beef stock and simmer for 2–3 minutes.

Carve the beef into 1 cm (½ in) slices. Spoon the pea and carrot purées onto two plates. Top with a few slices of beef, spoon on the red wine sauce and serve.

Serves 2

RIB OF BEEF WITH RED WINE SAUCE

Côte de boeuf à la Bordelaise

FROM THE BORDEAUX/SOUTH WEST REGION	BY PHILIPPE MOUCHEL

It's a matter of taste, but for many people there are no better red wines in the world than the fine wines of Bordeaux in the south west of France. This dish of beef ribs with red wine sauce is a perfect match for the Bordeaux wines. It's lovely served with sautéed mushrooms.

2 tablespoons vegetable oil

2 x 400 g (14 oz) beef ribs, each about 5 cm (2 in) thick

sea salt

freshly cracked black pepper

55 g (2 oz) salted butter

2 French shallots, chopped

100 ml (3½ fl oz) Bordeaux (or another red wine)

125 ml (4 fl oz/½ cup) rich veal or beef stock

a few parsley sprigs

85 g (3 oz) bone marrow

Heat the oil in a heavy frying pan and cook the beef ribs on one side for 4–5 minutes. Season with salt and pepper, turn and cook for 4–5 minutes on the other side, adding 1 tablespoon of butter to the pan and basting the meat from time to time. Transfer the cooked beef ribs to a dish, cover with foil and leave to rest in a warm place.

Tip out any excess fat from the frying pan then add another tablespoon of butter. Add the shallots and stir over a medium heat for a few minutes. Add the wine and boil for a few minutes until reduced by at least half. Add the stock and simmer for 5 minutes. Whisk in the remaining butter and add the parsley.

Meanwhile, put the bone marrow in a small saucepan of cold salted water and bring to a simmer. Poach over a low heat for 5 minutes, then drain well.

Cut each rib into slices, arrange on plates and serve with thin slices of the bone marrow. Spoon on the red wine sauce and serve.

Serves 3

BEEF BURGUNDY

Boeuf Bourguignon

FROM THE BURGUNDY REGION

This is one of the most famous French regional dishes. Allow enough time to cook the dish slowly and well. It's perfect for a winter dinner party as it can be prepared in advance and enjoyed with a great red wine.

800 g (1 lb 12 oz) beef cheek (or another casserole cut such as oyster blade)

1 medium brown onion, thinly sliced

2 French shallots, thinly sliced

2 garlic cloves, crushed

1 thyme sprig or a 6 cm (2½ in) rosemary sprig

300 ml (10 fl oz) red wine

3 tablespoons olive oil

salt

freshly ground black pepper

2 teaspoons butter

1 tablespoon plain (all-purpose) flour

125 g (4½ oz) bacon, finely chopped

16 baby onions

25 small mushrooms

4 tablespoons chopped parsley

The day before you cook the dish, trim the beef of excess fat and sinews and cut it into 4–6 pieces. Place in a bowl with the onion, shallots, garlic and the thyme or rosemary. Cover with wine and stir in 1 tablespoon of the olive oil.

The following day lift the meat, onion, garlic and shallots from the wine and place on a cloth to dry. Reserve the wine and herbs as well. Season the meat with salt and pepper.

Preheat the oven to 140°C (275°F).

Heat 1 tablespoon of the oil in an ovenproof saucepan or casserole dish and brown the meat on all sides. Add the butter to the pan, followed by the reserved onion, shallots and garlic, and stir well. Sprinkle on the flour and stir well. Add the reserved wine and stir well, then add the reserved herbs. Cover with a lid and cook for about 2 hours, or until the meat is tender.

Meanwhile, heat the remaining olive oil in a frying pan and sauté the bacon over a medium heat for a few minutes. Remove the bacon and set aside. Add the baby onions and brown well all over. Remove the onions, set aside and cook the mushrooms in the same pan for 2 minutes.

Towards the end of the 2 hours, add the bacon, onions and mushrooms to the casserole and stir in well.
Return to the oven and cook for a further 20 minutes.

Serve sprinkled with chopped parsley.

Serves 4

BEEF AND BEER STEW

Carbonnade de boeuf

| FROM THE NORTHERN REGION | BY PHILIPPE MOUCHEL |

In the north of France, beer is much more popular than wine.
It is often used in cooking, as in this flavoursome winter beef casserole.
It is traditional to serve this stew with large croutons spread with mustard.

3 tablespoons vegetable oil

55 g (2 oz) salted butter

4 beef cheeks or 1 kg (2 lb 3 oz) oyster blade steak, trimmed of excess fat and sinews

3 large onions, thinly sliced

2 teaspoons brown sugar

2 tablespoons red wine vinegar

40 g (1½ oz) plain (all-purpose) flour

750 ml (25½ fl oz/3 cups) beer (dark beer is often used in France)

250 ml (8½ fl oz/1 cup) beef stock

salt

freshly ground black pepper

a pinch of nutmeg

2 thyme sprigs

a few parsley sprigs

1 bay leaf

12 baby carrots

3 tablespoons chopped parsley

Preheat the oven to 140°C (275°F).

Heat half the oil and half the butter in a cast-iron saucepan or casserole dish and brown the beef on all sides. Transfer the beef to a plate.

Add the remaining oil and butter to the pan and cook the onions over a medium heat for about 10 minutes, or until they are soft and lightly browned. Sprinkle in the brown sugar and add the vinegar. Stir in the flour and cook for a few minutes. Add the beer, stock, salt, pepper and nutmeg.

Use kitchen string to tie the thyme, parsley and bay leaf together to make a bouquet garni. Add to the pan with the meat and bring to a simmer. Skim the surface then transfer to the oven for 3 hours, or until the meat is very tender.

Remove the casserole from the oven and add the baby carrots. Cook on top of the stove for 10–12 minutes, or until the carrots are tender. Sprinkle with chopped parsley and serve.

Serves 4

BEEF CHEEK STEW IN MADIRAN WINE

Estoufat de joue de boeuf au Madiran

FROM THE MIDI-PYRÉNÉES REGION

One of the great characteristics of French cuisine is the use of red wine in meat dishes. The wine tenderises the meat and adds rich flavour to the gravy of delicious slow-cooked cuts, like beef cheek.

½ brown onion, diced

2 bacon rashers, diced

3 garlic cloves, sliced

1 medium carrot, sliced

salt

freshly ground pepper

2 cloves, sliced

a pinch of cinnamon

a pinch of grated nutmeg

1 very thin slice of pork fat, about 15 cm (6 in) square (alternatively, use slices of bacon fat)

3 beef cheeks, trimmed

bouquet garni, made up of 6 sprigs of parsley, 2 thyme sprigs and 1 bay leaf, tied together with kitchen string

125 ml (4 fl oz/½ cup) Madiran red wine or another full-bodied red wine

125 ml (4 fl oz/½ cup) rich beef stock or broth

3 tablespoons chopped parsley

Preheat the oven to 140°C (275°F).

In a bowl, mix together the onion, bacon, garlic, carrot, salt, pepper, cloves, cinnamon and nutmeg.

Line the base of a medium casserole dish with the pork fat. Top with half of the vegetable mix, then cover with the beef cheeks. Add the bouquet garni, then sprinkle the remaining vegetables on top. Add the wine and beef stock, and cover with foil and a lid.

Bake in the preheated oven for about 3 hours or until the beef is very tender.

Place a beef cheek onto each plate and spoon over the sauce and vegetables, then garnish with chopped parsley.

It is delicious served with mashed potato.

Serves 3

BEEF STEW WITH OLIVES & FENNEL

Paleron de boeuf aux olives

FROM THE LANGUEDOC-ROUSSILLON REGION

This hearty winter beef casserole is delicious and a superb match with a full-bodied shiraz. It may take a few hours in the oven, but that gives you the perfect excuse to kick back and relax while your dinner bubbles away.

---

4 x 250 g (9 oz) oyster blade beef slices

1 brown onion, sliced

1 carrot, sliced

2 garlic cloves, crushed

4 thyme sprigs

2 cloves

1 tablespoon Pernod

125 ml (4 fl oz/½ cup) full-bodied red wine

2 tablespoons plain (all-purpose) flour

125 ml (4 fl oz/½ cup) strong beef stock

3 anchovies, chopped

20 black olives

2 fennel bulbs, each cut into 6 segments

4 tablespoons chopped parsley

In a large bowl place the beef slices, onion, carrot, garlic, thyme, cloves, Pernod and red wine. Cover with plastic wrap and marinate overnight in the refrigerator.

Preheat the oven to 120°C (250°F).

Place the flour in an ovenproof pan. Stir in the marinade liquid, then add the vegetables and beef. Add stock and stir gently. Cover with foil and a lid and cook in the preheated oven for about 3 hours until the meat is almost tender.

Stir in the anchovies, olives and fennel. Cover again with foil and a lid and cook for at least 20 minutes until the meat is tender.

Sprinkle with parsley.

Serves 4

VEAL & MUSHROOM SAUTÉ WITH RÖSTI

Veau sauté aux champignons et rösti

FROM THE ALPS AND SWISS REGION

Veal is an extremely popular meat in the Alps, especially Switzerland and in France along the Swiss border. This recipe is popular all over the world and is sure to please.

2 medium all-purpose potatoes, boiled in their skins

1 brown onion, chopped

salt

freshly ground pepper

2 tablespoons vegetable oil

60 g (2 oz) salted butter

450 g (1 lb) veal tenderloin, well trimmed and finely sliced

250 g (9 oz) Swiss brown mushrooms, sliced

50 ml (1¾ fl oz) dry white wine

125 ml (4 fl oz/½ cup) pouring cream

3 tablespoons chopped parsley

Peel and grate the potatoes. Mix them in a bowl with half the onion and season with salt and pepper.

In a medium non-stick frying pan, heat half the oil and half the butter. Place three mounds of grated potato in the pan, pressing them down to form three rösti (in the shape of a burger), each about 1 cm (½ in) thick. Cook for several minutes then very gently turn them over and cook the other side. Put aside and keep warm.

Heat the remaining oil and butter in a large non-stick pan and brown the veal on a high heat for a short time. Transfer the veal to a plate.

Add the remaining chopped onion to the pan and stir for 1 minute. Add the mushrooms and cook for a few minutes. Add the white wine, bring to the boil and evaporate the wine a little. Stir in the cream, bring to the boil and boil for 1 minute. Season well with salt and pepper.

Add the veal to the pan and reheat briefly.

Place a rösti in the centre of each plate and arrange the veal and the mushroom sauce around it. Sprinkle with parsley and serve.

Serves 3

VEAL CUTLETS WITH MUSHROOMS & COMTÉ

Côtes de veau panés aux champignons et Comté

FROM THE FRENCH JURA REGION | BY PHILIPPE MOUCHEL

The huge Comté cheese from the Jura region is so delicious that it's one of the three or four most popular cheeses in France. It's also a superb cooking cheese and is wonderful in this veal dish.

3 veal cutlets

salt

freshly ground pepper

6 prosciutto-style ham slices

6 Swiss-style cheese slices

plain (all-purpose) flour

1 egg, beaten

50 g (1¾ oz/½ cup) fine dry breadcrumbs

2 tablespoons extra-virgin olive oil

60 g (2 oz) salted butter

3 thyme sprigs

5 garlic cloves (2 whole, 2 crushed, 1 chopped)

270 g (9½ oz/3 cups) mixed mushrooms, chopped

1 shallot, chopped

3 tablespoons chopped parsley

juice of ½ lemon

Make a horizontal cut through the centre of the veal cutlets, from the edge to the bone. Butterfly and season the cutlets with salt and pepper.

On one side of each cutlet, place a thin slice of ham, then two slices of cheese and lastly another slice of ham, then fold the meat on top like a sandwich and press together.

Set up three plates, one with flour, one with beaten egg and one with breadcrumbs. Dust each cutlet with a little plain flour, then dip each side in the beaten egg. Lastly, coat each cutlet with a thin layer of breadcrumbs.

Heat 1 tablespoon of olive oil and 1 tablespoon of butter in a frying pan. Add the thyme, 2 whole cloves of garlic and the veal and cook the cutlets on each side for 5 minutes.

Heat 1 tablespoon of olive oil and 1 tablespoon of butter in a second frying pan. Add 2 crushed cloves of garlic and the mushrooms, season with a little salt and pepper and cook for a few minutes on a medium heat. Add the chopped shallot, the remaining clove of chopped garlic and some of the parsley.

Spoon the mushrooms onto each plate and top with a veal cutlet.

Melt the remaining butter in a pan, then add the lemon juice and remaining parsley. Spoon the sauce over the meat and serve.

Serves 3

VEAL BLANQUETTE WITH VEGETABLES

Blanquette de veau aux petits légumes

FROM THE NORMANDY REGION

This classic French veal stew takes its name from the fact the meat is not browned prior to stewing, so the dish remains pale in colour. A little crème fraîche, combined with an egg yolk, is used to enhance the pale creaminess and to lightly thicken the sauce.

10 g (¼ oz) salted butter

800 g (1 lb 12 oz) trimmed cubed veal, from the shoulder or shank

1 tablespoon plain (all-purpose) flour

50 ml (1¾ fl oz) dry white wine

250 ml (8½ fl oz/1 cup) strong chicken stock

140 g (5 oz/1 cup) diced celery

salt

freshly ground black pepper

2 carrots, cut into small bite-size pieces

15 washed baby mushrooms

125 ml (4 fl oz/½ cup) crème fraîche

1 egg yolk

2 tablespoons chopped parsley

Heat the butter in a large saucepan, add the veal pieces and stir for a few minutes without browning.

Sprinkle in the flour until combined, then add the wine and stir for 10 seconds before adding the chicken stock and celery. Season with salt and pepper and stir well. Cover with foil and a lid and simmer on a low heat for about 1 hour.

When the veal is almost tender, add the carrot pieces and the mushrooms and simmer for about 15 minutes.

In a small bowl combine the crème fraîche with the egg yolk, then stir this into the liquid of the veal casserole to thicken it. The sauce must not boil or it will split.

Serve sprinkled with chopped parsley.

Serves 3–5

GRILLED LOIN OF LAMB WITH RATATOUILLE & TAPENADE

Agneau grillé avec ratatouille et tapenade

FROM THE PROVENCE REGION

This superb lamb dish is a perfect example of the flavoursome cuisine of Provence. The ratatouille is also wonderful served on its own.

---

4 loins of lamb, each about 12 cm (4¾ in) long

2 tablespoons olive oil, plus extra for drizzling

freshly ground black pepper

1 garlic clove, finely chopped

2 tablespoons finely chopped rosemary leaves

salt

Ratatouille

3 tablespoons olive oil

½ brown onion, finely diced

2 thyme sprigs, chopped

1 garlic clove, finely chopped

1 small red capsicum (pepper), diced

1 small zucchini (courgette), diced

1 small eggplant (aubergine), diced

3 tomatoes, diced

Tapenade

100 g (3½ oz) pitted black olives

3 anchovies

1 tablespoon capers

2 tablespoons olive oil

To make the ratatouille, heat the oil in a saucepan over a medium heat. Add the onion and thyme and fry for a few minutes. Stir in the garlic, then add the capsicum and stir for a few minutes. Add the zucchini, eggplant and tomatoes, bring to a simmer and cook over a low heat for 20–30 minutes until the vegetables are soft. Refrigerate until required. It may be reheated as you need it.

To make the tapenade, blend all ingredients to a paste. Store in the refrigerator until 10 minutes before serving.

Season the lamb loins with oil, pepper, garlic and rosemary, then marinate in the refrigerator for at least 30 minutes. Grill the lamb for 3–4 minutes on each side. Turn off the heat, cover the meat and leave it to rest for at least 5 minutes before slicing.

Serve the lamb loins on a bed of hot ratatouille. Season with salt and top each loin with a tablespoon of tapenade. Drizzle with the extra olive oil and serve.

Serves 4

GRILLED LOIN OF LAMB WITH OLIVES & CAPSICUM

Filet d'agneau rôti aux olives et poivrons

FROM THE PROVENCE/LANGUEDOC REGION

The lamb from the north of Provence, around the beautiful town of Sisteron, is known for being very flavoursome and is superb served with Provençale vegetables.

3 tablespoons olive oil

1 red capsicum (pepper), cut into fine strips

1 yellow capsicum (pepper), cut into fine strips

100 g (3½ oz) baby English spinach leaves

salt

freshly ground black pepper

1 garlic clove, finely chopped

8 green olives, pitted

8 black olives, pitted

2 pieces of deboned loin of lamb, each about 10 cm (4 in) long

2 teaspoons cracked pepper

3 thyme sprigs, finely chopped

Heat half the olive oil in a saucepan over a medium–high heat. Add the capsicum and cook for 2–3 minutes until soft. Add the spinach leaves and cook for 1 minute or until wilted. Season with salt and pepper and add the garlic. Mix in the olives, then remove from the heat. Allow the vegetables to cool.

Using a sharp knife with a long, thin blade, make a small incision lengthwise into the centre of each lamb loin to form a pocket. Fill each pocket with a little of the vegetable mix.

Season the meat with the remaining oil, some salt, cracked pepper and the thyme.

Cook the lamb on a hot grill or barbecue for 3–4 minutes on each side. Rest the meat on a plate for 5 minutes.

Slice each loin into three and serve with the remaining vegetables.

Serves 2

LOIN OF LAMB WITH BROAD BEANS & FINE HERBS

Noisettes d'agneau aux fèves et aux fines herbes

FROM THE AQUITAINE/BORDEAUX REGION

The lamb from Paulliac in the Bordeaux region is known as some of the best in France. Open a bottle of your finest red wine to enjoy with this lovely dinner-party dish.

---

2 x 150 g (5½ oz) loins of lamb, trimmed of fat and skin

1 garlic clove, finely sliced

3–4 lemon thyme sprigs, chopped

freshly ground pepper

1½ tablespoons extra-virgin olive oil

6 baby carrots, peeled

3 tablespoons water

175 g (6 oz) shelled broad beans (fava)

salt

75 ml (2½ fl oz) dry white wine

10 g (¼ oz) salted butter

about 10 tarragon leaves

fresh herbs (mint leaves and chervil)

Cut each loin of lamb into five pieces. In French the cut is called noisette. In a bowl, season the noisettes with the garlic, lemon thyme, a little pepper and 1 tablespoon olive oil. Combine and then put aside for 30 minutes.

Place the carrots in a small saucepan with 2 teaspoons olive oil and 3 tablespoons water and simmer, covered, for about 8 minutes.

Place the shelled broad beans in a saucepan of boiling water. Drain after 3 minutes. When cool enough to handle, peel the broad beans and put aside in a bowl.

Heat a non-stick frying pan and cook the lamb noisettes, seasoned with salt, for about 2–3 minutes on each side. Transfer the noisettes to a dish.

Add the dry white wine to the pan and bring to the boil. Add the carrots and their cooking juices, the broad beans, the butter and the tarragon leaves.

Arrange five pieces of lamb on each plate. Spoon the vegetables and cooking juices in between the noisettes, garnish with a few mint leaves and chervil leaves and serve.

Serves 2

LAMB SHANKS WITH THYME & OLIVES

Jarret d'agneau au thym et aux olives

FROM THE NORTHERN PROVENCE REGION

Northern Provence is one of my favourite regions in my homeland. Just thinking of it evokes aromas of its colourful cuisine, packed with fresh herbs and tasty vegetables.

4 lamb shanks

salt

freshly ground pepper

4 lemon thyme sprigs, finely chopped

3 tablespoons extra-virgin olive oil

1 brown onion, diced

3 garlic cloves, crushed

2 medium fennel bulbs, each cut into 8 segments

1 green capsicum (pepper), cut into bite-sized pieces

1 red capsicum (pepper), cut into bite-size pieces

3 medium tomatoes, quartered

75 ml (2½ fl oz) dry white wine

30 baby olives

Preheat the oven to 140°C (275°F).

Season the lamb shanks with salt, pepper and the lemon thyme.

Heat the olive oil in an ovenproof pan and brown the meat for a few minutes.

Add the onion and garlic and stir briefly. Add the fennel, capsicum and tomatoes, making sure to distribute the vegetables evenly in the pan. Add the wine and bring to a simmer.

Cover the pan with a lid and cook in the preheated oven for about 2 hours until the meat is tender. During the cooking stir the vegetables and turn the meat a couple of times.

Transfer the cooked meat and vegetables to a dish.

Boil down the pan juices to a sauce consistency. Add the olives and stir for 10 seconds.

Spoon some of the vegetables onto each plate. Top with a lamb shank and spoon the sauce and olives over the top.

Serves 4

ROAST RACK OF LAMB WITH SPRING VEGETABLES

Carré d'agneau rôti aux légumes printaniers

FROM THE PARIS REGION

Paris is surrounded by large areas of farmland where vegetables are grown and then sold in the many superb markets dotted throughout the city. There are actually more than fifty open-air markets in Paris.

2 x 3-cutlet racks of lamb, trimmed of fat

2 tablespoons extra-virgin olive oil

freshly ground pepper

1 tablespoon chopped rosemary leaves

175 g (6 oz) shelled broad beans (fava)

4 baby carrots, peeled

75 g (2¾ oz) shelled peas

tips of 4 fat asparagus spears

20 g (¾ oz) salted butter

8 tarragon leaves

salt

Preheat the oven to 150°C (300°F).

Brush the racks of lamb with a little olive oil and season with pepper and rosemary leaves.

Heat a small ovenproof pan and brown the lamb racks for 1 minute. Bake in the preheated oven for about 10 minutes.

Remove the pan from the oven, cover the meat with foil and rest for 10 minutes.

Meanwhile, drop the broad beans into a small saucepan of boiling water and cook for 1 minute. Lift the broad beans out of the water and refresh in a bowl of cold water.

Place the baby carrots in the boiling water and cook for 2 minutes. Add the peas to the boiling carrots, cook for 5 minutes, then add the asparagus. Cook the vegetables for a further 2 minutes, then drain and transfer them to a frying pan.

Add the peeled broad beans, the butter and tarragon leaves and season with a little salt and pepper and reheat briefly.

On each plate, place the rack of lamb, which can be carved before plating if you wish, over the spring vegetables. Spoon the tarragon-flavoured butter over the lamb and serve.

Serves 2

ROAST LAMB WITH FLAGEOLETS

Gigot d'agneau aux flageolets

FROM THE NORMANDY REGION

The sheep that graze on the coastal fields of Normandy eat a rich, salty grass that gives the lamb meat a superb flavour. A tradition in the region is to bake lamb at Easter, often served with baked beans. Flageolets are small, delicate beans, light-green in colour.

12 garlic cloves

1 leg of spring lamb, trimmed of most of the fat

1 tablespoon extra-virgin olive oil

60 g (2 oz) salted butter, softened

salt

freshly ground pepper

4 medium carrots, cut into 1.5 cm (½ in) slices

75 ml (2½ fl oz) dry cider

550 g (1 lb 3 oz) drained cooked flageolet beans (alternatively, borlotti or haricot beans)

3 tablespoons chopped parsley

Preheat the oven to 180°C (350°F).

Peel four garlic cloves and cut each clove lengthways into four slivers.

Using the tip of a small knife blade, make 16 cuts into the lamb at regular intervals, ensuring the cuts are deep enough to hold the pieces of garlic. Push the slivers of garlic into the cuts.

Oil a roasting pan. Place the leg of lamb in the pan and rub it all over with half the butter. Season the lamb with salt and pepper and bake it in the preheated oven for about 45 minutes, turning it two or three times during the cooking so it cooks evenly.

After 20 minutes of cooking, add the carrot slices and remaining garlic cloves to the pan.

When the meat is done, remove it from the oven, transfer to a dish, cover with foil and leave to rest for about 10 minutes.

Remove the excess fat from the roasting pan, add the cider and bring to the boil. Add the flageolet beans and the remaining butter and heat. Stir in the chopped parsley.

Serve two or three tablespoons of beans and carrots on each plate and a few thin slices of lamb.

Serves 8

ROAST SADDLE OF LAMB WITH HERBS

Selle d'agneau rôti aux herbes

FROM THE NORTHERN PROVENCE REGION

The lamb of northern Provence has a delicate meat that marries well with herbs. The saddle is a cut comprising the racks that are deboned but still held together by the skin. Ask your butcher to debone it for you.

1 x 1.2 kg (2 lb 10 oz) deboned saddle of lamb

4 tablespoons chopped parsley

2 tablespoons chopped tarragon

4 tablespoons chopped thyme

salt

freshly ground pepper

50 g (1¾ oz) salted butter, softened

3 tablespoons dry breadcrumbs

2 tablespoons extra-virgin olive oil

3 different-coloured capsicums (peppers), cut into bite-sized pieces

6 garlic cloves, with the skin

a little extra olive oil

Preheat the oven to 180°C (350°F).

Without damaging the skin, remove some of the excess fat from the top of the saddle.

Place the parsley, tarragon and thyme in a bowl. Season with salt and pepper and mix in the butter and breadcrumbs.

Place the deboned rack of lamb, skin side down, on a board and spread the herb mixture over the meat. Roll the meat into a roast and tie it with about 10 rounds of kitchen string, 2 cm (¾ in) apart.

Heat the olive oil in a small ovenproof pan and gently brown the roast on all sides. Place the capsicums and garlic around the meat and roast in the preheated oven for 40 minutes.

Turn off the heat and rest the meat in the oven for about 10 minutes.

Cut the string and carve the meat into 3 cm (1¼ in) slices. Serve the meat with the capsicums and garlic, drizzle the meat with a little extra olive oil and pan juices.

Serves 5–6

ROAST LAMB WITH TARBAIS BEANS

Rôti d'agneau aux haricots Tarbais

FROM THE GASCOGNE-PYRÉNÉES REGION | BY PHILIPPE MOUCHEL

The cuisine north of the Pyrénées, around the city of Tarbes, is known as one of the most rustic in France and its tasty bean dishes are on offer on many restaurant menus as well as being very popular at home. If you are unable to find Tarbais beans, then use other dried beans of your choice, such as borlotti or cannellini. They need to be soaked for 24 hours in cold water.

Tarbais beans

85 g (3 oz) dried beans of your choice (Tarbais, borlotti, cannellini), soaked for 24 hours in cold water

1 small carrot, chopped

1 celery stalk, chopped

½ onion, left whole

1 garlic clove

1 thyme sprig

½ bay leaf

4–5 peppercorns

To prepare the Tarbais beans, drain the soaked beans and place them in a saucepan with plenty of cold water. Add the carrot, celery, onion, whole garlic clove, thyme, bay leaf and peppercorns. Bring to a simmer and cook over a low heat for about 1½ hours, or until the beans are tender.

Preheat the oven to 180°C (350°F).

1 x 6–8 cutlet lamb rack

salt

freshly ground black pepper

a little olive oil

2 garlic cloves

4 thyme sprigs, plus extra to garnish

20 g (¾ oz) salted butter

2 French shallots, finely chopped

2 teaspoons chopped thyme

2 teaspoons red wine vinegar

2 tablespoons chopped parsley

Season the lamb with salt and pepper. Heat a little oil in a roasting tin. Add the lamb rack and top with the whole garlic cloves and thyme sprigs. Roast the lamb for about 5 minutes, then turn it over and roast the other side for 5 minutes. Remove from the oven and leave to rest for 5 minutes in a warm place.

Meanwhile, drain the beans and remove the vegetables and herbs. Heat the butter in a saucepan. Add the shallots and chopped thyme and stir for 1 minute.

Add the beans and heat through well. Stir in the red wine vinegar and parsley and season to taste.

When ready to serve, slice the lamb rack in half. Divide the beans between two plates and top with the lamb. Garnish with thyme sprigs and drizzle a little olive oil over the top.

Serves 2

LAMB CASSEROLE WITH GREEN OLIVES

Ragoût de mouton aux olives vertes

FROM THE LANGUEDOC/PYRÉNÉES REGION | BY PHILIPPE MOUCHEL

The Pyrénées region is famous for its tasty lamb, and this delicious casserole benefits from being cooked for a long time at a moderate temperature. When it's ready, the meat should be soft and tender.

800 g–1 kg (about 2 lb) deboned lamb shoulder, trimmed of excess fat and cut into large cubes

salt

freshly ground black pepper

2 tablespoons olive oil, plus extra for drizzling

1 teaspoon butter

½ medium carrot, diced

½ medium onion, diced

2 teaspoons tomato paste (concentrated purée)

150 ml (5 fl oz) dry white wine

3 garlic cloves, crushed

3 x 5 cm (2 in) strips orange zest

15 green olives

300 ml (10 fl oz) chicken stock

1 large tomato, cut into 8 pieces

1 thyme sprig

1 bay leaf

a few basil leaves to garnish

Preheat the oven to 140°C (275°F).

Season the lamb with salt and pepper. Heat the oil in an ovenproof saucepan or casserole dish and brown the lamb on all sides over a high heat.

Add the butter, followed by the carrot and onion, and stir for 2 minutes. Add the tomato paste and stir well. Add the wine and bring to the boil. Add the garlic, orange zest, olives, chicken stock, tomato, thyme and bay leaf. Stir well and bring to a simmer. Cover with a lid and bake in the oven for about 3 hours, or until the meat is tender.

Garnish with basil leaves, drizzle with extra olive oil and serve.

Serves 4

SLOW-COOKED LEG OF LAMB

Gigot de sept heures

FROM THE PYRÉNÉES REGION	BY PHILIPPE MOUCHEL

*This speciality of the Pyrénées region translates as 'seven-hour lamb'.
You can cook it in a little less time at a higher temperature,
but it won't be quite as succulent.*

1 x 1.5 kg (3 lb 5 oz) leg of lamb, trimmed of most visible fat

2 garlic cloves, cut into slivers

a little olive oil

2 thyme sprigs

a few parsley sprigs

1 bay leaf

sea salt

freshly ground black pepper

3 litres (101 fl oz/12 cups) water or beef stock

3 carrots, cut into 2 cm (¾ in) slices

2 small turnips, quartered

2 leeks, washed and cut into 2 cm (¾ in) pieces

1 onion, sliced

3 celery stalks, cut into 2 cm (¾ in) pieces

8 garlic cloves, chopped

Preheat the oven to 100–120°C (200–235°F).

Stud the lamb with the garlic slivers and tie with string. Heat the oil in a cast-iron casserole dish and brown the lamb all over.

Use kitchen string to tie the thyme, parsley and bay leaf together. Add to the casserole dish and season the lamb with a little salt and pepper. Add the water or stock and bring to a simmer on top of the stove. Cover with a lid, then transfer to the oven for 5–6 hours. Turn the lamb over in the casserole after 1 hour. During the cooking, the liquid may simmer very gently, but must not boil.

After 5–6 hours, tuck the carrots, turnips, leeks, onion, celery and chopped garlic around the meat and cook for another hour.

Remove the casserole from the oven and transfer the meat and vegetables to a warm serving platter. Discard the bouquet garni and cover the platter with foil. On top of the stove, reduce the remaining juices to about 500 ml (17 fl oz/2 cups).

When ready to serve, remove the string from the lamb. Pour sauce over the meat and vegetables and season with a little salt and pepper before carving at the table.

Serves 8

LAMB STEW WITH SPRING VEGETABLES

Navarin d'agneau printanier

FROM THE PYRÉNÉES REGION	BY PHILIPPE MOUCHEL

I love to visit the stunning Pyrénées region at the end of spring when most of the snow has melted. The grass looks so rich that it's easy to understand why the local lamb is so good.

2 tablespoons extra-virgin olive oil

20 g (¾ oz) salted butter

1 kg (2 lb 3 oz) deboned lamb shoulder or neck, cut into 15–20 pieces

1 medium carrot, diced

1 medium onion, diced

2 tablespoons plain (all-purpose) flour

3 ripe tomatoes, diced

750 ml (25½ fl oz/3 cups) chicken stock

2 garlic cloves, chopped

bouquet garni, made up of a few sprigs of parsley, thyme and a bay leaf, tied together with kitchen string

salt

freshly ground pepper

8 baby carrots

8 small turnips

230 g (8 oz/1½ cups) shelled peas

8 small onions

8 baby potatoes

chopped parsley

Preheat the oven to 150°C (300°F).

Heat the oil and butter in a flameproof casserole and brown the lamb pieces on all sides for a few minutes. Add the diced carrot and onion and stir for 2 minutes. Stir in the flour to coat the meat well, then add the tomatoes and stir for 1 minute. Add the stock, garlic and bouquet garni. Mix well and season with salt and pepper.

Cover with a lid and cook in the preheated oven for about 2 hours.

Meanwhile, steam the baby carrots, turnips, peas, small onions and potatoes in a saucepan until tender.

Add the vegetables to the tender meat, stir well and reheat.

Serve sprinkled with chopped parsley.

Serves 4

LAMB & BEAN STEW

Pistache de mouton

FROM THE PYRÉNÉES REGION

The mountain range between France and Spain is called the Pyrénées, and the cuisine of this region is very hearty, perfect for the cold weather in the mountains. This delicious local dish takes a few hours to cook but is easy to prepare and really worth it.

20 g (¾ oz) salted butter

50 g (1¾ oz) fatty bacon, diced

3 thyme sprigs, chopped

12 pieces of lamb from the shoulder, each about 80 g (2¾ oz)

1 small onion, diced

4 garlic cloves, crushed

1 bay leaf

salt

freshly ground pepper

75 ml (2½ fl oz) dry white wine

2 tomatoes, diced

400 g (14 oz) cooked white beans, drained

4 tablespoons chopped parsley

35 g (1¼ oz/⅓ cup) dry breadcrumbs

Heat the butter and bacon in a wide, heavy saucepan. Add the thyme and stir well. Add the lamb pieces and brown the lamb on all sides for a few minutes.

Add the onion, garlic and bay leaf and season with salt and pepper. Cook for 4–5 minutes to lightly brown the onion.

Add the wine, bring to the boil, then add the tomatoes. Cover with foil and the lid and cook on a low heat for about 1½–2 hours until the meat is tender. Stir the stew a couple of times during the cooking to make sure it doesn't stick.

When the meat is cooked, add the beans. Stir gently and reheat for a few minutes. Transfer the stew to a wide gratin dish and sprinkle the top with the chopped parsley and breadcrumbs.

Place under a hot grill (broiler) and leave for a few minutes until golden brown. Serve immediately but take care as it is very hot.

Serves 4–6

LAMB NAVARIN WITH MUSHROOMS & PEAS

Navarin d'agneau aux champignons et petit pois

FROM THE NORMANDY REGION

This classic French lamb stew from Normandy uses pieces of boneless lamb shoulder, but you could use lamb neck if you prefer. While it traditionally incorporates turnips (navets), here I use mushrooms and peas.

---

2 tablespoons extra-virgin olive oil

800 g (1 lb 12 oz) lamb meat from the shoulder, trimmed and cut into about 12 pieces

salt

freshly ground black pepper

1 brown onion, diced

4 thyme sprigs, chopped

1 tablespoon plain (all-purpose) flour

250 ml (8½ fl oz/1 cup) strong chicken or beef stock

2 medium tomatoes, diced

2 garlic cloves, crushed

1 large carrot, diced

300 g (10½ oz) mushrooms, sliced

155 g (5½ oz/1 cup) fresh or frozen peas

3 tablespoons chopped parsley

Preheat the oven to 140°C (275°F).

Heat half the oil in a flameproof casserole dish over a high heat and brown the lamb pieces in batches for a few minutes until golden. Return all the meat to the pan and season with salt and pepper.

Add the onion and thyme and stir for 1 minute. Stir in the flour to coat the meat. Stir in the stock, tomatoes, garlic and carrot.

Cover with foil and a lid and cook in the preheated oven for about 2 hours or until the meat is very tender. Remove from the oven.

Just before the lamb is ready, heat the remaining oil in a frying pan over a medium heat and cook the mushrooms until golden and tender.

Meanwhile, cook the peas in lightly salted boiling water until tender, then drain.

Stir the mushrooms and peas into the stew. If the sauce is too runny, simmer the stew uncovered for 10 minutes to evaporate the excess liquid.

Sprinkle with chopped parsley.

Serves 3–4

HAM KNUCKLE WITH BRAISED GREEN CABBAGE

Jambonneau braisé aux choux

FROM THE ALSATIAN REGION

The Alsatian people love pork meat and cabbage, and this dish of cooked knuckles and braised cabbage, a superb winter warmer, is often served with steamed potatoes.

1 tablespoon vegetable oil

½ onion, diced

about 150 g (5½ oz) speck or smoked bacon, cut into 8 pieces

1 celery stalk, diced

1 medium carrot, sliced

½ cabbage, finely sliced

15 juniper berries

100 ml (3½ fl oz) riesling

salt

freshly ground black pepper

1 cooked ham knuckle, from the hind leg

8 small potatoes, skin on

3 tablespoons chopped parsley

Heat the oil in a cast-iron pan over a medium heat and cook the onion, speck, celery and carrot for 3 minutes or until tender. Add the cabbage, juniper berries and riesling and season with salt and pepper. Stir to combine.

Add the ham knuckle and cover with the cabbage mixture. Cover the dish with a lid and cook for about 45 minutes, stirring the vegetables a couple of times during the cooking.

Steam the potatoes in the skins for 45 minutes or until cooked, then peel them.

Place the cabbage mixture in a dish and top with the ham knuckle. Garnish with steamed potatoes and sprinkle with chopped parsley.

Serves 4

SLOW-COOKED SALTED PORK WITH LENTILS

Petit salé aux lentilles

FROM THE AUVERGNE REGION | BY PHILIPPE MOUCHEL

The central mountainous region of Auvergne is famous for its charcuterie and pork. This slow-cooked pork belly and lentil dish is popular with the locals and is often served in Parisian brasseries. You need to plan ahead when preparing this dish.

500 g (1 lb) pork belly

3 tablespoons sea salt

2 teaspoons cracked pepper

3 thyme sprigs

1 onion, pierced with a clove

2 garlic cloves, whole

2 carrots

1 piece of leek, 10 cm (4 in) long

2 bouquet garni, each made up of a few parsley sprigs, thyme and a bay leaf, tied together with kitchen string

30 g (1 oz) pork fat

2 shallots, chopped

80 g (2¾ oz) bacon, diced

280 g (10 oz/1½ cups) lentils, boiled for 2 minutes then drained

750 ml (25½ fl oz/3 cups) chicken stock

1 garlic clove extra, crushed

20 g (¾ oz) salted butter

2 tablespoons chopped parsley

Place the pork belly on a plate and rub generously with sea salt. Season with cracked pepper and thyme, then cover in plastic wrap and refrigerate for at least 8 hours.

Remove the salted pork from the plastic wrap and place in a saucepan. Add the onion pierced with a clove, the whole garlic cloves, carrots, leek and 1 bouquet garni. Cover with water, bring to a simmer and cook for 2–3 hours until tender.

Heat the pork fat in a saucepan. Add the shallots and stir for 1 minute. Add the bacon, stir well, then add the lentils. Cover with the chicken stock, add the extra garlic and remaining bouquet garni, and simmer until the lentils are soft, by which time the lentils will have absorbed almost all the stock. Stir in the butter.

Drain and slice the pork.

On each plate, place the lentils with a few carrots and some of the sliced pork. Sprinkle with parsley. If you wish, serve with mustard or drizzle a salad dressing with herbs over the dish.

Serves 2–3

PAN-FRIED PORK CUTLETS WITH CABBAGE

Côtes de porc aux choux

FROM THE ALSACE REGION	BY PHILIPPE MOUCHEL

*Alsatians love their food and take their cooking very seriously.
Pork is the most popular meat at home and cabbage is the great specialty
of this beautiful region.*

10 cabbage leaves

2 free-range pork cutlets

salt

cracked black pepper

3 tablespoons olive oil

55 g (2 oz) salted butter

2 thyme sprigs

¼ medium onion, chopped

60 ml (2 fl oz/¼ cup) dry white wine

2 tablespoons veal glaze (available from good butchers and delicatessens)

1 tablespoon dijon mustard

5 gherkins (pickles), cut into julienne strips

1 bacon slice, diced

Preheat the oven to 170°C (340°F).

Cook the cabbage leaves in a large saucepan of boiling water for 3 minutes. Transfer them to a bowl of cold water and ice cubes, which helps them to cool quickly and keep their colour.

Season the pork cutlets with salt and pepper. Heat the oil and 1 tablespoon of the butter in an ovenproof frying pan. Add the thyme and fry the pork cutlets for 1 minute on each side, then cook in the oven for about 5 minutes. Transfer the cutlets to a warm dish, cover with foil and leave to rest.

Heat another tablespoon of butter in the frying pan and cook the onion for 1 minute. Add the wine and boil until reduced to about 2 tablespoons. Stir in the veal glaze and bring to a simmer. Add the mustard and gherkins and stir well.

Meanwhile, cook the cabbage leaves again in boiling water for about 5 minutes, then drain.

Heat the remaining butter in a separate frying pan. Fry the bacon, stirring, for 2 minutes. Add the cabbage leaves and cook together for a few minutes.

Divide the cabbage between two plates. Arrange the pork cutlets on top, spoon on the sauce and serve.

Serves 2

ALSATIAN SAUERKRAUT

La choucroûte Alsacienne

| FROM THE ALSACE REGION | BY PHILIPPE MOUCHEL |

Alsatian sauerkraut is one of the best-known French regional dishes. It's served in most Alsatian restaurants but also in many of the popular brasseries of Paris. It's often enjoyed with a glass of beer or Alsatian riesling. Sauerkraut, which literally means 'sour cabbage', is available at German-style delis and butchers, as are the pork cuts.

1 kg (2 lb 3 oz) sauerkraut

20 g (¾ oz) salted butter

1 large brown onion, sliced

2 bay leaves

3 cloves

12 juniper berries

600 g (1 lb 5 oz) kassler (smoked and salted pork loin), cut into 6 slices

6 x 1 cm (½ in) slices jagdwurst (or use strassburg or Polish sausage)

6 x 1 cm (½ in) slices kaiserfleisch (smoked pork belly)

375 ml (12½ fl oz/ 1½ cups) dry white wine, preferably Alsatian riesling

6 medium potatoes

salt

6 thin Viennese sausages

3 tablespoons chopped parsley

Rinse the sauerkraut in cold water and squeeze out the excess moisture. This removes some of the sour flavour.

Melt the butter in a wide saucepan and gently fry the onion for 3 minutes. Sprinkle on half the sauerkraut and add the bay leaves, cloves and 6 of the juniper berries. Arrange the slices of kassler, jagdwurst and kaiserfleisch on top then add the remaining sauerkraut and juniper berries. Pour on the wine, cover the pan tightly and simmer over a low heat for about 2 hours. This dish can also be cooked in a 150°C (300°F) oven for 2 hours.

Half an hour before serving, boil the potatoes in lightly salted water until tender. Cook the sausages in simmering water for about 10 minutes.

Spoon the cabbage onto a large platter. Arrange the cooked meats and sausages on top and surround with the potatoes. Sprinkle with parsley and serve at the table with mustard or your favourite condiments.

Serves 6

AIL VIOLET
"SPECIAL"
LONGUE
CONSERVATION

BEAN STEW WITH TOULOUSE SAUSAGES

Cassoulet Toulousain

FROM THE LANGUEDOC/GASCOGNE REGION │ BY STÉPHANE LANGLOIS

Every corner of south-west France has a different version of cassoulet. Around the town of Toulouse it's the local thick sausage that is the highlight of this popular French classic. Confit duck and duck fat are both available from specialist butchers and good delicatessens.

2 tablespoons duck fat

400 g (14 oz) salted pork belly or shoulder, cut into 6 pieces

1 onion, diced

3 garlic cloves, crushed

1 carrot, sliced

2–3 thyme sprigs, finely chopped

1 celery stalk, diced

3 tablespoons plain (all-purpose) flour

150 ml (5 fl oz) dry white wine

1 litre (34 fl oz/4 cups) chicken stock

750 g (1 lb 11 oz/3¾ cups) dried cannellini beans, soaked overnight in cold water

3 tablespoons tomato paste (concentrated purée)

salt

freshly ground pepper

6 Toulouse sausages or good-quality pork sausages

6 confit duck legs

3 tablespoons chopped parsley

Melt the duck fat in a cast-iron saucepan or casserole dish. Add the pork to the pan and brown for a few minutes. Stir in the onion and garlic, then the carrot and thyme, and stir again. Add the celery, sprinkle on the flour and stir for 30 seconds. Stir in the wine, then the stock. Add the beans, tomato paste, salt and pepper and bring to a simmer. Cover the pan and cook for about 1 hour over a low heat, or until the beans are almost cooked.

Add the sausages and simmer for a further 15 minutes. Add the duck legs and simmer gently for another 10 minutes. To serve, spoon the beans and sauce into 6 deep soup plates. Top with a piece of pork, a duck leg and a sausage, sprinkle with chopped parsley and serve.

Serves 6

Cakes & Sweet Morsels

BRIOCHE FROM VENDÉE

Brioche Vendéenne

FROM THE VENDÉE REGION	BY PIERRICK BOYER

As with many cakes, this special treat of Brioche Vendéenne is usually bought at the local pâtisserie or boulangerie by French families to serve to visitors. It's served with coffee and is often dunked in the coffee. Skilful home cooks will derive great pleasure from making brioche.

500 g (1 lb 2 oz) plain (all-purpose) flour

10 g (¼ oz) salt

150 g (5½ oz) caster (superfine) sugar

15 g (½ oz) dry yeast

4 eggs, at room temperature

1 teaspoon orange flower water

300 g (10½ oz) unsalted butter

2 egg yolks mixed with 1 tablespoon water

3 tablespoons sesame seeds

In the bowl of an electric beater, place the flour, salt, caster sugar, dry yeast, eggs and orange flower water and beat on medium speed until it forms a smooth, elastic dough.

Reduce to low speed, add the butter bit by bit and beat until well incorporated. This takes about 10 minutes.

Remove the dough from the bowl and form it into a long piece. Place it on a baking tray lined with baking paper, cover with a damp tea towel and leave to rise for 2 hours.

Flatten the dough into a long rectangle and cut it into three long pieces. Roll each piece into a long baguette shape and form a plait with the three pieces of dough. Place on another baking tray lined with baking paper and leave to prove for about 1 hour in a warm place.

Preheat the oven to 160°C (320°F).

Brush the risen dough lightly with the egg yolk mixture and sprinkle with sesame seeds. Bake in the preheated oven for about 30 minutes.

Cool the brioche before slicing.

Serves 10–15

FRENCH TOASTED BRIOCHE

Brioche perdue

FROM THE BEAUCE REGION

This easy-to-prepare French family classic was traditionally made using one-day-old bread but now it's often made with brioche as a breakfast treat. I serve it with red fruits, like raspberries.

250 ml (8½ fl oz/1 cup) milk

3 tablespoons caster (superfine) sugar

½ vanilla bean, split lengthways

1 egg

1 piece of brioche loaf, about 12 cm (4¾ in) long

40 g (1½ oz) unsalted butter

icing (confectioners') sugar for dusting

ground cinnamon for dusting

Place the milk, half the caster sugar and the vanilla bean in a small saucepan. Bring to a simmer, then transfer to a wide dish to cool.

Beat the egg with the remaining caster sugar in a bowl.

Cut the brioche into six thick slices. Dip each slice in the cooled milk then lightly coat with the egg mix.

Heat the butter in a large frying pan and cook the brioche on each side until golden brown.

Generously dust the brioche with icing sugar and a little cinnamon. Serve immediately on its own or with red fruits.

Serves 3

KOUIGN AMANN BRETON CAKE

Kouign Amann

FROM THE BRETAGNE REGION	BY JEAN-MARIE BLANCHOT

This Breton cake is quite unique — a cross between a croissant and puff pastry. Very few French people would make it at home. Preparing this recipe requires advanced pastry skills — and patience!

500 g (1 lb 2 oz) plain (all-purpose) flour, sifted

1 teaspoon bread improver

320 ml (11 fl oz) cold water

15 g (½ oz) salt

10 g (¼ oz) fresh compressed yeast

350 g (12½ oz) unsalted butter

300 g (10½ oz) sugar

Butter two cake tins, each about 24 cm (9½ in) in diameter.

In the bowl of an electric beater, place the flour, bread improver, water, salt and yeast and beat until it forms a dough. Shape the dough into a ball, cover with plastic wrap and refrigerate for about 1 hour.

On a floured bench, flatten the dough with a rolling pin to a square about 1 cm (½ in) thick and dust with flour.

Using the rolling pin, flatten the butter between two layers of baking paper to a 1 cm (½ in) thickness and place it in the centre of the dough. Fold the four edges of the dough into the middle to completely envelop the butter.

Roll the pastry out to a rectangular strip about 1 cm (½ in) thick. Take the lower end of the strip and fold it up one-third of the way towards the top. Now fold the top down to fit over the first fold to form a neat rectangle with no overlapping sides.

Refrigerate the dough for 30 minutes, then roll it out again to a long rectangle. Coat with a generous amount of sugar, then fold it into thirds as before, coating all sides with sugar. Place in the refrigerator to rest for 30 minutes.

Repeat the previous step of rolling, coating with sugar and folding one more time, then rest the dough in the refrigerator for 30 minutes.

Roll the pastry out to a 1 cm (½ in) thickness. Cut it in half, then fold the corners of the dough to meet in the centre. Place the two pieces of dough in buttered cake tins, pressing slightly so the dough fits the tins snugly.

Cover the cake tins with a towel and leave to rise for 2 hours in a warm place.

Bake in a preheated oven at 200°C (400°F) for about 30 minutes, then carefully turn out onto a rack. The cake will be beautifully caramelised. Cut into wedges.

Serves 12–16

CHOCOLATE CONCORDE CAKE

Gâteau Concorde au chocolat

FROM THE PARIS REGION	BY PIERRICK BOYER

This delicate cake was named after the Place de la Concorde in Paris.

9 egg whites

220 g (8 oz) caster (superfine) sugar

40 g (1½ oz) Dutch (unsweetened) cocoa, plus extra for dusting

150 g (5½ oz) icing (confectioners') sugar, plus extra for dusting

200 g (7 oz) dark chocolate, broken into small pieces

200 g (7 oz) unsalted butter, cut into pieces

Preheat the oven to 90°C (190°F). Line a baking tray with baking paper and draw two 18 cm (7 in) circles on the paper.

Place 5 of the egg whites in the bowl of an electric mixer and whisk to medium-stiff peaks. Gradually whisk in 125 g (4½ oz) of the caster sugar until well incorporated.

Mix the cocoa with the icing sugar and gently fold into the meringue mixture. Spoon into a piping bag fitted with a 1 cm (½ in) round nozzle. Pipe two 18 cm (7 in) spiral discs onto the prepared baking tray. Also pipe four 30 cm (12 in) long, thin 'sticks' of meringue. Bake for about 1 hour, then turn off the oven and leave the meringue for a further 30 minutes. Remove from the oven and leave to cool completely.

Place the chocolate and butter in a bowl set over a saucepan of medium-hot water. Stir together until smooth and well mixed. Set the bowl aside.

Meanwhile, whisk the remaining 4 egg whites to stiff peaks, then gradually whisk in the remaining caster sugar until well incorporated. Fold a little of the mixture into the melted chocolate, then gently fold in the remaining egg whites until just mixed. Spoon into a piping bag.

When ready to assemble, place a cake ring 18 cm (7 in) in diameter and 8 cm (3¼ in) high on a wire rack. Place one of the chocolate meringue discs inside, trimming the edges to fit, if necessary. Pipe a 5 cm (2 in) layer of chocolate mousse on top of the meringue, then place the second chocolate meringue disc on top. Spread the top and side of the cake with a thin layer of chocolate mousse then transfer to the freezer for about 20 minutes to set.

Transfer the cake to a serving plate and carefully lift away the cake ring. Break the thin meringue sticks into 3–4 cm (1¼ in–1½ in) pieces and stick them all over the sides and top of the cake. Take your time. The effect is stunning. Dust with a little icing sugar and cocoa powder.

Serves 8

RUM SAVARIN

Savarin au rhum

FROM THE LORRAINE REGION

The savarin, a yeast cake moistened with a rum-flavoured sugar syrup, is one of the great French gâteaux and a favourite of mine. Baking this recipe will need a little experience with using yeast.

---

1 x 7–10 g (¼ oz) sachet dry yeast

50 ml (1¾ fl oz) warm milk

200 g (7 oz) plain (all-purpose) flour, sifted

3 large eggs, at room temperature

90 g (3 oz) unsalted butter, slightly softened

345 g (12 oz) sugar

500 ml (17 fl oz/2 cups) water

zest of 1 lemon

75 ml (2½ fl oz) rum

375 ml (12½ fl oz/ 1½ cups) whipped cream

400 g (14 oz) raspberries

Dissolve the yeast in the warm milk.

In the bowl of an electric beater fitted with a beating attachment, place the flour, the yeast and milk mixture, and the eggs and beat for about 2 minutes until the mixture is elastic. If you do not have an electric beater, beat it with a wooden spoon. Cover with a cloth and allow to rise for about 1 hour.

Lightly butter a 20 cm (8 in) ring cake tin. Preheat the oven to 200°C (400°F).

Add the softened butter and 1 tablespoon of sugar to the risen dough and beat thoroughly with a wooden spoon. Place the mixture in a piping bag without a nozzle and pipe into the prepared tin, tapping the tin lightly to eliminate any air bubbles. Leave to rise uncovered for 30 minutes in a warm place, then bake in the preheated oven for 25 minutes.

In a saucepan, bring the water, remaining sugar and lemon zest to the boil and cook for 5 minutes.

When the cake is cooked, remove from the oven and wait about 3 minutes before turning it out onto a dish.

Stir the rum into the sugar syrup and pour this slowly over the cake. Allow the cake to absorb the syrup.

Serve the cake garnished with whipped cream and raspberries.

Serves 6–8

NANCY'S CHOCOLATE CAKE

Gâteau au chocolat de Nancy

FROM THE LORRAINE REGION

The charming town of Nancy has its own version of chocolate cake, which is really easy to make and popular with all chocolate lovers.

125 g (4½ oz) dark (70%) cooking chocolate

125 g (4½ oz) caster (superfine) sugar

125 g (4½ oz) very soft unsalted butter

4 eggs, separated

25 g (1 oz) plain (all-purpose) flour, sifted

100 g (3½ oz) almond meal

a pinch of cream of tartar

50 g (1¾ oz) toasted flaked almonds

a little icing (confectioners') sugar for dusting

250 ml (8½ fl oz/1 cup) whipped cream

80 g (2¾ oz/¼ cup) marmalade

Preheat the oven to 170°C (340°F). Butter and flour a 22 cm (8¾ in) cake mould.

Place the chocolate in a bowl and melt gently over a bath of hot water. Remove from the heat.

Mix half the sugar with the softened butter, then mix this well with the melted chocolate. Mix in the 4 egg yolks, then the flour and almond meal.

Beat the egg whites with a pinch of cream of tartar into stiff peaks. Beat in the remaining sugar, then fold the beaten whites into the chocolate preparation.

Pour the cake mix into the tin and gently flatten the top. Bake the cake in the preheated oven for about 35 minutes.

Remove the cake from the oven and after 10 minutes very carefully turn it out onto a rack to cool.

Sprinkle the cake with flaked almonds and dust with icing sugar.

Serve with whipped cream mixed with a little marmalade.

Serves 8

CHESTNUT CAKE

Gâteau aux marrons

FROM THE LANGUEDOC REGION | BY SÉBASTIEN BUROT

You find lovely layered cakes such as this in many French pâtisseries and they make wonderful desserts for special occasions. To create a great-looking cake you will need to assemble it in a cake ring that is the same size as your sponge cake. You can decorate it with chocolate curls, glacé chestnuts and even gold leaves.

Rum syrup

125 ml (4 fl oz/½ cup) water

120 g (4½ oz) caster (superfine) sugar

2 tablespoons rum

Cake

200 g (7 oz) unsweetened purée de marrons (chestnut purée, which is available from delicatessens)

350 g (12½ oz) Crème pâtissière (see page 418)

300 ml (10 fl oz) whipped cream

1 x 18 cm (7 in) plain or chocolate sponge cake

Chocolate icing

80 ml (2½ fl oz/⅓ cup) pouring cream

3 tablespoons rum syrup

200 g (7 oz) dark chocolate, cut into small pieces

To make the rum syrup, combine the water and caster sugar in a saucepan. Bring to a simmer and cook for 5 minutes. Stir in the rum, allow to cool, then refrigerate until ready to use.

Beat the chestnut purée and crème pâtissière until well combined. Fold in the whipped cream.

When ready to assemble, place a cake ring on a wire rack. Cut the sponge cake horizontally into three even layers and if necessary, trim them to fit into the cake ring. Place a layer of sponge cake into the base of the cake ring. Brush with a little rum syrup then spoon half the chestnut cream on top and smooth the surface. Top with another layer of sponge cake and brush with a little more syrup. Spoon in the remaining chestnut cream. Brush one side of the remaining sponge layer with syrup and place that side on top of the cream. Transfer the cake, still on the rack, to the freezer for 30 minutes to set.

While the cake is setting, make the icing. Combine the cream and rum syrup in a saucepan and bring to the boil. Stir in the chocolate until melted. Remove from heat and leave to cool slightly, stirring from time to time to keep it smooth.

Transfer the cake onto a serving plate and carefully lift away the cake ring. Use a flat spatula to glaze the cake all over with chocolate icing. Place in the refrigerator to allow the icing to set.

Serves 8–10

WALNUT CAKE

Gâteau aux noix

FROM THE ALPS REGION

*This family cake is very popular in the region of Grenoble,
famous for its large production of walnuts.*

Cake

165 g (6 oz) walnuts

150 g (5½ oz) unsalted butter

finely grated zest of 1 lemon

150 g (5½ oz) sugar

4 eggs, separated

75 g (2¾ oz/⅔ cup) dried breadcrumbs

a pinch of cream of tartar

Icing

55 ml (1¾ fl oz) water

100 g (3½ oz) sugar

2 drops red wine vinegar

10 walnut halves

a little icing (confectioners') sugar, for dusting

Preheat the oven to 150°C (300°F). Butter a 22 cm (8¾ in) cake tin, line the base with baking paper, then butter the paper.

Place the walnuts in a food processor and grind to a coarse meal.

Using an electric mixer, beat the butter, lemon zest and half the caster sugar until pale and creamy. Add the egg yolks, one at a time, beating on medium speed. Add the breadcrumbs and chopped walnuts and mix well.

Whisk the egg whites and cream of tartar to medium-stiff peaks. Gradually whisk in the rest of the caster sugar until well incorporated. Add a third of the egg whites to the batter and fold in well. Carefully fold in the remaining whites.

Pour into the prepared cake tin and smooth the surface. Bake for 1 hour.

Remove the cake from the oven and cool for 5 minutes before turning out onto a wire rack.

To make the icing, combine the water, sugar and vinegar in a small saucepan and bring to the boil. Cook to a light-brown caramel. Pour the icing slowly onto the centre of the cake and use a spatula to spread it out smoothly. Garnish with walnut halves and dust the edges of the cake with icing sugar.

Serves 8–10

STRAWBERRY SPONGE CAKE

Gâteau fraisier

FROM THE LANGUEDOC-ROUSSILLON REGION | BY PIERRICK BOYER

Many of the sweetest French strawberries are grown in the sunny region of Languedoc-Roussillon, and this gâteau is popular in the pâtisseries of the region and, naturellement, in the top pastry shops in Paris.
To make this exquisite cake you will need to be an experienced pastry cook and for perfect presentation you will need a few pieces of special equipment, such as a cake ring and acetate plastic. Both are available from specialist food stores.

Syrup

1½ tablespoons water

30 g (1 oz) caster (superfine) sugar

Custard filling

3 gelatine leaves

400 ml (13½ fl oz) milk

1 vanilla bean, split lengthways

2 eggs

50 g (1¾ oz) caster (superfine) sugar

50 g (1¾ oz) cornflour (cornstarch)

100 g (3½ oz) unsalted butter, cut into cubes

400 ml (13½ fl oz) whipped cream

To make the syrup, combine the water and sugar in a saucepan. Bring to a simmer and cook for 2 minutes to make a syrup. Set aside to cool.

To make the custard, first soak the gelatine leaves in a bowl of cold water for 5–10 minutes.

Combine the milk and vanilla bean in a saucepan and bring almost to the boil.

In a bowl, whisk the eggs, caster sugar and cornflour until well blended. Pour on the hot milk and whisk well until smooth. Return the mixture to the rinsed-out saucepan and cook over a medium heat, whisking constantly, until it thickens. Tip the mixture into a bowl, whisk briefly and leave to cool a little.

Squeeze the gelatine leaves to remove excess water then stir into the custard to dissolve. Whisk in the butter cubes until melted and smooth. Pour the custard into a tray so that it can cool quickly, but don't allow it to set firm. When the custard is cold, fold in the whipped cream. Transfer the custard to a piping bag fitted with a 1 cm (½ in) round nozzle.

When ready to assemble the cake, line the base and sides of a 22 cm (8¾ in) cake ring with plastic acetate, which stops the cake sticking. Place the cake ring on a baking tray lined with baking paper.

Cake

1 x 22 cm (8¾ in) plain sponge cake

500 g (1 lb 2 oz) medium–large strawberries, halved

a little icing (confectioners') sugar, for dusting

250 g (9 oz) marzipan

a few raspberries and/or strawberries, to serve

150 ml (5 fl oz) whipped cream, to serve

Cut the sponge cake horizontally to create two layers. Trim 1 cm (½ in) from the edge of each, so they are smaller than the cake ring. Place one of the sponge layers in the base of the cake ring. Pipe custard into the space between the sponge and the sides of the ring. Stick strawberry halves into the custard around the edge of the ring, with the flat edges facing outwards.

Pipe a layer of custard on top of the sponge and in between the strawberries. Use a small palette knife to spread the custard up the sides of the cake ring to the top. Arrange a layer of strawberry halves on top of the custard then sit the second layer of sponge cake on top. Brush with the sugar syrup. Finish with a layer of custard, smooth the surface and refrigerate for 2 hours to set.

Dust a work surface with a little icing sugar. Roll the marzipan out thinly and cut out a 22 cm (8¾ in) circle. Lift it carefully onto the top of the set cake.

Transfer the cake to a cake stand and very carefully lift away the cake ring. Decorate the cake with a few strawberries or raspberries and dust with icing sugar. Just before serving, remove the strip of acetate from the side of the cake. Cut into slices and serve with whipped cream.

Serves 8

RASPBERRY ICE CREAM CAKE WITH MERINGUE

Vacherin aux framboises

FROM THE ALSACE REGION

The region of Alsace is famous for this ice cream dessert, which combines fruit sorbet, vanilla ice cream, home-made meringues and whipped cream. It's one of my favourite desserts after a special dinner. To assemble the vacherin, you will need a 2-litre (68 fl oz) charlotte mould that should be well chilled in the freezer. Once the mould is filled, transfer to the freezer for a minimum of 1 hour before serving, so that it sets very firm.

Raspberry sorbet

500 g (1 lb 2 oz) raspberries

300 g (10½ oz) sugar

juice of 1 lemon

juice of 2 oranges

Meringues

whites of three large eggs

a pinch of cream of tartar

120 g (4½ oz) caster (superfine) sugar

50 g (1¾ oz) pure icing (confectioners') sugar, sifted

1 litre (34 fl oz/4 cups) good-quality vanilla ice cream

300 ml (10 fl oz) whipped cream

300 g (10½ oz) raspberries

To make the raspberry sorbet, combine the raspberries, sugar, lemon and orange juice in a food processor and blend to a purée. Strain through a fine sieve, then transfer to an ice cream machine and churn according to the manufacturer's instructions. When the sorbet is ready, transfer it to a pre-chilled container and place in the freezer.

If you don't have an ice cream maker, freeze the mixture in a stainless-steel bowl. When it starts to freeze, whisk for 10–15 seconds and return to freezer. Repeat at regular intervals until it becomes too firm to whisk. The whisking lightens the sorbet and prevents large ice crystals from forming.

To make the meringues, preheat the oven to 140°C (275°F). Line a baking tray with baking paper.

Place the egg whites and cream of tartar in the bowl of an electric mixer and whisk to soft peaks. Gradually whisk in half of the caster sugar until the meringue becomes shiny and stiffer. Whisk in the remaining caster sugar and the icing sugar until well incorporated.

Spoon 12 oval spoonfuls of meringue on the baking tray, leaving a little space between them. Don't worry if the shapes are not perfect, and avoid fiddling with them. Cook for 20 minutes, then reduce the oven temperature to 100°C (200°F) and cook for a further 60 minutes.

Turn off the oven and leave the meringues in the oven for a further hour to dry completely. Store in an airtight container.

To assemble the vacherin, spoon the vanilla ice cream into a chilled charlotte mould. Smooth the surface then top with the raspberry sorbet. Freeze for at least 1 hour to set well.

To unmould the vacherin, briefly dip the mould in warm water to loosen the ice cream, then invert it onto a serving dish. Stick meringues around the sides of the ice cream using a little whipped cream to attach them. Use as many meringues as necessary. Spoon the whipped cream into a piping bag fitted with a fluted nozzle and use to pipe rosettes of whipped cream in between the meringues. Top with raspberries.

Use a sharp knife to cut the vacherin into slices, so that everyone gets a meringue.

Serves 8–10

CHERRY MOUSSE CAKE

Charlotte aux cerises

FROM THE ALSACE/FRANCHE COMTÉ REGION

In the lovely green region of South Alsace and North Franche Comté, the sides of the road are often lined with cherry groves, and cherries feature in many local desserts, as well as being transformed into a superb cherry liqueur. This dessert is a sort of French trifle.

Custard filling

2 gelatine leaves

500 ml (17 fl oz/2 cups) milk

½ vanilla bean, split lengthways

5 egg yolks

150 g (5½ oz) caster (superfine) sugar

1 x 25 cm (10 in) square sponge cake, about 4 cm (1½ in) thick

300 ml (10 fl oz) whipped cream

600 g (1 lb 5 oz) cherries, pitted at the last moment

Raspberry sauce (page 361), to serve (optional)

To make the custard, first soak the gelatine leaves in a bowl of cold water for 5–10 minutes.

Combine the milk and vanilla bean in a saucepan and heat until nearly boiling.

In a bowl, whisk the egg yolks with the sugar until light and creamy – it takes at least 5 minutes. Pour on the hot milk and whisk well until smooth. Return the mixture to the rinsed-out saucepan and cook over a medium heat, stirring with a wooden spoon, until the custard lightly coats the back of the spoon. Strain the custard into a bowl and leave it to cool slightly.

Squeeze the gelatine leaves to remove excess water then stir into the warm custard to dissolve. Transfer to the fridge to cool for 20–30 minutes, but check to ensure the custard does not set.

Line a medium loaf (bar) tin with baking paper. Cut the sponge cake horizontally into three layers, then cut the layers into pieces and use to line the base and sides of the tin.

Fold the whipped cream into the cold custard. Pour a little custard over the sponge pieces, to about one-third of the way up the tin. Top with the pitted cherries to almost fill the tin.

Add more custard, then tap the tin lightly to help the ingredients to settle. Add more custard to fill the tin. Cover with a layer of sponge pieces to form a lid. Carefully wrap the tin in plastic wrap and refrigerate for at least 4 hours to set.

To serve, carefully remove the plastic wrap and unmould the cake. Use a sharp knife to cut it into about 10 thick slices and serve with raspberry sauce, if you wish.

Serves 8–10

CHERRY & HAZELNUT CAKE

Gâteau aux cerises et aux noisettes

FROM THE LIMOUSIN REGION

---

*The texture and flavour of the cherries are fabulous in this delicious cake,
and if you own a cherry pitter that will make things so much easier.
It's best to eat this cake within 24 hours of making it —
but that shouldn't be too difficult!*

---

150 g (5½ oz) unsalted butter, cut into small pieces

150 g (5½ oz) caster (superfine) sugar

zest of 1 lemon, finely grated

3 eggs, at room temperature

150 g (5½ oz) self-raising flour

3 tablespoons almond meal

80 g (2¾ oz) skinned roasted hazelnuts, each crushed into 2–3 pieces

about 30 large cherries, pitted

2 tablespoons extra caster (superfine) sugar

2 tablespoons smooth apricot jam, heated

Preheat the oven to 180°C (350°F). Butter and flour a 22 cm (8½ in) loose-based cake tin.

Using an electric beater, cream the butter, sugar and lemon zest for a few minutes until light and creamy.

Add the eggs one at a time to the creamed butter and beat well. Then on low speed carefully add the self-raising flour, almond meal and roasted hazelnut pieces, beating until just mixed.

Carefully pour the mixture into the prepared tin and flatten the top with a spatula. Press the pitted cherries about 5 mm (¼ in) into the mixture, keeping them about 1 cm (½ in) away from the sides of the tin. Dust the top with the extra caster sugar.

Bake in the preheated oven for about 50 minutes until the cake is cooked.

Remove the cake from the oven and rest it for 15 minutes before carefully turning it out onto a cake rack. Brush the top of the cake with the heated jam and allow the cake to cool before serving.

It's delicious served with cream or ice cream.

Serves 8

ALMOND & APRICOT CAKE

Gâteau aux amandes et aux abricots

FROM THE RHÔNE-ALPS REGION

I urge you to try this cake when apricots are at their best.
It's easy to make and I love it so much that I have planted
an apricot tree in my garden!

5 ripe apricots

150 g (5½ oz) unsalted butter

100 g (3½ oz) caster (superfine) sugar

3 eggs, at room temperature

75 ml (2½ fl oz) orange blossom honey

120 g (4½ oz) almond meal

100 g (3½ oz/⅔ cup) self-raising flour, sifted

1 tablespoon extra caster (superfine) sugar

2 tablespoons flaked almonds

icing (confectioners') sugar for dusting

Preheat the oven to 200°C (400°F). Butter and flour a 24 cm (9½ in) cake tin.

Wash and halve the apricots and remove the stones.

Cream the butter and caster sugar for a few minutes until light and creamy, using an electric beater. Beat in the eggs and whisk in the honey. Then fold in the almond meal and flour.

Carefully pour the cake mixture into the prepared cake tin and tap the tin to distribute the mixture evenly. Arrange the apricot halves, cut side up, attractively on top and sprinkle them with extra caster sugar. Sprinkle flaked almonds in the spaces between the apricots.

Bake the cake in the preheated oven for 45 minutes or until cooked.

Remove the cake from the oven and cool for 10 minutes before carefully turning out onto a wire rack. Allow to cool.

Dust the top with icing sugar just before serving.

Serves 8

PUFF PASTRY & ALMOND CREAM CAKE

Pithiviers

FROM THE LOIRE VALLEY REGION	BY SÉBASTIEN BUROT

This classic cake is also known as Galette des Rois and it is really popular on 6 January, when French Catholics celebrate the Epiphany — the arrival of the Three Wise Kings. The Kings' cake is usually purchased from the local pâtisserie.

2 x 25 cm (10 in) square sheets puff pastry (or 500 g/1 lb 2 oz) puff pastry)

1 egg yolk

2 tablespoons water

Almond cream

125 g (4½ oz) unsalted butter

125 g (4½ oz) caster (superfine) sugar

2 eggs

125 g (4½ oz) almond meal

2 tablespoons rum

30 g (1 oz) plain (all-purpose) flour

Preheat the oven to 220°C (400°F). Line a flat baking tray with baking paper.

To make the almond cream, combine the butter and sugar in the bowl of an electric mixer and beat until well combined. Add the eggs one at a time, mixing well after each addition. Add the almond meal and mix well. Add the rum and flour and mix well. Spoon the mixture into a piping bag without a nozzle.

Lay the pastry sheets out on a work surface, or roll out to a thickness of 5 mm (¼ in). Using a large plate or similar, cut out two 25 cm (10 in) rounds.

Carefully lift one pastry round onto the prepared baking tray. Use the tip of a knife to trace a smaller circle, about 17 cm (6¾ in) in diameter, on the pastry.

Mix the egg yolk and water together to make eggwash and use to brush the outer edge of the pastry. Pipe a generous mound of almond cream in the centre. Cover with the second pastry disc and press the edges together to seal. Brush with more eggwash. Use the blade of a small knife to mark the surface with curved lines that radiate from the centre to the edges in an attractive pattern.

Bake for 15 minutes, then reduce the oven temperature to 200°C (400°F) and bake for a further 20–25 minutes, or until the cake is browned underneath.

Serves 6–8

NOUGAT CAKE FROM TOURS

Nougat de Tours

FROM THE CENTRAL LOIRE VALLEY REGION

This lovely speciality from the Loire Valley town of Tours is actually not nougat but a cake filled with confit fruits and a type of almond meringue called macaronade (macaron mixture).

---

400 g (14 oz) Sweet shortcrust pastry (page 408)

60 g (2 oz) apricot jam

150 g (5½ oz) diced confit fruits
(3 or 4 varieties)

80 g (2¾ oz) almond meal

80 g (2¾ oz) caster (superfine) sugar

3 egg whites

a pinch of cream of tartar

icing (confectioners') sugar for dusting

Preheat the oven to 200°C (400°F).

Roll the pastry out thinly and line a 20 cm (8 in) loose-based flan (tart) tin. Spread the base of the pastry with apricot jam and cover with the confit fruits.

Mix the almond meal with the caster sugar and sift together.

Beat the egg whites and cream of tartar into stiff peaks, then gently fold in the almond meal and sugar preparation. Spread this on top of the confit fruits, finishing just short of the pastry edges. Smooth the top with a spatula.

Generously dust the top with icing sugar. Bake in the preheated oven for about 30 minutes until the pastry has browned and is cooked. Cool before serving.

Serves 8

PARIS BREST GÂTEAU

FROM THE PARIS REGION | BY PHILIPPE MOUCHEL

Named after a bicycle race from, you guessed it, Paris to Brest, this delicious French gâteau is made by most traditional French pâtissiers. You can prepare both the crème pâtissière pralinée and the choux pastry rings the day before you serve the dessert.

1 egg yolk

1 teaspoon water

about 55 g (2 oz) flaked almonds

icing (confectioners') sugar, for dusting

Crème pâtissière pralinée

55 g (2 oz) unsalted butter, softened

55 g (2 oz) hazelnut pralinée or chocolate pralinée (or use Nutella)

Crème pâtissière (page 418), chilled

Choux pastry

100 ml (3½ fl oz) water

150 ml (5 fl oz) milk

½ teaspoon salt

2 teaspoons sugar

85 g (3 oz) unsalted butter, cut into small pieces

150 g (5½ oz/1 cup) plain (all-purpose) flour, sifted

4 eggs

To make the crème pâtissière pralinée, beat the butter with the pralinée until combined. Add the crème pâtissière and mix well. Refrigerate until ready to use.

Preheat the oven to 200°C (400°F). Place a 20 cm (8 in) flan (tart) ring on a baking tray lined with baking paper.

To make the choux pastry, combine the water, milk, salt, sugar and butter in a medium saucepan and bring to a simmer. When the butter has dissolved, lower the heat and add all the flour, stirring vigorously with a wooden spoon for a few minutes until it forms a smooth mass.

Transfer the mixture to the bowl of an electric mixer fitted with the K beater and mix on medium speed. Add the eggs one at a time, mixing well after each addition, until the dough is smooth. Spoon into a large piping bag fitted with a 1 cm (½ in) nozzle.

Pipe a circle of dough inside the flan ring close to the edge. Pipe a second circle inside the first one then pipe a third circle on top of these two circles.

Mix the egg yolk and water together to make eggwash and brush over the pastry. Sprinkle on the flaked almonds and bake for 20 minutes. Reduce the oven temperature to 150°C (300°F) and bake for a further 25 minutes. Turn off the oven and leave the pastry in the oven to dry for about 1 hour. Remove from the oven and leave on a wire rack until completely cold. Carefully lift away the flan ring.

When nearly ready to serve, spoon the chilled crème pâtissière pralinée into a piping bag fitted with a serrated nozzle. Split the pastry in half horizontally and fill the base to a height of about 2.5 cm (1 in). Gently place the pastry lid on top. Dust with icing sugar and serve straight away. Alternatively, store in the refrigerator until 10 minutes before serving.

Serves 8

ST HONORÉ CAKE

Gâteau St Honoré

POPULAR ALL OVER FRANCE | BY PIERRICK BOYER

Pierrick Boyer, our team's talented pâtissier, prepared this popular and delicious French gâteau to celebrate Bastille Day, the French national day on 14 July. It is a rather elaborate cake and to make it you will need good baking skills and some specialist equipment, such as a St Honoré nozzle.

Choux pastry

250 ml (8½ fl oz/1 cup) water

100 g (3½ oz) unsalted butter

a pinch of salt

165 g (6 oz) plain (all-purpose) flour, sifted

5 large eggs

20 cm (8 in) square rolled puff pastry

200 g (7 oz) fondant (available from specialist food stores)

Preheat the oven to 180°C (350°F). Line two baking trays with baking paper.

To make the choux pastry combine the water, butter and salt in a medium saucepan and bring to a simmer. When the butter has dissolved, lower the heat and add the flour in one go, stirring vigorously with a wooden spoon for a few minutes until it forms a smooth mass.

Transfer the mixture to the bowl of an electric mixer fitted with the K beater and mix on medium speed. Add the eggs one at a time, mixing well after each addition, until the dough is smooth. Spoon into a large piping bag fitted with a 1 cm (½ in) nozzle.

Place the puff pastry square on a floured surface and cut out a 20 cm (8 in) disc. Lift it carefully onto the prepared baking tray. Pipe a circle of choux pastry around the edge of the puff pastry disc. Now pipe a loose spiral shape, starting from the centre and working to the edge.

Pipe twelve 3 cm (1¼ in) choux puffs onto the second prepared baking tray. Place both trays in the oven and cook for about 20 minutes, until the pastries are golden brown and cooked. Remove from the oven and cool the cake and choux puffs on a wire rack.

Place the fondant and glucose syrup in a small saucepan. Bring to the boil and cook to a caramel. Very carefully dip the choux puffs into the hot caramel then place them, caramel side down, on a non-stick baking tray to cool. When cold they will have a nice smooth caramel edge.

250 g (9 oz) glucose syrup

300 g (10½ oz) Crème patissière (page 418)

300 g (10½ oz) whipping cream

a few halved strawberries

icing (confectioners') sugar, for dusting

Dip the opposite sides of the choux puffs into the caramel, then stick them onto the cake, in a circle around the edge, so the flat caramel sides are uppermost. Make sure you set one choux puff aside.

In a bowl fold together the crème pâtissière and the whipped cream and spoon into a piping bag fitted with a special St Honoré nozzle. Pipe a generous amount into the centre of the cake, forming the traditional little rounded peaks. (If you don't have a special nozzle, pipe it in as attractively as you can.)

Using a serrated knife, slice the choux puffs in half horizontally and remove the caramelised lids. Carefully fill the choux halves that are attached to the cake, then replace the lids. Place the reserved choux puff in the centre of the cake. As a final flourish, decorate the top with strawberry halves and dust with icing sugar.

Serves 8

SAVOIE SPONGE CAKE

Gâteau de Savoie

FROM THE ALPS REGION

My grandmother, who inspired me to become a chef, baked one of these lovely gâteaux each time we had a special family celebration. I love to serve it with a runny custard and fresh fruits.

---

85 g (3 oz) plain (all-purpose) flour

85 g (3 oz) cornflour (cornstarch)

6 eggs, separated

grated zest of 1 lemon

300 g (10½ oz) caster (superfine) sugar

a pinch of cream of tartar

icing (confectioners') sugar, for dusting

Preheat the oven to 180°C (350°F). Butter a 25 cm (10 in) round cake tin.

Sift the flours together.

Put the egg yolks, lemon zest and 150 g (5½ oz) of the caster sugar in the bowl of an electric mixer and beat until very pale and mousse-like.

Add the cream of tartar to the egg whites and whisk them to stiff peaks. Gradually whisk in the remaining caster sugar until well incorporated. Gently fold the egg whites into the egg yolks. Lastly, fold in the sifted flours, being careful not to over-mix.

Pour the cake mixture into the prepared tin and smooth the surface. Dust with a little icing sugar and bake for 35–40 minutes. Remove from the oven and cool for about 10 minutes on a wire rack. Turn out of the tin and cool completely before serving.

Serves 10–12

ROLLED SAVOY SPONGE WITH BLUEBERRIES

Biscuit de Savoie roulées aux myrtilles

FROM THE ALPS/SAVOIE REGION

The Biscuit de Savoie is a regional sponge cake that is very popular for celebrating family birthdays and name days. Wild blueberries are plentiful in the Alps and so the sponge is rolled with blueberry jam.

3 eggs, separated, at room temperature

zest of 1 lemon, grated

150 g (5½ oz) caster (superfine) sugar

a pinch of cream of tartar

45 g (1½ oz) plain (all-purpose) flour

45 g (1½ oz) cornflour (cornstarch)

3 tablespoons brandy

200 g (7 oz) blueberry jam

100 g (3½ oz) toasted flaked almonds

icing (confectioners') sugar for dusting

Preheat the oven to 180°C (350°F).

Butter a 36 cm (14 in) x 26 cm (10¼ in) Swiss roll tin (jelly roll tin) and line it with baking paper. Butter and flour the baking paper.

Place the egg yolks, lemon zest and half the sugar in the bowl of an electric mixer and beat until foamy.

In a separate bowl, add the cream of tartar to the egg whites and whisk into firm peaks. Gradually whisk in the remaining sugar until well incorporated.

Gently fold the egg whites into the beaten yolks. Sift together the plain flour and the cornflour and then fold into the egg preparation. Avoid over-mixing the flour. Pour the mixture into the prepared tin and spread to the edges.

Bake in the preheated oven for about 8 minutes or until firm to the touch.

Turn the warm sponge out onto a clean tea towel. Peel off the baking paper and roll the sponge up by gradually lifting the tea towel. Set aside to cool.

Unroll the sponge, sprinkle it with the brandy and spread three-quarters of the jam over the sponge. Carefully roll up the sponge firmly.

Brush the remaining jam over the roll and refrigerate if not serving immediately.

Sprinkle with toasted almonds, dust with icing sugar and serve.

Serves 10

KOUGELHOPF GÂTEAU

FROM THE ALSACE REGION | BY PHILIPPE MOUCHEL

This wonderful yeast cake is a great speciality of Alsace. You can find it in every pâtisserie and bakery in the region and at the better hotels it is usually on offer for breakfast. You will need a special kougelhopf mould to create the traditional fluted, curved shape.

100 g (3½ oz) raisins

55 ml (1¾ fl oz) rum

12 g (½ oz) fresh yeast

60 ml (2 fl oz/¼ cup) milk, boiled and cooled to lukewarm

250 g (9 oz/1⅔ cups) plain (all-purpose) flour

40 g (1½ oz) caster (superfine) sugar

1 teaspoon salt

4 eggs

185 g (6½ oz) unsalted butter, at room temperature, plus extra for greasing

100 g (3½ oz) whole or flaked almonds

1 egg yolk

1 tablespoon water

icing (confectioners') sugar, for dusting (optional)

Put the raisins in a bowl with the rum and leave to macerate overnight.

Mix the yeast with the warm milk in a small bowl.

Combine the flour, caster sugar, salt and yeast mixture in the bowl of an electric mixer fitted with the dough hook. Beat on medium speed. Add the eggs, one at a time, beating well after each addition. Beat for about 5 minutes until the dough is smooth and elastic.

Turn the mixer speed to low and add the butter, bit by bit. Once it's all incorporated, increase the speed to medium again and beat for about 8 minutes until the dough comes away from the sides of the bowl. Briefly mix in the macerated raisins.

Transfer the dough to a bowl, cover with a clean cloth and leave to rise at room temperature for about 2 hours.

Knock back the dough by punching it lightly with your fists a few times. Roll it out to a rectangle and fold it onto itself to form a sausage shape.

Butter a kougelhopf mould with the extra butter and scatter the flaked almonds onto the sides and base. Place the dough into the mould, adjusting it gently to fit. Mix the egg yolk and water together and use to seal the ends together. Leave to rise in a warm place (about 25°C/75°F is ideal) for another 2 hours.

Preheat the oven to 200°C (400°F). Bake the kougelhopf for 20 minutes, then cover with baking paper and cook for a further 20 minutes. Remove the cake from the oven and place on a rack to cool. Turn out after about 15 minutes and leave to cool completely. Dust with icing sugar just before serving.

Serves 8–10

MACAROONS

Macarons

These delicious small, round cakes are crunchy on the outside and smooth and soft in the centre. They were made famous by the great Parisian pâtisserie Ladurée, where every year a new flavour of macaroon is created. A little experience is required to make macaroons well, so you may need to make a few batches to perfect the technique.

150 g (5½ oz) caster (superfine) sugar

50 ml (1¾ fl oz) water

120 g (4½ oz) egg whites

2 vanilla beans, split lengthways and seeds scraped

160 g (5½ oz) almond meal

160 g (5½ oz) icing (confectioners') sugar

160 ml (5½ fl oz) pouring cream

160 g (5½ oz) dark chocolate

Preheat the oven to 145°C (280°F). Line two baking trays with baking paper.

Combine the caster sugar and water in a saucepan and bring to a simmer. Place a sugar thermometer in the pan and cook until the syrup reaches 121°C (250°F).

Just before the syrup reaches temperature, place 2 of the egg whites in an electric mixer and whisk to stiff peaks. With the motor running, slowly drizzle in the hot syrup. Continue whisking at a low speed for a few minutes.

In a mixing bowl, combine the remaining egg whites with the vanilla seeds, almond meal and icing sugar. Mix in a spoonful of the beaten egg whites to loosen the mixture. Then use a plastic scraper to mix in the remaining egg whites. Transfer the mixture to a piping bag fitted with a 1 cm (½ in) nozzle.

Pipe small 3 cm (1¼ in) mounds of the mixture onto the baking trays, spacing them evenly. Tap the trays lightly on a work surface to settle the mixture. Leave to rest for 1 hour, then bake for 8–10 minutes.

Meanwhile, bring the cream to the boil. Pour the hot cream onto the chocolate and stir until very smooth. Leave the chocolate to cool and firm up a little, but don't allow it to set. Spoon into a piping bag.

Pipe neat dollops of chocolate onto the flat sides of half the macarons. Top each with a macaron and sandwich together. Store in an airtight container.

Makes 30–35

MONT BLANC CHESTNUT CAKES

Petits gâteaux Mont Blanc

FROM THE ALPS REGION	BY PIERRICK BOYER

The French are mad about chestnuts and this dessert, using a luscious chestnut cream, was created to celebrate the beauty of the alpine Mont Blanc peak. You need special pastry equipment, in particular a piping bag fitted with a Mont Blanc nozzle.

250 g (9 oz) Sweet shortcrust pastry (page 408)

55 g (2 oz) almond meal

55 g (2 oz) icing (confectioners') sugar, plus extra for dusting

55 g (2 oz) plain (all-purpose) flour, sifted

55 g (2 oz) unsalted butter, softened

1 egg

1½ tablespoons orange marmalade

6 small meringues, the size of a ball of cotton wool

100 g (3½ oz) sweet chestnut cream (crème de marrons, which is available from delicatessens)

100 g (3½ oz) unsweetened chestnut purée (purée de marrons, which is available from delicatessens)

100 ml (3½ fl oz) whipped cream

Preheat the oven to 170°C (340°F). Lightly grease six 6 cm (2½ in) tartlet rings. Arrange the rings on a flat baking tray.

Roll the pastry out to a thickness of 3 mm (⅛ in). Cut out six 10 cm (4 in) discs of pastry and use to line the tartlet rings, pushing the pastry in gently. Trim the edges neatly.

In a bowl, combine the almond meal, sugar, flour and butter. Add the egg and mix until smooth. Spoon into a piping bag and neatly fill the pastry cases three-quarters full. Bake for about 15 minutes or until the pastry is cooked and golden brown. Remove from the oven and leave to cool, then turn the tartlets out.

Spread 1 teaspoon of marmalade on each tartlet, and top with a small meringue.

In a bowl, combine the chestnut cream and chestnut purée. Spoon the mixture into a piping bag fitted with a special Mont Blanc nozzle and use it to pipe the traditional vermicelli-like icing over the top of the meringues to cover them well. Dust with icing sugar. Use a piping bag fitted with a star nozzle to pipe whipped cream rosettes of 'snow' on the summit of your mini Mont Blanc cakes. Refrigerate until 10 minutes before serving.

Makes 6 little cakes

RASPBERRY MILLEFEUILLES

Millefeuilles aux framboises

FROM THE ÎLE-DE-FRANCE REGION

I love caramelised puff pastry and can never resist these delicious raspberry millefeuilles when I see them on display in the best Parisian pâtisseries.

about 500 g (1 lb 2 oz) puff pastry

50 g (1¾ oz) caster (superfine) sugar

30 g (1 oz) icing (confectioners') sugar

30 g (1 oz) finely chopped pistachio nuts

2 tablespoons Calvados liqueur

300 ml (10 fl oz) whipped cream

400 g (14 oz) raspberries

Preheat the oven to 200°C (400°F).

Line a flat 25 x 35 cm (10 x 13½ in) baking tray with baking paper and lightly brush the paper with water.

Roll the puff pastry out to about 2 mm (⅓ in) thick and to fit the size of the baking tray. Carefully lift the pastry onto the tray and chill in the refrigerator for 30 minutes.

Dust the pastry with caster sugar, then bake in the preheated oven. After about 8 minutes, top the pastry with a grill or heavy tray to prevent it from rising too much, then bake it for a further 5 minutes.

Remove the pastry from the oven and remove the grill. Turn the pastry out onto a second baking tray lined with baking paper and dust the top with 10 g (¼ oz) of the icing sugar. Increase the oven temperature to 250°C (480°F) and bake the pastry for a further 8 minutes to glaze it. Remove the pastry from the oven and allow it to cool.

Cut the pastry into three long strips, then cut each strip into six equal pieces.

Mix the pistachio nuts with the remaining 20 g (¾ oz) of icing sugar.

Whisk the Calvados into the cream, then mix in the pistachio nuts.

Place 12 pieces of pastry on a dish and spread the top with some pistachio cream. Top six of the pastry pieces with raspberries, then place the six remaining cream-topped pastry pieces on top. Garnish with raspberries and top with the pastry pieces (without cream).

Serves 6

RASPBERRY FRUIT JELLIES

Pâte de fruit aux framboises

FROM THE LIMOUSIN REGION	BY PHILIPPE MOUCHEL

You find these exquisite, soft and flavoursome fruit jellies in the best French pâtisseries and they are often served with coffee in top restaurants. Making these jellies requires some experience and you will need a few items of specialist equipment, such as a sugar thermometer and a fruit jelly frame.

1.2 kg (2 lb 10 oz) strained raspberry purée

1.1 kg (2 lb 7 oz) caster (superfine) sugar

30 g (1 oz) apple pectin

200 g (7 oz) liquid glucose

3 tablespoons citric acid

2 tablespoons raspberry liqueur

200 g (7 oz) sugar

Line a tray with baking paper and place a 40 cm (15¾ in) square fruit jelly frame on top.

Place the strained raspberry purée in a saucepan and bring to a simmer.

Mix 100 g (3½ oz) of the caster sugar with the apple pectin and stir into the raspberry purée. Add the liquid glucose and the remaining sugar and bring to a slow boil.

Place a sugar thermometer in the pan and cook until the syrup reaches 108°C (226°F). Stir from time to time and brush the side of the pan with a little water if necessary, to keep it clean.

Dissolve the citric acid in the raspberry liqueur and add it to the purée once it reaches 108°C (226°F). Very carefully pour the jelly mixture into the frame and spread it evenly. Allow to cool, then refrigerate for at least 2 hours to set.

Gently remove the frame and cut the fruit jelly into 3 cm (1¼ in) squares. Place the jellies onto a plate of sugar and coat delicately with sugar. Store in a dry cake tin in layers separated with baking paper.

Makes about 150 jellies

BORDEAUX CANELÉS

Canelés de Bordeaux

FROM THE BORDEAUX/AQUITAINE REGION | BY PIERRICK BOYER

*In France most people buy these little cakes at the pâtisserie,
but experienced dessert makers will have fun making them.
You will need special metal canelé moulds, and the cake mix needs to rest
overnight in the fridge before being baked.*

1 litre (34 fl oz/4 cups) milk

1 vanilla bean, split lengthways

60 g (2 oz) unsalted butter

620 g (1 lb 6 oz) caster (superfine) sugar

310 g (11 oz) plain (all-purpose) flour

1 egg, at room temperature

8 egg yolks, at room temperature

125 ml (4½ fl oz/½ cup) rum

200 g (7 oz) beeswax, melted

Pour three-quarters of the milk into a saucepan. Scrape the seeds of the vanilla bean into the milk and then add the vanilla bean. Heat the milk to almost boiling point. Add the butter to melt. Remove the pan from the heat and add the remaining cold milk.

Combine the caster sugar and flour in a bowl.

In another bowl, whisk the egg with the 8 egg yolks. Mix in the rum, the flour and sugar mixture and about a quarter of the warm milk, mixing until smooth. Little by little, add the remaining milk.

Refrigerate the preparation overnight. The next day, preheat the oven to 220°C (430°F).

Brush the canelé moulds lightly with melted beeswax. Fill the moulds with the mixture to about 5 mm (¼ in) below the rim. Place the filled moulds in the preheated oven and then reduce the oven to 180°C (350°F). Bake for about 45–50 minutes.

Carefully turn the canelés out onto a cake rack while still hot. Allow to cool.

Makes about 50

ALMOND & APRICOT FRIANDS

Financiers aux amandes et abricots

FROM THE LANGUEDOC-ROUSSILLON REGION

The Languedoc/Roussillon region enjoys superb weather, and almond and apricot trees thrive. I like to use special rectangular financier moulds, but you can also use small muffin moulds (you need eight buttered moulds).

---

juice of 1 lemon

80 g (2¾ oz/⅓ cup) caster (superfine) sugar

1 vanilla bean, split lengthways

12 apricots, halved

50 g (1¾ oz) almond meal

50 g (1¾ oz/⅓ cup) plain (all-purpose) flour, sifted

4 egg whites

90 g (3 oz) good quality unsalted butter

8 raspberries

24 pistachio nuts, halved

2 tablespoons toasted flaked almonds

icing (confectioners') sugar for dusting

In a small saucepan over a low heat, combine the lemon juice with 30 g (1 oz) of the sugar and half a vanilla bean.

Add the apricot halves without the stones. Cover and cook on a low heat until the apricots are soft. Transfer the apricots to a bowl to cool.

Preheat the oven to 180°C (350°F). Butter 8 muffin moulds or rectangular financier moulds.

Scrape the black seeds from the remaining vanilla bean half and mix them with the remaining sugar.

In a bowl, mix the vanilla sugar with the almond meal, then mix in the flour and the egg whites until smooth.

Heat the butter in a saucepan over a medium–high heat for 2–3 minutes until it just begins to brown. Combine the butter with the mixture.

Spoon or pipe the cake mixture into the buttered moulds.

Top each friand with 1 raspberry and 6 pistachio halves. Bake in the preheated oven for about 12–15 minutes.

Place three apricot halves on each plate. Then add a friand or two, scatter with a few toasted flaked almonds and dust with icing sugar.

Serves 4-8

ALMOND & HONEY NOUGAT

Nougat aux amandes et au miel

Nougat is the speciality of the town of Montélimar at the northern border of Provence and this festive sweet is one of the thirteen traditional Provençal Christmas desserts.

450 g (1 lb) raw almonds (skins on)

100 g (3½ oz) pistachio nuts, skinned and roughly chopped

100 g (3½ oz) hazelnuts, skins removed if possible

125 ml (4 fl oz/½ cup) water

375 g (13 oz) caster (superfine) sugar

185 g (6½ oz) liquid glucose

250 g (9 oz) honey

2 large egg whites

a pinch of cream of tartar

6 sheets edible rice paper

Preheat the oven to 150°C (300°F). Line a roasting tin with baking paper. Line a 35 x 25 x 2.5 cm (14 x 10 x 1 in) Swiss roll (jelly roll) tin with baking paper.

Put all the nuts in the prepared roasting tin and dry-roast in the oven for about 20 minutes, stirring occasionally. Remove the nuts from the oven and keep warm until ready to use.

Reduce the oven temperature to 100°C (200°F).

To make a syrup, combine the water, sugar and glucose in a saucepan and bring to the boil over a medium heat. Place a sugar thermometer in the pan and cook until the syrup reaches 150°C (300°F).

At the same time, heat the honey in a second saucepan. Bring to the boil over a medium heat and cook to 135°C (275°F).

Just before the honey and syrup reach temperature, combine the egg whites and cream of tartar in an electric mixer and whisk to soft peaks. With the motor running, slowly drizzle in the honey. Then drizzle in the hot syrup. Continue whisking at a low speed for about 5 minutes. Fold the roasted nuts into the nougat.

Arrange 3 sheets of rice paper in the prepared tin. Tip in the nougat mixture and smooth the surface with a wet metal spoon. Lay the remaining three sheets of rice paper on top and leave the nougat to cool before covering with plastic wrap. Refrigerate when cold.

Remove the plastic wrap and turn the nougat out onto a chopping board. Use a large knife to cut into 2.5 cm (1 in) squares. The nougat becomes softer at room temperature.

Makes about 100 pieces

BRITTANY CRÊPES WITH STRAWBERRIES

Crêpes de Bretagne aux framboises

FROM THE BRITTANY REGION

Brittany is regarded as the birthplace of these lovely delicate pancakes, so much so that every family in Brittany knows how to cook them. You can fill the crêpes with almost anything, but make sure you rest the batter prior to cooking, as this allows the gluten to relax and makes for a tender, delicate pancake.

---

150 g (5½ oz/1 cup) plain (all-purpose) flour, sifted

1 large egg

about 375 ml (12½ fl oz/ 1½ cups) milk

10 g (¼ oz) unsalted butter

about 60 g (2 oz) apricot jam or other jam

80 ml (2½ fl oz/⅓ cup) rich cream

250 g (9 oz) strawberries, sliced

icing (confectioners') sugar for dusting

Place the flour in a bowl and make a well in the centre. Drop the egg into the well and add a little milk. Using a whisk, mix the egg and milk together, then gradually incorporate the flour, slowly adding more milk until you obtain a smooth, thin mixture.

Strain the mixture through a fine strainer and leave it to rest for at least 10 minutes before cooking the crêpes.

Heat the butter in a crêpe pan. Pour this hot, melted butter into the pancake mixture.

Pour enough mixture into the hot pan to thinly cover the base. When the upper half of the crêpe starts to become dry, turn the pancake over and cook the second side. Make all the crêpes the same way.

To assemble, spread each crêpe with a little jam and cream and top with 4 or 5 slices of strawberry. Fold the crêpes and, just before serving, dust them with icing sugar.

Makes 8 small crêpes

Desserts &
Tarts

CHAMPAGNE JELLY WITH RED FRUITS

Gelée de Champagne aux fruits rouges

FROM THE CHAMPAGNE REGION | BY PIERRICK BOYER

Made with Champagne, this jelly is a very special adult indulgence. It's nice at the end of a dinner party as it's light, fruity and … because it's Champagne!

4 gelatine leaves or 1 x 7 g (¼ oz) sachet powdered gelatine

500 ml (17 fl oz/2 cups) French Champagne

juice of ½ lemon

55 g (2 oz/¼ cup) caster (superfine) sugar

250 g (9 oz) strawberries, hulled

100 g (3½ oz/⅔ cup) blueberries

200 g (7 oz) raspberries (or blackberries)

icing (confectioners') sugar for dusting

Drop the gelatine leaves in a large bowl of cold water to soften.

Pour 190 ml (6½ fl oz/¾ cup) of Champagne into a saucepan and mix in the lemon juice and sugar. Bring almost to simmering point, then remove from the heat.

Drain the softened gelatine leaves, squeezing them by hand to remove excess water, then add them (or add the powdered gelatine) to the warm Champagne and mix until dissolved. Stir in the remaining Champagne.

Carefully pour the preparation into attractive glasses and refrigerate for at least 2 hours or place in the freezer for about 15 minutes.

Wash the strawberries, cutting large ones into halves or quarters.

Garnish the top of the set jelly with strawberries, blueberries and raspberries. Dust with icing sugar and serve.

Serves 6

RED FRUIT GRATIN WITH PEAR WILLIAMS LIQUEUR

gratin de fruits rouge à l'eau de vie de poire williams

FROM THE ALSACE REGION

Alsace makes some of the most delicious fruit liqueurs in the world. I particularly like Pear Williams liqueur in this lovely dessert.

about 500 g (1 lb 2 oz) red fruits (strawberries, blueberries, raspberries, red currants, blackberries, cherries)

2 egg yolks

30 g (1 oz) caster (superfine) sugar

2 tablespoons Pear Williams liqueur or spirit

125 ml (4 fl oz/½ cup) whipped cream

a little icing (confectioners') sugar for dusting

Wash the fruits and cut large strawberries in half. Spoon the fruits into four individual gratin dishes.

Place the egg yolks in a bowl and mix in the sugar. Place the bowl over a bath of hot water and beat with a whisk until it becomes foamy. Then gradually add the Pear Williams liqueur.

Remove the bowl from the heat and gently fold in the whipped cream.

Spread the creamy mixture over the fruits and dust with icing sugar. Place under a hot grill (broiler) (broiler) and leave until the top is golden. Serve immediately.

Serves 4

CHERRY & BEAUJOLAIS SYRUP WITH ALMONDS

Soupe aux cerises au beaujolais et aux amandes

FROM THE RHÔNE-ALPS REGION

Beaujolais is a wonderfully fruity red wine, and it marries so well with cooked cherries. This recipe is spiced with vanilla, pepper, cinnamon and ginger, and finished with flaked almonds, for a sensational flavour combination.

---

about 600 ml (20½ fl oz) beaujolais wine (I love brouilly wine)

80 g (2¾ oz/⅓ cup) caster (superfine) sugar

½ vanilla bean

3 cm (1¼ in) cinnamon stick

4 cracked peppercorns

2 small slices of ginger

peel of ½ orange

peel of ½ lemon

800 g (1 lb 12 oz) pitted cherries

60 g (2 oz/⅔ cup) toasted flaked almonds

a little icing (confectioners') sugar for dusting

Place the red wine in a saucepan with the caster sugar, vanilla bean, cinnamon stick, peppercorns, ginger and orange and lemon peel. Bring to a simmer and cook for 5 minutes, then strain the liquid into a bowl.

Return this wine syrup to the saucepan. Add the cherries, bring to a simmer and cook for 3 minutes. Transfer to a clean bowl and allow to cool, then refrigerate for at least 3 hours.

Spoon the cherries and beaujolais syrup into bowls or glasses. Sprinkle some toasted flaked almonds on top and dust with icing sugar. Serve.

Serves 4

GREEN CHARTREUSE ICED PARFAIT

Soufflé glacé à la Chartreuse verte

FROM THE ALPS REGION | BY PHILIPPE MOUCHEL

Tasting of exotic herbs and plants, green chartreuse is a unique liqueur. This adult-only dessert is popular, relatively easy to prepare and looks good served in whisky-style glasses.

250 ml (8½ fl oz/1 cup) milk

1 vanilla bean, split lengthways

9 egg yolks

300 g (10½ oz) caster (superfine) sugar

150 ml (5 fl oz) green chartreuse liqueur

435 ml (15 fl oz/1¾ cups) whipped cream

a selection of red fruits or other fresh fruits

icing (confectioners') sugar for dusting

In a medium saucepan, heat the milk with the vanilla bean. Remove the vanilla bean.

Beat the egg yolks with the caster sugar in a bowl for at least 1 minute until well combined. Whisk in the hot milk and transfer back to the saucepan. Cook over a medium heat, stirring with a wooden spoon until the custard thickens just slightly and coats the spoon. The custard must not boil; otherwise it will curdle.

Transfer the custard to the bowl of an electric mixer and beat with the whisk attachment for about 10 minutes until it doubles in volume and has cooled.

Mix in 100 ml (3½ fl oz) of green chartreuse and fold in the whipped cream.

Pour a little of the remaining chartreuse into each glass and top with the parfait preparation. Place in the freezer for at least 6 hours.

Garnish the top of each parfait with a selection of red fruits and dust with icing sugar.

Serves 10

APPLE FRITTERS

Beignets aux pommes

FROM THE RHÔNE-ALPS REGION

The valley of the southern part of the Alps provides some of the best apples in France, and apple fritters are a really popular regional winter dessert.

250 g (9 oz/1⅔ cups) plain
(all-purpose) flour

1 x 7–10 g (¼ oz) sachet dry yeast

a pinch of salt

2 eggs, separated

about 400 ml (13½ fl oz) milk

1 tablespoon Calvados liqueur or other liqueur

a pinch of cream of tartar

4 apples (golden delicious, granny smith or royal gala)

2 litres (68 fl oz/8 cups) vegetable oil

caster (superfine) sugar for dusting

Place the plain flour, yeast and salt in a bowl. Make a hollow in the centre and pour the egg yolks into the hollow. Add a little milk, then use a whisk to slowly combine the wet ingredients. Gradually incorporate the flour, adding the remaining milk, until the mixture is smooth. Mix in the Calvados.

Beat the two egg whites and a pinch of cream of tartar into stiff peaks. Mix the beaten whites into the batter.

Peel and core the apples, then cut them into 1 cm (½ in) slices.

Heat the oil in a large saucepan over a medium heat until 180°C (350°F). If you don't have a thermometer, you'll know the oil is ready when a cube of bread turns brown in 20 seconds.

Dip the apple slices in the batter, then carefully place them in the hot oil. Cook the fritters for 2–3 minutes on each side or until golden brown. Transfer to a plate lined with paper towel to drain.

Dust the fritters with caster sugar before serving. They're best eaten straight away, but take care as they're very hot.

Serves 4–6

4 pommes
2,50€
le litre

6 B

APRICOT COMPOTE WITH ALMONDS & ARMAGNAC WITH EWE'S MILK YOGHURT

Compote d'abricots à l'Armagnac et aux amandes avec un yaourt de brebis

FROM THE NORTH PYRÉNÉES REGION

Using seasonal fruits, this simple French dessert is easy to prepare, and the ewe's milk yoghurt is a little more exotic than regular yoghurt. You can replace the Armagnac with another liqueur if you wish, or omit it altogether.

juice of 1 orange

juice of 1 lemon

115 g (4 oz/½ cup) caster (superfine) sugar, plus extra 2 tablespoons

⅓ vanilla bean, split lengthways

12 ripe apricots, halved and stoned

2 tablespoons Armagnac

500 g (1 lb 2 oz) sheep's milk yoghurt

100 ml (3½ fl oz) pouring cream

20 blanched almonds, toasted

Combine the orange and lemon juice in a saucepan with the sugar and vanilla bean. Bring to a simmer. Add the apricots and return to a simmer. Cover the pan and cook the apricots over a low heat until soft. Transfer the apricots and syrup to a bowl, stir in the Armagnac and leave to cool. Refrigerate until 10 minutes before serving.

Whip the yoghurt with the cream and extra sugar until smooth.

When ready to serve, add the almonds to the apricots. Spoon a little yoghurt onto four serving plates. Top with the apricots and almonds and spoon on the syrup.

Serves 4

PEACHES POACHED IN SWEET WINE

Pêches poêlées au vin doux

FROM THE LANGUEDOC/PROVENCE REGIONS | BY MICHAEL GATÉ

These peaches poached in sweet wine make a superb finish to a summer dinner party. Make sure the peaches are very sweet and just ripe when you buy them.

4 just-ripe peaches, washed

30 g (1 oz) unsalted butter

55 g (2 oz/¼ cup) sugar

100 ml (3½ fl oz) Muscat de Rivesaltes or another sweet white wine

200 g (7 oz) raspberries

2 tablespoons chopped, pistachios

icing (confectioners') sugar for dusting

whipped cream or ice cream, to serve

Three-quarters fill a medium saucepan with water and bring to the boil. Gently drop in the peaches and simmer for 2 minutes. Drain the peaches and put them in a bowl of cold water to cool. When cold, carefully peel the peaches. Cut them in half and remove the stones.

Melt the butter in a frying pan large enough to hold all the peaches. Add the sugar and stir briefly with a wooden spoon. When the sugar starts to brown, add the peach halves. Cook for 1–2 minutes then turn the peaches and shake the pan well. Add the muscat and bring to a simmer. Cover the pan with foil and cook for a few minutes until the peaches are cooked through.

To serve, place two peach halves on each plate. Garnish with raspberries and spoon on a little wine sauce. Sprinkle with pistachios and dust with icing sugar. If you wish, serve with whipped cream or ice cream.

Serves 4

CHERRY FRUIT SALAD WITH LANGUEDOC BRANDY

Salade de cerises au marc de Languedoc

FROM THE LANGUEDOC REGION

The sunny region of Languedoc produces very sweet fruit, including grapes for wine and brandy, and delicious plump cherries. This easy fruit salad makes a perfect finish to a special dinner and looks stunning. Eau de vie de marc du Languedoc is a regional grape brandy.

100 g (3½ oz) raspberries

100 g (3½ oz) strawberries, hulled

juice of 1 lemon

juice of 2 oranges

115 g (4 oz/½ cup) caster (superfine) sugar

1 tablespoon eau de vie de marc du Languedoc (grape brandy)

30 cherries

3 ripe peaches

3 tablespoons toasted flaked almonds

icing (confectioners') sugar for dusting

Place the raspberries and strawberries in a blender with the lemon juice, orange juice and sugar and blend to a purée. Strain into a bowl and discard the raspberry seeds. Mix in the eau de vie de marc.

Pit the cherries and add them to the berry purée.

Wash the peaches, cut each into eight segments and add to the fruit salad.

Spoon the fruit salad into deep plates. Decorate with the toasted almonds and dust with the icing sugar.

Serves 8–10

POACHED PEACHES WITH STRAWBERRIES & SPARKLING VOUVRAY SAUCE

Pêches pochées sauce aux fraises et au Vouvray pétillant

FROM THE TOURS/LOIRE VALLEY REGION

The region around the Loire is often referred to as the 'garden of France' because fruits and vegetables grow very well in the mild climate. This simple recipe is traditionally made with the delicious local sparkling wine, vouvray.

6 lovely ripe peaches

500 ml (17 fl oz/2 cups) water

400 g (14 oz) sugar

½ vanilla bean, split lengthways

3 tablespoons whipped cream

500 g (1 lb 2 oz) strawberries, hulled (wild strawberries are excellent)

125 ml (4 fl oz/½ cup) sparkling vouvray wine

3 tablespoons pistachio nuts, finely chopped

Gently drop the peaches into a saucepan of boiling water and cook for 1 minute. Drain the peaches and peel them carefully.

In a medium saucepan, combine the water with 350 g (12½ oz) of the sugar and the vanilla bean, and bring to the boil. Add the peeled peaches and simmer for about 10 minutes. Allow the peaches to cool in the syrup.

In a bowl, whisk the remaining sugar and the whipped cream.

Blend the strawberries into a coarse purée. Fold the strawberries and the sparkling wine into the cream and refrigerate until needed.

Place the drained peaches in a serving bowl. Spoon the strawberry sauce over the fruit, sprinkle with pistachio nuts and serve.

Serves 6

PEACHES & APRICOTS POACHED IN JURANÇON WINE

Verrine de pêches et abricots au vin de Jurançon

FROM THE BÉARN/PYRÉNÉES REGION

In France in the last few years, chefs have been serving this delightful summer dessert in glasses. The French word for glass is 'verre' which is why this dessert is called a 'verrine'. It's a refreshing way to finish a rich meal.

4 apricots

4 peaches

250 ml (8½ fl oz/1 cup) fresh orange juice

115 g (4 oz/½ cup) sugar

150 ml (5 fl oz) sweet Jurançon wine or another sweet wine

200 ml (7 fl oz) (whipping) cream

3 tablespoons sweetened chestnut cream (crème de marrons)

2 tablespoons toasted flaked almonds

icing (confectioners') sugar for dusting

Wash and halve the apricots and peaches and remove the stones. Quarter the peaches.

Heat the orange juice, sugar and sweet Jurançon wine in a saucepan and add the apricots and peaches. Stir gently, bring to a simmer and poach the fruits for about 15 minutes or until soft.

Transfer to a bowl and allow to cool, then cover with plastic wrap and refrigerate.

Whip the cream until firm. Gently combine the whipped cream with the chestnut cream, then transfer to a piping bag fitted with a serrated nozzle.

Carefully spoon the cold fruit into four glasses and pipe some chestnut cream on top of the fruit. Refrigerate if not serving immediately. Just before serving, sprinkle the top with toasted flaked almonds and dust with icing sugar.

Serves 4

POACHED PEACH & CHERRY COUPE IN A LEMON SYRUP

Coupe de pêches et de cerises au citron

FROM THE LANGUEDOC REGION

You can find this type of luscious, fruity dessert in the Languedoc region around the stunning city of Albi, the birthplace of French painter Toulouse-Lautrec.

juice of 4 lemons

220 g (8 oz/1 cup) sugar

½ vanilla bean, split lengthways

6 peaches, washed and stoned

500 g (1 lb 2 oz) cherries, pitted

200 ml (7 fl oz) whipping cream

2 tablespoons full-cream milk

2 tablespoons sugar

sweet biscuits (such as waffles, cats' tongues, sponge fingers)

Combine the lemon juice, sugar and vanilla bean in a medium saucepan. Bring to a boil and cook for 30 seconds.

Cut each peach into 6–8 slices, but do not peel. Place in the simmering syrup and poach for 5–8 minutes. Use a slotted spoon to transfer the peach segments to a large bowl.

Return the syrup to a simmer and add the cherries. Stir gently then turn off the heat. The syrup must not boil. Pour the cherries and syrup over the peaches. Shake the bowl well then leave to cool. Once cold, refrigerate until 10 minutes before serving.

Whip the cream and milk together until light and firm, but not too stiff. Mix in the sugar.

Spoon the sweet cream into a piping bag fitted with a small serrated nozzle. Pipe a little cream into six serving glasses and top with a few peach segments and cherries. Top with a little more piped cream and finish with fruit. Serve straight away with your choice of sweet biscuits.

Serves 6

PEACH MELBA
Pêche Melba

FROM THE PROVENCE REGION

Pêche Melba, one of the best-known French desserts, was created in 1892 by the super-talented Provençal chef Auguste Escoffier in honour of Dame Nellie Melba, the Australian opera diva.

1.5 litres (51 fl oz/6 cups) water

440 g (15½ oz/2 cups) sugar

½ vanilla bean, split lengthways

thinly peeled zest of about ⅔ of a lemon

6 just-ripe peaches, washed

1 litre (34 fl oz/4 cups) good-quality vanilla ice cream

45 g (1½ oz) flaked almonds, toasted

a little icing (confectioners') sugar for dusting

Raspberry sauce

300 g (10½ oz) raspberries, fresh or frozen

juice of 1 lemon

juice of 1 orange

3 tablespoons caster (superfine) sugar

Combine the water, sugar, vanilla and lemon zest in a saucepan large enough to hold the peaches. Bring to a simmer and cook for 5 minutes.

Gently drop the peaches into the syrup. Bring to a slow simmer and poach the peaches for 10 minutes, until just tender. Transfer the peaches and syrup to a bowl and leave to cool. Once cold, refrigerate until 10 minutes before serving.

To make the raspberry sauce, blend all the ingredients to a purée. Strain through a fine sieve and refrigerate until ready to use.

When ready to serve, lift the peaches out of the syrup and peel them carefully. Place six scoops of ice cream in a deep serving dish. Gently place the peeled peaches on top and spoon the raspberry sauce over. Sprinkle with toasted flaked almonds, dust with icing sugar and serve immediately. Alternatively, serve the Pêche Melba in individual bowls.

Serves 6

ROAST FIGS WITH CARAMELISED NUTS

Figues rôties aux noix caramélisées

FROM THE RHÔNE VALLEY REGION

The Rhône Valley, well known for its fruity red wines, enjoys plenty of sunshine and the local figs are sweet and juicy. This luscious dessert is a cinch to make, but take care not to burn yourself with the caramelised nuts.

6 large ripe figs

30 g (1 oz) unsalted butter

½ star anise

2 tablespoons sugar

12 walnut halves

12 roasted hazelnuts

12 almonds, halved

20 grapes

60 ml (2 fl oz/¼ cup) pouring cream

Cut the figs into quarters.

Heat the butter in a large frying pan. Add the star anise and the figs and cook for 3–4 minutes on a medium heat, turning the figs gently.

Transfer the figs to four plates, arranging them attractively. Leave the star anise in the pan.

Add the sugar to the pan and stir, lightly caramelising the sugar. Add the walnuts, hazelnuts, almonds and grapes and stir for 2 minutes. Add the cream and mix well to obtain a sauce texture.

Spoon the nuts and grapes around and over the figs.

It's lovely served with vanilla ice cream.

Serves 4

RHUBARB RASPBERRY GRATIN

Gratin à la rhubarbe et aux framboises

FROM THE PICARDY REGION

Many French people living in rural areas in the north grow fruit trees, berries and rhubarb. This easy dessert is sure to please everyone.

1 kg (2 lb 3 oz) rhubarb

50 g (1¾ oz) unsalted butter, melted

50 g (1¾ oz) sugar

250 g (9 oz/2 cups) raspberries

2 tablepoons orange juice

2 tablepoons finely grated lemon zest

2 egg yolks

250 ml (8½ fl oz/1 cup) whipped cream

icing (confectioners') sugar for dusting

Preheat the oven to 180°C (350°F). Butter six individual gratin dishes.

Trim the rhubarb and peel away the hard skin. Cut the rhubarb into about 5 cm (2 in) pieces. In a bowl, toss the rhubarb with the melted butter and then with the sugar.

Place the rhubarb neatly in an ovenproof dish and bake in the preheated oven for about 10 minutes until the rhubarb is soft. Transfer the rhubarb to the six gratin dishes and fill the gaps with a few raspberries.

Combine the orange juice, lemon zest and egg yolks in a bowl. Place the bowl over a saucepan of almost simmering water and whisk the yolks continuously until the preparation is creamy and light. It takes a few minutes.

Remove the bowl from the heat and gently fold in the whipped cream.

Spread the egg and cream mixture over the top of the fruit and dust with icing sugar.

Place under a hot grill (broiler) until the top becomes golden. Serve immediately.

Serves 6

RASPBERRY TRIFLES

Verrine aux framboises

FROM THE LOIRE VALLEY REGION

The Loire Valley is known as the garden of France and red fruits are a speciality. The climate is so pleasant that the kings of France and their entourage chose to spend their summer holidays there. They built many stunning châteaux that are now the pride of the region.

250 ml (8½ fl oz/1 cup) milk

½ vanilla bean, split lengthways

2 egg yolks

55 g (2 oz/¼ cup) caster (superfine) sugar

25 g (1 oz) plain (all-purpose) flour, sifted

2 oranges

2 tablespoons Cointreau

300 ml (10 fl oz) whipped cream

6 savoiardi (lady fingers), cut in half

600 g (1 lb 5 oz) raspberries

a little icing (confectioners') sugar

To make the custard, heat the milk and vanilla bean in a saucepan.

In a bowl, whisk the egg yolks with the caster sugar until well combined. Gently stir in the flour. Pour on the hot milk and whisk well until smooth. Return the mixture to the rinsed-out saucepan and cook over a medium heat, whisking constantly, until it begins to thicken. Tip into a bowl, whisk briefly and leave to cool. Remove the vanilla bean. When cold, cover with plastic wrap and refrigerate.

Use a serrated knife to slice all the skin and pith from the oranges. Cut the oranges into 5 mm (¼ in) slices and lay them in a bowl. Drizzle with Cointreau.

Fold the whipped cream into the cold custard, then spoon into a piping bag without a nozzle. Pipe a little custard cream into six serving glasses. Top with a piece of savoiardi, then with two slices of orange and a few raspberries. Pipe on a little more custard cream and finish with another savoiardi and a few more raspberries. Dust with icing sugar and serve.

Serves 6

BLUEBERRY & CHERRY COUPE

Verrine de myrtilles et cerises

FROM THE ALPS REGION

In winter, the stunning, snow-covered mountains of the French Alps have a magical atmosphere. In summer, it's great fun to harvest the wild forest berries and wander among the fruit trees that grow in the valleys.

1 gelatine leaf
(or 1 teaspoon
powdered gelatine)

36 cherries, pitted

juice of 1 lemon

400 g (14 oz) blueberries

110 g (4 oz) caster
(superfine) sugar

2 egg yolks

1 tablespoon plain
(all-purpose) flour

1 tablespoon finely
grated lemon zest

250 ml (8½ fl oz/1 cup)
hot milk

2 egg whites

1 small layer of sponge
cake, 1 cm (½ in) thick,
cut into 6 circles (using
one of the serving
glasses)

icing (confectioners')
sugar for dusting

Drop the gelatine leaf into a large bowl of cold water to soften it.

Meanwhile, place 30 of the pitted cherries in a saucepan with the lemon juice, blueberries and 40 g (1½ oz) of the caster sugar. Bring to a simmer, stir gently and cook for about 2 minutes. Transfer the fruit to a bowl to cool.

In a bowl combine the 2 egg yolks with 20 g (¾ oz) sugar. Stir in the flour and grated lemon zest. Whisk in the hot milk, then pour the preparation into a saucepan and cook on a low heat, stirring until it thickens. Transfer to a bowl and whisk in the drained gelatine leaf (or the powdered gelatine). Allow to cool.

Beat the egg whites with 25 g (1 oz) caster sugar until firm and shiny. Beat in an extra 25 g (1 oz) caster sugar, then gently fold this into the cold custard. This preparation is called a crème chiboust. Transfer the mixture into a piping bag.

Spoon a little red fruit and juice into glasses and top with the circle of sponge cake. Pipe a 3 cm (1 in) layer of crème chiboust and add a bit more fruit and juice.

Garnish with a whole cherry and dust with icing sugar.

Serves 6

BLUEBERRY MOUSSE

Mousse aux myrtilles

FROM THE ALPS REGION

This type of fruit mousse served in a glass has become very fashionable. The wild blueberries that grow in the Alps are used in many desserts. Begin making this dessert at least 8 hours before you serve it.

juice of 1 lemon

150 g (5½ oz) caster (superfine) sugar

½ vanilla bean (split lengthways and seeds scraped)

400 g (14 oz) blueberries

10 g (¼ oz) gelatine powder

2 egg whites

a pinch of cream of tartar

100 ml (3½ fl oz) whipped cream

6 berry macaroons of your choice

Place the lemon juice, 100 g (3½ oz) of the caster sugar, the vanilla bean, scraped seeds and the blueberries in a small saucepan and bring to a simmer over a low heat. Cook for 5 minutes, then remove from the heat. Transfer half of the cooked blueberries to a bowl to cool and press the remaining berries through a fine strainer to obtain a purée.

Whisk the gelatine into the purée until it has all melted, then refrigerate the preparation to cool (but not set).

Beat the egg whites with the cream of tartar into stiff peaks. Mix in the remaining caster sugar.

Fold the whipped cream into the cold blueberry purée, then fold in the beaten egg whites. Pipe the preparation into six whisky-type glasses and refrigerate for at least 6 hours to set.

Just before serving, top each mousse with blueberry compote and serve with a macaroon.

Serves 6

SUMMER FRUIT MOUSSE

Mousse de fruits d'été

FROM THE LOIRE VALLEY REGION

This is a lovely, delicate dinner party dessert. You will need to have some cooking experience and know how to use a sugar thermometer. For a beautiful presentation, you will also need four 10 cm (4 in) rings.

---

juice of 1 lemon

juice of ½ orange

150 g (5½ oz) raspberries

⅓ vanilla bean, split lengthways

2 gelatine leaves

100 g (3½ oz) caster (superfine) sugar

2 tablespoons cold water

2 egg whites

a pinch of cream of tartar

120 ml (4 fl oz) whipped cream

100 g (3½ oz) each raspberries, blackberries and strawberries, to serve

icing (confectioners') sugar, for dusting

Combine the juices, raspberries and vanilla bean in a small saucepan and bring to the boil. Boil for 5 minutes then strain through a fine sieve into a bowl. Set aside.

Soak the gelatine in a bowl of cold water for 5–10 minutes. Squeeze to remove excess water then stir into the raspberry mixture to dissolve. Set aside to cool.

Combine the sugar and water in a saucepan and bring to a simmer. Place a sugar thermometer in the pan and cook until the syrup reaches nearly 120°C (245°F). Just before the syrup reaches temperature, combine the egg whites and cream of tartar in an electric mixer and whisk to stiff peaks. With the motor running, slowly drizzle in the hot syrup. Continue whisking at a low speed for about 8 minutes, or until cool. Use a large spoon to carefully fold in the cold raspberry mixture, then the whipped cream.

Arrange the PVC rings on dessert plates. Spoon the mousse mixture into the rings, smooth the surface and refrigerate for at least 2 hours to set.

To serve, carefully run a knife blade around the inside of the rings. Top each mousse with a mixture of the berries and dust with icing sugar. Carefully lift the rings away. It looks spectacular!

Serves 4

COFFEE PARFAIT WITH PRUNES IN ARMAGNAC

Parfait au café et aux pruneaux à l'Armagnac

FROM THE SOUTH WEST REGION

Armagnac is a wonderful spirit made from grapes and matches very well with the prunes. Pay attention not to over-cook the sugar syrup or you'll have to start again.

15 prunes, pitted and halved

50 ml (1¾ fl oz) Armagnac

200 g (7 oz) caster (superfine) sugar

125 ml (4 fl oz/½ cup) water

6 egg yolks

2 teaspoons coffee essence

310 ml (10½ fl oz/1¼ cups) whipped cream

Place the prunes and Armagnac in a bowl, stir well and leave to macerate for at least 1 hour.

Heat the sugar and water in a small saucepan. Bring to a simmer and cook until the sugar syrup takes on a slight yellow tinge.

Place the egg yolks in the bowl of an electric beater and, while beating over a medium heat, pour the sugar syrup in bit by bit over a period of about 20–30 seconds. Continue beating for about 10 minutes until it's creamy and cold.

Gently mix in the macerated prunes and coffee essence, then fold in the whipped cream. Transfer to a mould, cover with plastic wrap and freeze for at least 8 hours.

To unmould, dip the mould briefly in warm water and then turn out the parfait onto a platter.

It is lovely garnished with crystallised violets and, if you wish, a few extra prunes soaked in Armagnac.

Serves 8

COGNAC & GLACÉ FRUIT ICE CREAM

Glace plombières au cognac

FROM THE SOUTH WEST REGION AROUND COGNAC

One of my favourite tools in the kitchen is my ice cream maker, which allows me to prepare this dessert that is to die for. Once the ice cream is made, the dessert is frozen in a chilled mould (I like to use an attractive cake or jelly mould) and it looks spectacular when it is turned out. It can be made up to three days ahead of time.

---

110 g (4 oz) mixed glacé fruit, diced

2 tablespoons cognac

500 ml (17 fl oz/2 cups) milk

¼ vanilla bean, split lengthways

55 g (2 oz/½ cup) almond meal

4 egg yolks

150 g (5½ oz) caster (superfine) sugar

250 ml (8½ fl oz/1 cup) whipped cream

1 kg (2 lb 3 oz) mixed summer berries

Place the glacé fruits in a bowl with the cognac and macerate for at least 20 minutes, or overnight if you wish.

Gently heat the milk, vanilla bean and almond meal in a large saucepan.

Put the egg yolks and sugar in the bowl of an electric mixer and beat for about 5 minutes or until pale and creamy. Pour on the warm milk, whisking well. Return the mixture to the rinsed-out saucepan. Cook over a medium heat, stirring in a figure-eight motion with a wooden spoon. Once the mixture thickens to coat the back of the spoon, remove the pan from the heat. Strain through a fine sieve and discard the almond meal and the vanilla bean. Whisk the custard briefly and leave to cool.

Tip the custard into an ice cream machine and churn according to the manufacturer's instructions. When the ice cream is quite firm, add the macerated fruits and churn briefly. Add the whipped cream and churn again until well incorporated. Transfer the ice cream to a pre-chilled 2-litre (68 fl oz/8-cup) mould and place in the freezer for at least 2 hours before serving.

When ready to serve, briefly dip the mould in warm water to loosen the ice cream, then invert it onto a deep serving platter. Cut into slices and serve with seasonal berries of your choice.

Serves 6–8

APRICOT ICE CREAM WITH CARAMELISED ALMONDS

Glace à l'abricot aux amandes caramélisées

FROM THE NORTHERN PROVENCE REGION

The northern Provence countryside has hills dotted with vineyards, olive and almond trees, and trees producing a variety of stone fruits. It is a place of great beauty.

---

1 kg (2 lb 3 oz) apricots

230 g (8 oz/1 cup) caster (superfine) sugar

125 ml (4 fl oz/½ cup) orange juice

½ vanilla bean, split lengthways

juice of 1 lemon

250 ml (8½ fl oz/1 cup) whipped cream

2 tablespoons water

3 drops red wine vinegar

155 g (5½ oz/1 cup) almonds

Wash the apricots and remove the stones. Place the fruit in a saucepan with half the caster sugar, the orange juice and vanilla bean. Cover with a lid and simmer until the apricots are soft. Discard the vanilla bean and blend the apricots and liquid to a fine purée. Strain the purée into a bowl and allow to cool.

Add the lemon juice to the purée and fold in half the whipped cream. Transfer the preparation to an ice cream maker and churn until done. Transfer to a mould, cover with plastic wrap and place in the freezer.

In a saucepan, heat the 2 tablespoons water, the remaining caster sugar and the vinegar. Bring to the boil and cook until lightly caramelised. Add the almonds and stir with a wooden spatula for 1–2 minutes until the almonds are well coated with dark caramel.

Place the caramelised almonds on a lightly oiled square of baking paper and leave to cool. Cut the cooled almonds into small pieces.

To unmould, dip the mould briefly in warm water and turn out the ice cream onto a cold platter.

Decorate the ice cream with the almond pieces and the remaining whipped cream and serve.

Serves 6–8

NOUGAT ICE CREAM WITH RASPBERRY SAUCE

Nougat glacé avec un coulis de framboises

FROM THE NORTH PROVENCE REGION

This is one of my favourite desserts, but it does require some cooking experience as you need to make a caramel and use a sugar thermometer.

70 g (2½ oz) caster (superfine) sugar

1 tablespoon water

125 g (4½ oz) hazelnuts, toasted and skinned

55 g (2 oz) honey

30 g (1 oz) liquid glucose

3 egg whites

a pinch of cream of tartar

150 g (5½ oz) glacé apricots, cut into 1 cm (½ in) squares

30 g (1 oz) glacé cherries, cut into 5 mm (¼ in) squares

300 ml (10 fl oz) whipped cream

Raspberry sauce (page 361), to serve

Combine 40 g (1½ oz) of the sugar with the water in a small saucepan and cook over a medium heat until it darkens to a caramel. Add the hazelnuts and stir for 2 minutes to coat them with the caramel. Very carefully tip the caramelised nuts onto a piece of lightly oiled baking paper and spread them out. When cold, roughly chop three-quarters of the caramelised nuts. Reserve the remaining whole nuts to garnish.

Combine the honey, liquid glucose and remaining sugar in a small saucepan over a medium heat. Place a sugar (candy) thermometer in the pan and cook until the syrup reaches 100°C (200°F).

Once the syrup reaches temperature, combine the egg whites and cream of tartar in an electric mixer and whisk to stiff peaks.

Continue cooking the syrup until it reaches 120°C (245°F) then slowly drizzle it onto the egg whites, whisking continuously. Continue whisking at a low speed for about 10 minutes. Transfer the ice cream mixture to the refrigerator for 10 minutes to cool.

Carefully fold the chopped hazelnuts and glacé fruits into the cooled ice cream mixture. Fold in the whipped cream then tip into a 22 cm (8¾ in) cake tin lined with plastic wrap. Cover the surface with plastic wrap and freeze for at least 6 hours.

When ready to serve, dip the mould briefly in warm water to loosen the ice cream, then invert it onto a serving dish. Peel away the plastic wrap and cut into slices. Top with caramelised nuts and serve with the raspberry sauce.

Serves 8–10

Nougat aux
...houri et ama...
...90/100 g...

Nougat aux
Macarons
Amaretti
5,90/100 g

Calissons
de
provence

Nougat au

Nougat à la
Crème de Citron
(lemon curd)
5,90/100 g

NOUGAT ICE CREAM WITH PISTACHIO NUTS AND GLACÉ FRUITS

Nougat glacé à la pistache

FROM THE RHÔNE-ALPS REGION

You won't need an ice-cream machine for this dessert — just some fragrant honey and good-quality glacé fruits. It's a great recipe for entertaining as all the work is done long before the guests arrive.

---

60 g (2 oz) almonds, each cut into about 3 pieces

30 g (1 oz) pistachio nuts

55 g (2 oz/¼ cup) caster (superfine) sugar

2 eggs, separated

50 g (1¾ oz) honey (orange blossom goes well with this)

100 ml (3½ fl oz) whipped cream

3 tablespoons diced mixed glacé fruits

300 g (10½ oz) raspberries

juice of ½ lemon

juice of 1 orange

Lightly grease six 250 ml (8½ fl oz/1 cup) capacity moulds or a 1.5-litre (51 fl oz/6 cup) capacity rectangular mould, then line with plastic wrap, leaving the sides overhanging.

Place the almonds and pistachio nuts in a frying pan over a medium heat and toast them lightly without browning them. Add 1 tablespoon of caster sugar and stir until it caramelises and coats the nuts.

Transfer the nuts to a tray lined with baking paper and set aside to cool. Once cool, break up the nuts until separated.

Beat the egg whites until just before stiff peaks form.

At the same time, bring the honey to the boil in a saucepan and boil for 10 seconds. Pour the honey slowly onto the beaten egg whites as you beat them, and continue beating until the whites are almost cold.

Beat the egg yolks with 1 tablespoon of caster sugar, then fold this into the cold beaten egg whites. Fold in the whipped cream, glacé fruits and three-quarters of the caramelised nuts.

Spoon or pipe the preparation into the prepared moulds. Cover the top with plastic wrap and place in the freezer for at least 10 hours.

Meanwhile, to make the raspberry coulis, blend the raspberries, lemon juice, orange juice and 2 tablespoons of caster sugar to a purée. Strain the preparation and refrigerate until required.

To serve, unmould the desserts onto cold plates and remove the plastic wrap. Scatter with the remaining nuts and serve with the raspberry coulis.

Serves 6

CHOCOLATE & HAZELNUT ICE CREAM CAKE

Glacé au chocolat et aux noisettes

FROM THE ALPS/ITALIAN BORDER REGION

The Italian influence is strong in this Alps region. This ice cream cake is ideal for a special dinner party as it can be prepared in advance. You need an ice cream maker to prepare this dessert.

---

5 egg yolks

200 g (7 oz) caster (superfine) sugar

500 ml (17 fl oz/2 cups) hot milk

2 teaspoons bitter cocoa powder

100 g (3½ oz) dark chocolate, cut into small pieces

375 ml (12½ fl oz/1½ cups) whipped cream

2 tablespoons water

3 drops red wine vinegar

100 g (3½ oz) roasted hazelnuts

16 Italian biscuits (e.g. sfogiatine or savoiardi)

Beat the egg yolks in a bowl with 150 g (5½ oz) of the caster sugar for about 5 minutes until light and pale.

Stir in the hot milk, then transfer to a saucepan and cook on a medium heat without boiling, stirring with a wooden spoon until the custard lightly coats the spoon. Transfer the preparation to a bowl and stir in the cocoa powder and chocolate pieces. Allow to cool.

When cold, fold in 1 cup of the whipped cream, then churn the preparation in an ice cream maker.

While the ice cream is churning, place the remaining caster sugar, 2 tablespoons of water and the red wine vinegar in a small saucepan. Bring to the boil and cook until it caramelises. Stir in the hazelnuts until the nuts are well coated.

Transfer the hazelnuts to a tray lined with baking paper. After 2 minutes or so, crush about half of the hazelnuts (this can be done between two layers of baking paper using a rolling pin) and add the crushed nuts to the churning ice cream.

Transfer the firm ice cream to a mould, cover and place in the freezer for a few hours.

To unmould, dip the mould in warm water and turn the ice cream out onto a cold platter.

Pipe a little of the remaining whipped cream around the sides of the ice cream and attach the biscuits to the sides. Decorate the top with the remaining cream and the whole caramelised hazelnuts.

Serves 8

HAZELNUT MERINGUE WITH CHESTNUT CREAM & RASPBERRIES

Meringue aux noisettes et crème de marrons avec framboises

FROM THE ALPS REGION

A French cousin of the pavlova, this dessert uses sweetened chestnut cream, which has a lovely strong flavour and contrasts wonderfully with the meringue and fresh raspberries.

---

30 g (1 oz/¼ cup) ground hazelnuts

85 g (3 oz) caster (superfine) sugar

2 teaspoons cornflour (cornstarch)

2 egg whites

a pinch of cream of tartar

¼ teaspoon white vinegar

200 ml (7 fl oz) whipping cream

100 g (3½ oz) crème de marrons (sweetened chestnut cream, which is available from delicatessens)

500 g (1 lb 2 oz) raspberries

80 g (2¾ oz/¼ cup) apricot jam

2 teaspoons water

a little icing (confectioners') sugar for dusting

Preheat the oven to 180°C (350°F). Line a baking tray with baking paper and draw a 25 cm (10 in) circle on the paper.

Place the ground hazelnuts in a small frying pan over a medium heat and toast until lightly browned. Mix with half the sugar and the cornflour.

Place the egg whites and cream of tartar in the bowl of an electric mixer and whisk to medium-stiff peaks. With the motor turned to low, gradually whisk in the remaining sugar and the vinegar, to form stiff peaks.

Fold the hazelnut mixture into the meringue then spoon into a piping bag fitted with a 1 cm (½ in) round nozzle. Pipe a 25 cm (10 in) spiral disc onto the prepared baking tray, working from the outer edge in to the centre. Bake for about 25 minutes. When cooked, the meringue should be dry and firm. Remove from the oven and leave to cool.

Whip the cream, then gently fold in the crème de marrons. Spread onto the meringue and top with the raspberries. Heat the apricot jam with the water to make a runny glaze. Brush the raspberries with the glaze. Just before serving, dust with icing sugar.

Serves 6

CHOCOLATE CREAM WITH GLACÉ CHESTNUTS & RASPBERRIES

crème de chocolat et marrons glacés aux framboises

FROM THE RHÔNE-ALPS REGION

This Valrhona chocolate dessert with glacé chestnuts is out of this world. Served with raspberries, it's a perfect match! If you can't get Valrhona chocolate, make sure you use a good-quality chocolate with at least 70 per cent cocoa solids.

60 ml (2 fl oz/¼ cup) milk

60 ml (2 fl oz/¼ cup) cream

100 g (3½ oz) Valrhona cooking chocolate, broken into small pieces

about 60 g (2 oz) glacé chestnuts, in small pieces

2 tablespoons raspberry jam

about 30 raspberries

icing (confectioners') sugar for dusting

4 whole glacé chestnuts, extra

Bring the milk and cream to a simmer in a small saucepan. Place the chocolate in a heat-proof bowl, pour over the hot cream and whisk until it is very well combined.

Pour the chocolate cream onto 4 small porcelain plates with an edge or into small bowls. To each one, add 5 small pieces of glacé chestnuts. Refrigerate for at least 3 hours or until firm.

Place the raspberry jam in a small plastic piping bag and pipe a little jam into the cavity of each raspberry. Dust the raspberries with icing sugar.

Just before serving, decorate the chocolate cream with the raspberries and one whole glacé chestnut.

Serves 4

CORSICAN CHEESE CAKE

Fiadone Corse

FROM THE ISLAND OF CORSICA

This popular Corsican family cake is made with brocciu, a fresh ewe's milk cheese that resembles ricotta but is a bit stronger in flavour.

---

500 g (1 lb 2 oz) fresh brocciu cheese (or ricotta or ewe's milk ricotta)

200 g (7 oz) caster (superfine) sugar

zest of 1 lemon, finely grated

2 tablespoons lemon juice

1 tablespoon alcohol of your choice (grappa is nice)

5 x 60 g (2 oz) eggs, at room temperature

Place the fresh cheese in a muslin cloth over a colander or bowl and refrigerate for 1 hour to drain off the excess liquid.

Preheat the oven to 180°C (350°F). Butter a 20 cm (8 in) cake tin.

Take the drained cheese out of the refrigerator. Combine the cheese with 50 g (1¾ oz) of caster sugar and the lemon zest in a bowl. Stir until smooth, then mix in the lemon juice and alcohol.

In another bowl, whisk the eggs with the remaining sugar for about 5 minutes until foamy. Slowly whisk the cheese preparation into the eggs, beating until the texture is creamy.

Transfer the mixture to the prepared cake tin and bake in the preheated oven for about 45 minutes.

Allow it to cool before turning out.

It's lovely served with fresh berries and dusted with sugar.

Serves 8–10

PEPPERMINT CRÈME BRÛLÉE

Crème brûlée à la menthe

FROM THE NORTHERN REGION

The north of France produces sugar from beetroots, and this world-famous dessert is very popular. I have added a little peppermint to the custard, as this is also a popular local flavour. I like to use small porcelain moulds of 125 ml or less.

200 ml (7 fl oz) cream

200 ml (7 fl oz) milk

½ vanilla bean, split lengthways

1 tablespoon peppermint syrup (crème de menthe)

4 egg yolks

80 g (2¾ oz/⅓ cup) caster (superfine) sugar, plus extra 2 tablespoons

2 tablespoons brown sugar

Preheat the oven to 120°C (245°F). Place eight 125 ml (4 fl oz/½ cup) porcelain moulds in a baking tray.

Pour the cream and milk into a saucepan. Add the vanilla bean and peppermint syrup and bring to the boil. Turn off the heat. Remove the vanilla bean.

In a bowl, thoroughly whisk the egg yolks and caster sugar. Whisking continuously, gradually pour the hot milk mixture onto the egg and sugar mix, and combine well.

Pour this preparation carefully into the eight moulds and bake the custard in the preheated oven for about 30 minutes until just set. Remove from the oven and let it stand to cool. When cold, refrigerate the custard until a few minutes before serving.

Preheat the oven grill (broiler).

Combine 2 tablespoons of brown sugar with 2 tablespoons of caster sugar. Sprinkle a small layer of the sugar mixture over the custards, then place them under the grill (broiler) until just caramelised.

Stand for 5 minutes before serving.

Serves 4–8

BELGIAN CHOCOLATE MOUSSE WITH RASPBERRIES

Mousse au chocolat Belge et framboises

FROM THE NORTHERN FRANCE/BELGIUM REGION

Chocolate mousse is one of the most popular desserts in the world. It's easy to make and recently I've served it in elegant glasses topped with raspberries. Irresistible!

2 tablespoons pouring cream

200 g (7 oz) dark cooking chocolate, cut into pieces

4 egg yolks

6 egg whites

a pinch of cream of tartar

1 tablespoon caster (superfine) sugar

375 ml (12½ oz/1½ cups) whipped cream

500 g (1 lb 2 oz) raspberries

Place the cream and chocolate pieces in a bowl resting over a pan of simmering water (bain-marie) on a medium heat and whisk until the chocolate melts and is smooth. Remove the bowl from the bain-marie and stir in the egg yolks.

Place the egg whites and a pinch of cream of tartar in a separate bowl and beat until fairly firm. Add the sugar and continue beating the whites into stiff peaks.

Using a whisk, gently incorporate a quarter of the beaten egg whites into the chocolate preparation, then carefully fold in the rest of the whites.

Spoon the mixture into a piping bag and pipe it into the glasses. Cover with plastic wrap and place in the refrigerator to set for at least 4 hours.

When ready to serve, pipe a little whipped cream on top of each mousse and garnish with raspberries.

Serves 6

CHERRY CLAFOUTIS

Clafoutis aux cerises

FROM THE LIMOUSIN REGION | BY ELISABETH KERDELHUÉ

A clafoutis is a traditional French dessert in which fresh fruit — usually cherries — are baked in a batter. It is rather like a fruit flan without the pastry. In France many people have cherry trees in their backyard — we had several at our home — and the fruit is used in desserts like this one.

700 g (1 lb 9 oz) cherries, pitted

40 g (1½ oz) plain (all-purpose) flour, sifted

55 g (2 oz/¼ cup) caster (superfine) sugar

a pinch of salt

4 eggs

600 ml (20½ fl oz) full-cream milk

2 egg yolks

2 tablespoons cognac or kirsch

a little icing (confectioners') sugar, for dusting

Preheat the oven to 180°C (350°F). Lightly butter a porcelain flan (tart) dish 28 cm (11 in) in diameter and at least 3 cm (1¼ in) deep. Arrange the cherries over the base.

Combine the flour, sugar, salt and 2 of the eggs in a bowl and mix together well. Add a little milk and mix well. Mix in the 2 remaining whole eggs and the egg yolks. Lastly, mix in the remaining milk.

Carefully strain the mixture into the dish over the cherries. Drizzle the liqueur evenly over the top. Carefully place in the oven and bake for about 45 minutes.

Remove from the oven and dust with icing sugar before serving. Take care, as it is very hot.

Serves 8

BLACKCURRANT & ALMOND CLAFOUTIS

Clafoutis au cassis et aux amandes

FROM THE BURGUNDY REGION | BY PIERRICK BOYER

Blackcurrants, or as the French say cassis, are plentiful in Burgundy. Clafoutis is a type of pudding made with fruits. It's easy to make and a perfect family dessert.

225 g (8 oz) creamed cottage cheese or quark – in France it is called fromage frais (smooth, low-fat, unripened fresh cheese)

4 egg yolks

30 g (1 oz) cornflour (cornstarch)

250 g (9 oz) caster (superfine) sugar

200 g (7 oz) almond meal

250 g (9 oz/2 cups) blackcurrants, fresh or frozen

icing (confectioners') sugar for dusting

8 scoops vanilla ice cream (or a flavour of your choice)

Preheat the oven to 160°C (320°F).

In a large bowl mix the cottage cheese with the egg yolks and cornflour. Stir in the caster sugar and almond meal. Transfer the mixture to a piping bag and pipe into eight individual porcelain baking dishes.

Dot the top with blackcurrants and bake in the preheated oven for about 20 minutes.

Remove from the oven and allow to cool a little.

Dust with icing sugar and serve with vanilla ice cream.

Serves 8

Gateau au foie de volaille   foivre au poivre verte

La Charcuterie Artisanale

Jambon cru Serrano   Columbus Crespone

Jambon de Paris   Zoé's Meats Salami

Saucissons séchés à l'huile

wine available Les Patisseries

in take away   pommes

purchase   frites $5

Brioche,
pain au chocolat,
& hot crossed buns

Les Desserts $6

Nougat Glace   Cinnamon Ice Cream

Brioche Beignets   Lemon-Thyme Sorbet

Chocolat Chaud

APPLE TART FLAMED WITH CALVADOS

Tarte aux pommes flambée au Calvados

| FROM THE NORMANDY REGION | BY ANGIE GATÉ |

Normandy is famous for its cream, apples and a beautiful apple liqueur called Calvados

8 apples (red delicious, granny smith or another variety of your choice)

2 tablespoons water

250 g (9 oz) puff pastry

1 egg yolk

1 tablespoon water

2 tablespoons pouring cream

2 tablespoons caster (superfine) sugar

3 tablespoons Calvados

Preheat the oven to 200°C (400°F). Line a baking tray with baking paper.

Peel 4 of the apples, then cut them into eighths and remove the cores. Cook with the 2 tablespoons of water in a covered saucepan until tender. Mash the apple to a purée and leave it to cool.

Roll out the pastry on a floured surface until it is about 30 cm (12 in) round and about 3 mm (⅛ in) thick.

Carefully lift the pastry onto the prepared baking tray. Prick the pastry with a fork to prevent shrinkage. Use the tip of a knife blade to trace a smaller circle on the pastry, leaving a 2.5 cm (1 in) edge. Mix the egg yolk and water together and use to brush the edge.

Spread the apple purée over the pastry, leaving the edge free. Spread the cream over the purée.

Peel, quarter and core the remaining apples and cut each quarter into four wedges. Starting at the outer edge, arrange the apple wedges on top of the purée, forming a spiral towards the centre. Overlap the slices a little and make sure you leave no gaps.

Sprinkle on the sugar and bake for about 20 minutes. Reduce the oven temperature to 150°C (300°F) and bake for a further 30 minutes. The tart is cooked when the pastry is golden brown and crisp and the edges of the apples are lightly browned. The pastry base should be dry and lightly browned.

Carefully transfer the tart to a serving platter.

In a small saucepan, bring the Calvados to the boil. Remove the pan from the heat and away from the stove, then carefully flame the Calvados. Carefully pour the flaming liqueur over the tart and serve when the flames have subsided.

Serves 8

APPLE PIE WITH ARMAGNAC

Tarte aux pommes à l'Armagnac

FROM THE NORTH PYRÉNÉES REGION

The Armagnac in this pie makes a difference, but you could also use brandy or a liqueur such as Drambuie or kirsch. It's a delicious rustic dessert and is also perfect for afternoon tea.

4 dried figs, cut into 1 cm (½ in) cubes

2 tablespoons Armagnac

1 tablespoon finely grated lemon zest

20 g (¾ oz) unsalted butter

55 g (2 oz/¼ up) caster (superfine) sugar

4 apples, peeled, cored and cut into 1 cm (½ in) rings

1 egg yolk

1 teaspoon water

2 x 22 cm (9 in) squares rolled puff pastry

250 ml (8½ fl oz/1 cup) pouring cream

Place the fig pieces in a bowl with the Armagnac and lemon zest and macerate for at least 1 hour or overnight.

Melt the butter in a large non-stick frying pan over a medium heat. Add the sugar and when it has melted, add the apple slices. Cook until the apple slices have caramelised on one side, then turn and caramelise the other side. Add the figs and Armagnac to the pan and stir in. Remove the pan from the heat and away from the stove, then carefully flame the mixture for a few seconds. Transfer the fruit to a shallow dish and leave to cool.

Lightly grease a 22 cm (8¾ in) loose-based flan (tart) tin. Mix the egg yolk and water together to make eggwash.

Place the pastry squares on a floured work surface and cut out two circles to the size of the flan tin. Lay one pastry circle in the tin and brush the edges with the eggwash. Arrange the cold apple in the centre of the pastry, leaving an edge of about 2.5 cm (1 in).

Carefully place the second pastry circle on top and pinch the edges together to seal. Use the tip of a knife blade to make a hole in the centre of the pastry and brush the pastry with eggwash. Make a criss-cross pattern on the pastry using the tines of a fork. Place the tart in the refrigerator for 15 minutes.

Preheat the oven to 180°C (350°F).

Bake the tart for about 30 minutes, or until the pastry is cooked and golden brown. Allow to cool slightly before carefully removing from the tin. Cut the tart into wedges and serve with cream.

Serves 8

UPSIDE DOWN PEACH TART

Tarte aux pêches

FROM THE MIDI-PYRÉNÉES REGION

This sweet tart is really superb in summer when the peaches are ripe and delicious. With so few ingredients in this dessert, it's important you use the best quality peaches and pastry you can find. Look for puff pastry made with butter, not margarine. At home I use a 27 cm cast-iron frying pan to cook it, but if you don't have one exactly the same size don't worry — just adjust the size of the pastry and the number of peaches to fit.

about 350 g (12½ oz) quality puff pastry

50 g (1¾ oz) unsalted butter

120 g (4½ oz) caster (superfine) sugar

1 star anise

4 perfectly ripe peaches, each cut into 8 segments

Roll the puff pastry out to a thickness of about 3 mm (⅛ in). Cut a 27 cm (10¾ in) circle of pastry and place this on a tray to cool in the fridge.

Preheat the oven to 200°C (400°F).

Place the butter in the ovenproof frying pan with the caster sugar and star anise and cook over a medium heat until it just starts to become lightly golden. Carefully remove the star anise.

Arrange a neat layer of peach segments on top of the syrup in the frying pan – they can overlap each other but must cover the base of the pan. Cook the peaches on top of the stove over a low heat for 5 minutes.

Remove the pastry circle from the fridge and place on top of the peaches, using the back of a spoon to ease the edges of the pastry down between the peaches and the pan. Bake in the preheated oven for at least 15 minutes, or until the pastry is cooked on top.

Rest the tart for 10 minutes before carefully turning it out on a serving plate.

Serves 6–8

PRUNE & PEAR FLAN

Flan aux pruneaux et aux poires

FROM THE BRITTANY REGION | BY PIERRICK BOYER

Almost every French bakery and pastry shop sells one or several varieties of this classic tart from Brittany.

25 cm (10 in) square sheet puff pastry

200 g (7 oz) caster (superfine) sugar

40 g (1½ oz) plain (all-purpose) flour, sifted

4 eggs

250 ml (8½ fl oz/1 cup) pouring cream

250 ml (8½ fl oz/1 cup) milk

1 large or 2 small poached pears, cored and cut into thin slices

6 pitted prunes, cut into small pieces

a little icing (confectioners') sugar, for dusting

Preheat the oven to 180°C (350°F). Grease an 18 cm (7 in) loose-based flan (tart) tin and arrange it on a flat baking tray.

Carefully lift the pastry onto the prepared flan tin, pushing it in gently. Don't trim the edges as the pastry may shrink in the oven. Arrange a sheet of baking paper on top of the pastry and fill with rice. Bake for 10–15 minutes or until the pastry is just cooked. Remove the paper and rice.

In a bowl, mix the sugar and flour. Beat in 2 of the eggs until smooth. Beat in the remaining 2 eggs, followed by the cream and milk to form a smooth custard.

Arrange the pears and prunes in the tart shell then carefully pour in the custard. (Any leftover custard can be baked separately in an ovenproof porcelain dish.) Bake for 15–20 minutes or until set and beginning to brown.

Trim the edges of the pastry. Remove the flan from the tin and transfer to a cake stand or serving plate. Decorate with extra pears or prunes, if you wish. Dust with icing sugar just before serving.

Serves 8

PEAR & ALMOND TART

Tarte Bourdalou

FROM THE PARIS REGION	BY PIERRICK BOYER

*Many Parisian families buy this popular French dessert from the
local patisserie but it is fun to make at home.
The almond cream goes beautifully with the poached pears.*

Pastry

160 g (5½ oz) plain (all-purpose) flour

120 g (4½ oz) unsalted butter

50 g (1¾ oz) caster (superfine) sugar

¼ teaspoon salt

2 egg yolks

Almond cream

50 g (1¾ oz) unsalted butter

50 g (1¾ oz) almond meal

50 g (1¾ oz) caster (superfine) sugar

2 large eggs

50 ml (1¾ fl oz) pouring cream

3 large pears, poached, cored and each cut into 6 segments

icing (confectioners') sugar for dusting

Butter a 25 cm (10 in) loose-based flan (tart) tin.

To make the pastry, mix together the flour, butter, caster sugar and salt in the bowl of an electric beater. Lastly, beat in the egg yolks.

Form the dough into a ball, cover it in plastic wrap and place in the refrigerator to rest for at least 1 hour.

Preheat the oven to 160°C (320°F).

Roll the pastry thinly and line the tart tin. Trim the edges of the pastry then place the tin in the freezer for a few minutes.

To make the almond cream, mix the butter with the almond meal, caster sugar and the eggs in a blender. Lastly, mix in the cream.

Spread the almond cream over the pastry shell and then arrange the segments of poached pears on top.

Bake in the preheated oven for at least 20 minutes or until the pastry is cooked and browned. Allow to cool.

Dust the tart with icing sugar and remove it from the tin.

Serves 8

PLUM TART

Tarte aux prunes

FROM THE ALPS REGION | BY MICHAEL GATÉ

The Alpine region is famous for its wonderful fruit tarts, prepared throughout summer and autumn with local fruits and a dash of liqueur made from the same fruit. The sweet shortcrust pastry is my favourite for sweet tarts and pies, with the almonds providing a pleasant crunch. The pastry needs time to rest, so you will need to make it at least 1 hour before using.

8 large plums, halved and stoned (blood plums are lovely)

a little icing (confectioners') sugar, for dusting

Sweet shortcrust pastry

55 g (2 oz) whole blanched almonds

150 g (5½ oz) unsalted butter, cubed

1 large egg

2 drops pure vanilla essence

a pinch of salt

100 g (3½ oz) icing (confectioners') sugar

250 g (9 oz/1⅔ cups) plain (all-purpose) flour

To make the sweet shortcrust pastry, chop the almonds coarsely but evenly in a food processor. Add the butter, egg, vanilla and salt and process briefly until the butter has softened slightly. Continue to blend, gradually adding the icing sugar and flour until the pastry is well mixed. Tip the pastry out onto a work surface and use your hands to shape it into a ball. Wrap in plastic wrap. Flatten slightly and refrigerate for at least 1 hour before using.

Preheat the oven to 200°C (400°F). Grease a 25 cm (10 in) square or a 28 cm (11 in) round flan (tart) tin and place it on a flat baking tray.

Combine the sugar and butter in a small food processor and blend until well combined and creamy. Add the egg and egg yolk and blend. Add the liqueur, then the almond meal and flour, and blend until combined. Transfer the almond cream to a bowl.

Remove the pastry from the fridge and knead slightly to soften. Lightly flour two 30 cm (12 in) squares of baking paper. Place the pastry between them and roll out to a thickness of about 3 mm (⅛ in). Carefully lift the pastry into the prepared flan tin, pushing it in gently. Don't trim the edges as the pastry may shrink in the oven.

Almond cream

85 g (3 oz) sugar

85 g (3 oz) unsalted butter

1 whole egg

1 egg yolk

2 tablespoons plum liqueur (or use kirsch, Pear William or brandy)

85 g (3 oz) almond meal

1 tablespoon plain (all-purpose) flour, sifted

Spread the almond cream over the pastry base and up the sides. Arrange the plum halves on top, skin side down, working from the edge to the centre. Bake for 20 minutes, then trim the pastry edges neatly.

Reduce the oven temperature to 150°C (300°F) and bake for a further 35–40 minutes or until the pastry base is dry and lightly browned. Just before serving, dust the tart with icing sugar.

Serves 6–8

PRUNE TART FROM LORRAINE

Tarte aux quetches

FROM THE ALSACE-LORRAINE REGION

The region of Lorraine abounds in plum trees, and with the glut of plums in summer, many are dried and used in desserts.

about 350 g (12½ oz)
Sweet shortcrust pastry
(page 408), rolled out to
about 3 mm (⅛ in) thick

1 egg

110 g (4 oz/½ cup) caster
(superfine) sugar, plus
extra for dusting

55 g (2 oz/½ cup)
almond meal

2 tablespoons plum
liqueur

2 tablespoons crème
fraîche

about 800 g (1 lb 12 oz)
moist pitted prunes

icing sugar for dusting

Preheat the oven to 180°C (350°F).

Line the base and sides of a 25 cm (10 in) flan tin with the rolled pastry.

In a mixing bowl, combine the egg with the caster sugar, almond meal, plum liqueur and the crème fraîche.

Pour this mixture onto the pastry base, then top with pitted prunes. Dust a little caster sugar over the plums and bake the tart in the preheated oven for about 40–45 minutes or until the pastry is cooked.

Remove the tart from the oven and leave for at least 10 minutes before unmoulding.

Dust with icing sugar just before serving.

Serves 8

CHERRY & ALMOND TART

La tarte amandine aux cerises

FROM THE PARIS REGION

This appetising cherry and almond tart was traditionally made with cherries grown in orchards just outside Paris. If cherries aren't in season, you can use frozen or tinned, but make sure you defrost or drain them to get rid of any excess liquid. I use a 25 cm (10 in) tart mould.

2 eggs

50 g (1¾ oz) caster (superfine) sugar

50 ml (1¾ fl oz) cream

70 g (2½ oz) softened unsalted butter

100 g (3½ oz/1 cup) almond meal

about 350 g (12½ oz) Sweet shortcrust pastry (page 408), rolled out to about 3 mm (⅛ in) thick

about 600 g (1 lb 5 oz) pitted cherries

icing (confectioners') sugar for dusting

Preheat the oven to 180°C (350°F).

Mix the eggs with the caster sugar, cream, 60 g (2 oz) of the softened butter and the almond meal until well combined.

Butter a tart mould with the remaining butter and carefully line the mould with the pastry. Spread the almond cream over the pastry, then top generously with the pitted cherries, pressing the cherries in slightly.

Bake the tart in the preheated oven for about 25 minutes or until the pastry is golden.

Remove the tart from the oven and allow to cool.

It looks lovely dusted with icing sugar.

Serves 6–8

BLUEBERRY TART

Tarte aux myrtilles

FROM THE FRENCH ALPS REGION

*The French love to serve fruit tarts for a special family occasion.
It's great to bake your own rather than buying one from a pastry shop
as beautiful fresh fruits are so readily available.*

2 egg yolks

50 g (1¾ oz) caster (superfine) sugar, plus extra 2 tablespoons

25 g (1 oz) plain (all-purpose) flour

250 ml (8½ fl oz/1 cup) milk

⅓ vanilla bean, split lengthways

200 g (7 oz) block ready-made puff pastry, thawed

2 tablespoons whipping cream, whipped and chilled

250 g (9 oz) fresh blueberries

icing (confectioners') sugar for dusting

6 dollops of thick (heavy) cream

a few mint leaves

I like to make this tart in a loose-based rectangular flan (tart) tin about 30 cm (12 in) long.

Preheat the oven to 200°C (400°F).

Cream the egg yolks with the caster sugar in a bowl, then mix in the plain flour.

In a small saucepan, heat the milk with the vanilla bean to almost boiling point. Remove the vanilla bean.

Add the hot milk to the egg yolk preparation and mix, then transfer this to a saucepan and cook on a medium heat until it thickens. Return the preparation to the bowl, whisk for 10 seconds and allow to cool.

Roll out the puff pastry to a thickness of about 3 mm (⅛ in) and to measure about 35 cm x 15 cm (14 in). Lift the pastry and line the base and sides of the rectangular tin.

Mix the cooled, whipped cream into the cold custard and spread it over the base of the pastry. Garnish the top with blueberries and sprinkle with the extra caster sugar. Trim the edges of the pastry.

Bake the tart in the preheated oven for about 40–45 minutes or until the pastry is cooked and browned.

Remove the tart from the oven and allow to cool.

Slice the tart into six portions. Dust with icing sugar and garnish with a dollop of cream and a few mint leaves.

Serves 6

STRAWBERRY TART

Tarte aux fraises

FROM THE LOIRE VALLEY REGION

This dessert takes me back to my youth in my native Loire Valley. In summer, my father grew large quantities of strawberries in our family garden and my mum and grandmother made beautiful fruit tarts.

a little plain (all-purpose) flour

400 g (14 oz) Sweet shortcrust pastry (page 408)

300 ml (10 fl oz) crème fraîche

1 tablespoon Cointreau

2 tablespoons milk

2 tablespoons icing (confectioners') sugar

2 punnets (500 g/1 lb 2 oz) strawberries, hulled, washed and halved

4 tablespoons smooth apricot jam

3 tablespoons peeled pistachio nuts, cut into small pieces

Preheat the oven to 180°C (350°F). You will need a 25 cm (10 in) loose-based flan (tart) tin.

Dust the bench with plain flour and roll the pastry out thinly to about 4 mm (⅕ in).

Line the flan tin with the pastry and cover it with foil. Top the foil with pastry weights to stop the pastry from shrinking during cooking. Bake the pastry in the preheated oven for about 20 minutes.

In a bowl, beat the crème fraîche with the Cointreau and milk until almost firm. Add the icing sugar and mix well. This is called a chantilly cream.

Spread the chantilly cream over the cooled pastry shell. Top gently with strawberry halves and brush the berries lightly with apricot jam. Sprinkle pistachio nuts around the edge of the tart and refrigerate until ready to slice and serve.

Serves 8

RASPBERRY TARTLETS

Tartelettes aux framboises

FROM THE LOIRE VALLEY REGION

I prepared this dessert hundreds of times during my chef's apprenticeship in the Loire Valley. The pastry shells and crème pâtissière can both be made ahead of time. Avoid assembling the tartlets more than two hours before serving as the pastry will become soggy.

250 ml (8½ fl oz/1 cup) milk

2 egg yolks

⅓ vanilla bean, split lengthways

55 g (2 oz/¼ cup) caster (superfine) sugar

30 g (1 oz) plain (all-purpose) flour, sifted

Sweet shortcrust pastry (page 408), chilled

3 tablespoons pouring cream

3 tablespoons apricot jam

a splash of water

600 g (1 lb 5 oz) raspberries

To make the crème pâtissière, bring the milk to a boil in a medium saucepan.

In a bowl, whisk the egg yolks, vanilla bean and sugar for 2 minutes. When well blended, whisk in the flour. Pour on the hot milk and whisk well until smooth.

Return the mixture to the rinsed-out saucepan and cook over a medium heat, whisking constantly, until the mixture thickens and comes to a boil. Tip the mixture into a bowl. Whisk briefly and leave to cool. When cold, discard the vanilla bean, cover the crème pâtissière with plastic wrap and refrigerate until ready to use.

When ready to make the tartlets, preheat the oven to 200°C (400°F). Grease twenty 6 cm (2½ in) loose-based tartlet tins and arrange them on a baking tray.

Flour a work surface. Remove the pastry from the fridge and knead lightly. Roll out the pastry to about 3 mm (⅛ in) thick and cut into squares to fit the tartlet moulds. Line the moulds with the pastry, pushing it in gently. Trim the edges with your fingertips, taking care not to make them too thin and fragile. Cook for about 10 minutes, or until the edges have browned and the pastry is cooked. Remove from the oven and leave to cool before unmoulding.

Mix the crème patissière with the cream.

Heat the apricot jam with a little water to make a glaze.

To assemble the tartlets, place a spoonful of pastry cream into each pastry shell and spread it a little. Arrange the raspberries decoratively over the cream, working from the edge to the centre. Brush lightly with the apricot glaze and chill until ready to serve.

Makes about twenty 6 cm (2½ in) tartlets

INDEX

ACKNOWLEDGEMENTS

I wish to express my special thanks to SBS television, particularly Ken Shipp, Erik Dwyer and Nicki Roller for commissioning me to produce *Taste Le Tour with Gabriel Gaté*.

I thank my wife, Angie Gaté, who has been involved in all aspects of the project. I'm also grateful to Peter Warren, who produces the series with us.

A grand 'merci' to the French chefs, pastry cooks and charcutiers who have contributed recipes published in this book, especially Philippe Mouchel, Pierrick Boyer, Stéphane Langlois, Francis Dumas, Bernard Mure-Ravaud, Alain Gegnani, Nicolas Poelaert and Jean-Marie Blanchot.

Lastly, thanks to Hardie Grant's publishing team, especially publisher, Pam Brewster.